Love in America

ALSO BY LAWRENCE R. SAMUEL
AND FROM MCFARLAND

*The American Writer: Literary Life in the United States
from the 1920s to the Present* (2018)

New York City 1964: A Cultural History (2014)

Love in America
A Cultural History of the Past Century

Lawrence R. Samuel

McFarland & Company, Inc., Publishers
Jefferson, North Carolina

ISBN (print) 978-1-4766-7987-7
ISBN (ebook) 978-1-4766-3807-2

LIBRARY OF CONGRESS AND BRITISH LIBRARY
CATALOGUING DATA ARE AVAILABLE

© 2020 Lawrence R. Samuel. All rights reserved

No part of this book may be reproduced or transmitted in any form or by any means, electronic or mechanical, including photocopying or recording, or by any information storage and retrieval system, without permission in writing from the publisher.

Front cover image © 2020 Shutterstock

Printed in the United States of America

McFarland & Company, Inc., Publishers
Box 611, Jefferson, North Carolina 28640
www.mcfarlandpub.com

To Baylor, with love

Table of Contents

Preface   1

Introduction   5

1. Our National Melancholia, 1920–1939   15
2. America's No. 1 Problem?, 1940–1959   35
3. Revolt Against Love, 1960–1979   56
4. Are You Lovable?, 1980–1999   78
5. Your Brain on Love, 2000–2009   99
6. Ex Machina, 2010–   119

Conclusion   140

Chapter Notes   149

Bibliography   159

Index   163

Preface

Anyone and everyone who has experienced it can, for better and often worse, testify to its tremendous power over mind, body, and soul. Love is perhaps the strongest and most enduring of the human emotions, rooted in our biology and widely celebrated (and scorned) across our cultural landscape. Every year we set aside a special day for all things love, issue postal stamps dedicated to it, and wear t-shirts praising its wonderfulness. The high value we place on love in American society belies the fact that the emotion remains largely an enigma despite rigorous attempts to grasp its full meaning. Poets and philosophers of all stripes have over the centuries struggled to comprehend the true nature of love, but the subject continues to be in many respects a puzzle frustratingly difficult to solve. Scientists too have approached love as an increasingly respected field of study, but even they freely admit much more work needs to be done to have a thorough understanding of what is often prosaically defined as an intense feeling of deep affection.

Love in America is, as its title makes clear, the story of love in the United States. No such book exists, a surprising thing given the prominent role that the idea and pursuit of romantic love has played in this country since we became one. (While there are many legitimate forms of love—parental, theological, material, and many others—this work focuses on its romantic expression. Limiting the book's scope to romantic love in the United States over the past century is a deliberate means to contain what is obviously an immense subject.[1]) Love conquers all, the proverb tells us, but few know the full and fascinating history of the emotion in this country. Love has both shaped and reflected our core values, with its expression at any given time an open window into the prevailing cultural zeitgeist. As well, love is widely recognized as the most complex of human emotions, this alone making a history of the subject in the United States a worthy endeavor. By charting the course of love within American culture, we gain key insights not just into the history of emotions but into our national character, offering us a greater understanding of who we are as a people. Most important, however, taking a long view of the subject allows us to hear a good number of real love stories of real people, each one a case study of how the emotion has operated at the individual, personal level.

The wide range of arenas in which love intersects reflects the subject's centrality in everyday life in America these past one hundred years. Love overlaps with psychology, science, religion and spirituality, business, medicine and health, relationships, philosophy, sociology, child raising, and politics, making this work truly multi- and interdisciplinary. Love became a legitimate field of inquiry in the 20th century, with a relatively small but enthusiastic group of researchers dedicating their careers to learning more about what was considered a mysterious subject. Science and psychology are clearly the disciplinary pillars of the story, offering a complementary mix of solid research and practical advice based on prevailing theories. Romantic love has long been a mainstay of popular culture, of course, with movies, television shows, and songs often spouting the power of the emotion. The gap separating fictitious narratives of love and real ones has been wide, however, with Americans' expectations for the emotion frequently exceeding its actual possibilities. The disparity between the illusion and reality of love has proved to be a major problem for many over the years, in fact, making this the central theme of the book.

Based on this important finding, *Love in America* offers readers a provocative argument that challenges standard thinking and makes a contribution to mainstream scholarship. Despite popular belief, Americans have for the most part been largely critical of love, the work demonstrates, with abundant anecdotal evidence and hard research backing up that bold claim. Love has often been seen as something to be avoided because of the emotional mayhem it can cause in one's life, with more practical concerns prioritized over getting caught in the whirlwind of romance. A host of powerful forces—the emergence of the "modern woman" in the 1920s, the economic pressures and social instability of the Depression and World War II, the significant domestic discord of the postwar era, and the feminist movement and sexual revolution of the counterculture—each served to turn the emotion into somewhat of an unwanted guest in this country. More recently, many young women have rejected the idea and practice of love, thinking that "falling" under the spell of the emotion (and for another person) is a sign of weakness and vulnerability. The low marriage rate among millennials reflects this "down with love" attitude, something that presents major social and cultural implications for the nation's future. Rather than a happy tale as one might expect, the story of love in America is thus, as they say on Facebook, a "complicated" one, filled with contradictions and ambiguity.

From a wider perspective, *Love in America* joins an impressive and growing body of literature dedicated to the expanding field of the history of emotions.[2] Recent advances in neuroscience are revealing the degree to which emotions dictate our actions, evidence suggesting that we are often not the rational beings that we like to believe we are. Interdisciplinary and cross-cultural in nature, the field addresses the key question of whether emotions are learned and are subject to the values of a particular time and place or are rather universal to the human experience. While steeped in theory, the area of study also lends itself nicely to the examination of the emotional life of a specific society or community, making it no wonder that more historians are being attracted to the field. As well, scholars typically consider the emotional set of both the individual and the group in their research, another one of the discipline's more appealing aspects. Emotions have both shaped and reflected history to a greater degree than most people realize, we learn from published works including those focused on shame, sympathy, fear, and happiness, a finding that resonates within this study of love in America.[3]

The structure of *Love in America* is first and foremost designed to help tell an interesting and informative story. I find that a chronological approach works best for telling history because it provides readers with a compelling narrative. Based on clear shifts in the overall attitude and behavior among Americans, the book's chapters are defined by recognizable historical eras or periods, i.e., between-the-world-wars (1920-1939), wartime and postwar (1940-1959), counterculture (1960-1979), neo-conservative (1980-1999), and, for lack of a better word, digital (2000 to today, split into two decades and chapters in order to emphasize more recent events). Some cultural context is provided in each chapter to frame that era's particular chronicle of love. As a universal emotion, love offers the welcome opportunity to ignore our socially constructed divisions of race, class, age, sexual preference, and political affiliation, something of which I've taken full advantage in writing the book. Too much history is about how we have been purportedly different, I believe, making the chance to tell a story about something that we all share a very fortuitous thing.[4]

Regarding the work's scope, it was immediately after World War I when the modern concept of love was born, I posit, making 1920 a good place to begin the story. Everything changed in America after that war, as the disparate forces of modernity took hold. This was certainly true of love, as there was a decided shift in how the emotion was perceived and expressed, particularly among youth culture of the Roaring Twenties. All kinds of factors—greater sexual freedoms, women's new rights and opportunities, the rise of corporate culture, the popularity of radio, movies, and mass culture in general, to name just a few—influenced how Americans decided to pursue their romantic relationships.

In terms of sources, the work mostly draws upon period newspaper and magazine articles as well as other books, both trade and scholarly. I'm a firm believer that journalists really do write the first draft of history, as it is often said, as they are on the frontlines in reporting news about a particular subject. Knowing that love was a popular topic among readers, the mainstream media thoroughly covered that beat, with the resulting paper trail offering a compelling narrative of the role that the emotion played in American culture over the years. Hundreds of different sources are used, so the result is a balanced perspective that doesn't lean any particular way in terms of ideology or political bent. Journalists often interviewed experts in science and psychology and authors of recently published books on the subject in writing their articles, giving us a very full understanding of the state of love in the country at a particular moment in time. Although the sources are thus primarily "popular," the material is typically grounded in some kind of scientific or academic finding. While the subject is vast, my hope here is to offer interested readers some additional understanding of what has, as it has been said, made the world go 'round.

Introduction

"I'm thru with love, I'll never fall again.
Said adieu to love, don't ever call again."
—Charles Tobias/Cliff Friend

First things first: while romantic love is not a uniquely American idea, a fair argument can be made that it was the United States where it found its widest and most compelling expression. Love as we define it was simply not an emotion that most people throughout history have experienced or even thought possible. "The idea of romantic love—as cherished by Americans— the belief in passion and desire as the key to happy marriage and the good life—is relatively new and still largely confined to the Christian world," Arthur Schlesinger, Jr., observed in the *Saturday Evening Post* in 1966. Americanization was sweeping across both Europe and Asia in the postwar years, and with it our concept of romantic love, but until recently people in other parts of the world had had a distinctly different view of and approach to marriage and family. Love as we knew it was unlikely to be found in life, Europeans and Asians generally believed, and if it was it was not likely to end well. "Only the Americans have attempted on a large scale the singular experiment of trying to incorporate romantic love into the staid and stolid framework of marriage and family," he wrote, making this important aspect of life one of the distinguishing aspects of our national character.[1]

Although the Puritans were apparently more amorous than we give them credit for, rational thought and Victorian attitudes prevailed in the United States through the 19th century, according to Schlesinger, putting a damper on romantic love. Events of the early 20th century allowed love to rush in, however, marking a new era in the history of the emotion in the nation. "For most of history it was inconceivable that people would choose their mates on the basis of something as fragile and irrational as love," Stephanie Coontz wrote in her 2006 *Marriage, a History: How Love Conquered Marriage*; what had been considered an irrational and frivolous pursuit of the ruling class became normalized, democratized, and socially sanctioned.[2] The sexual experiences to be had during World War I (especially among soldiers who had been to France) and a host of factors in the 1920s including the feminist movement, the popularity of Freudian psychology, the booming economy, the mobility and privacy of the automobile, and affordable contraceptives all allowed romance of different forms to flourish. Consumer and popular culture, i.e., advertising, music, movies, and novels, reinforced this cultural climate that celebrated both love and sex, as did the hedonism and vices that defined the Jazz Age. "The American experience was at last in full tide," Schlesinger wrote, reprising psychologist and science writer Morton Hunt's declaration that the country had entered "The Age of Love."[3]

Other aspects of modernism contributed to the blossoming of romantic love in the United States after World War I. Work for many was becoming increasingly dull and monotonous, a function of rising bureaucracy and corporatization. The transition from farm to factory had begun during the Industrial Revolution, but now it was members of the burgeoning middle class of the early 20th century who were finding their office jobs to be an unfulfilling but necessary part of life. Intensifying urbanization too was making many feel like they were just cogs in a machine, encouraging Americans to look to their private lives, specifically romance and marriage, for emotional contentment. Love for another person could deliver the intimacy lacking in the public sphere, this thinking goes, turning committed relationships from socially sanctioned institutions of procreation into sanctuaries of affection in an increasingly impersonal and anonymous world.[4]

While it is of course impossible to pinpoint precisely when our interpretation of romantic love was born, scholars generally agree that modern America offered an ideal cultural climate for it to take shape. "During the late 1800s and the first half of the 1900s the traditional 'love story,' in which two young people see themselves as 'in love' and start to build an enduring relationship, became a popular social convention, at least in the United States," wrote the social psychologists Kenneth Gergen and Mary Gergen in 1988. Women spearheaded the notion of romantic love, the pair argued, a means of cementing relationships that might otherwise end should men decide to seek out greener pastures. "It was greatly to women's advantage if sexual desire could be interpreted as 'love' and a man's desire for her could result in lasting commitment and economic security," they explained, the romanticizing of lust employed as a form of control. Love was thus a "tale" that a couple would choose to believe in, according to this theory, mirroring other arguments that the emotion is a learned or constructed device rather than a biological determined response.[5]

In his 1993 *The Culture of Love: Victorians to Moderns*, Stephen Kern also posited that it was women of the early 20th century who created a new narrative of love that served social and economic ends. Love in the Victorian era was treated as trite and idealistic, he argued, while women of the modern era took a more realistic and "authentic" view of the emotion. As well, women gained greater access to the workplace and to public spaces after World War I, allowing them to meet men directly rather than have to be introduced through more formal measures such as matchmakers. Advances in science, changes in law, increasing secularism, declining parental influence, and a more flexible morality too encouraged both men and women to gain greater control over their love lives between the world wars, Kern showed, these gains outweighing the delicacy and politeness that defined the emotion for Victorians.[6]

A pair of self-help books published in the twenties illustrated the new, modern form of love that Americans were embracing as the more naïve and fanciful one from the previous generation faded further into history. Theodore Hendrik Van de Velde's *Ideal Marriage: Its Physiology and Technique* was a forthright guide to sex complete with charts and diagrams, making it *The Joy of Sex* of its day. (First published in London in 1926, it took four years for an American press to make it available in the States.) The author, a Dutch gynecologist, argued that eroticism was both a science and an art, making a greater understanding of it a valuable thing in order to realize a "normal marital relationship." While the book was officially aimed at medical professionals and other scientists (much like *The Kinsey Reports*), it reportedly ultimately became the best-selling sex manual of all time, and helped millions of people navigate what was largely unfamiliar territory. Romantic love could and should accompany sex, according to *Ideal Marriage*, marking an important milestone in the history of each subject.[7]

Doris Langley Moore's 1925 *The Technique of the Love Affair* (also originally published in London) similarly approached the dynamics of romantic relationships with a kind of directness that had to that point in time not been utilized in mainstream non-fiction. Foreshadowing the dedicated literary genre designed to empower women in their love lives (most notably represented by Ellen Fein's and Sherrie Schneider's 1995 *The Rules: Time-tested Secrets for Capturing the Heart of Mr. Right*), *The Technique of the Love Affair* showed readers how to get what they wanted out of their associations with men. The rules of both dating and marriage had changed after the Great War (in part because there were simply fewer men around), helping to explain why the book was an immediate bestseller on both sides of the Atlantic. ("The New Woman of the 1920s did not reject marriage, although she rejected her elders' advice about how to find and keep a husband," Coontz noted.[8]) "The whole etiquette of 'at homes,' of a man making calls on a woman and then progressing to unchaperoned walks with her—all those courtship conventions became obsolete," observed Norrie Epstein, editor of Pantheon Books, which published an updated version of the book in 1999.[9] "Skillfully handled, it constitutes an art, a delicate and genial art," Moore wrote of the love affair, offering women a "technique" grounded in the more female friendly social landscape of the Roaring Twenties.[10]

The re-release of a three-quarters-century old guide to love illustrates that the more we seem to know about the emotion, the more we seem to not know. As it always has, romantic love remains a challenge for individuals in the 21st century, with arguably no pursuit more difficult than successfully and happily managing a relationship predicated on mutually shared strong feelings between two people. Living one's life as a single person is itself a complex affair these days, making the addition of possessing love for and hopefully with another person yet another thing we must handle with great care. Then why do it, one has to ask? "It's the cornerstone of our humanity," Hara Estroff Marano plainly put in *Psychology Today* in 2004, thinking that "only love protects us enough to grow and change." Love has to be worth the effort for so many to willingly enter into it despite all the work and risks involved, we have to conclude, suggesting there is a basic human need to be part of something bigger than or outside of oneself. "Anyone who has come within waltzing distance of it, read Jane Austen or Danielle Steele, or listened to Frank Sinatra or Celine Dion, knows there's no elixir like love," Marano wrote, making the safe bet that it wasn't about to disappear anytime soon.[11]

Alongside our individual and collective love affair with love has existed, paradoxically, a deep distrust of and antipathy towards the emotion. "A lethal combination of Hollywood sentimentality, Victorian romanticism and bridal-magazine kitsch has placed an impossible burden on love," wrote Judith Hertog in her "un–Valentine" published in the online edition of the *New York Times* on Valentine's Day 2019, going on to explain how and why she resented "the tyranny of perfect romance."[12] Many women, especially millennials (those born after 1980 and the first generation to become young adults in the 21st century), have in fact resisted entering into serious relationships because they may involve love. Such a thing is, however, nothing new. As early as the 1930s, some scientists were describing romantic love as an emotion that mature adults had no business clinging to. Such love was a vestige of children's imagination, they declared, and a sentimental state of mind that served little useful purpose. Psychotherapists, notably Alfred Adler, also dismissed romantic love, thinking that marriages would be much better off without it. Many feminists of the 1970s, particularly Marilyn French, argued that romantic love presented a real and present danger to women's independence and ability to lead lives with real meaning. Later scholars such as Pepper Schwartz have made a convincing case for "peer marriage" predicated on equality and "deep friendship" in place of passion and stereotypical gender roles.[13] In short, love in America has been a contentious, highly charged site, simultaneously aggressively pursued for its emotional rewards and just as assertively avoided due to the havoc it could wreak on one's psyche.[14]

A recurrent theme in these pages is how Americans have consistently relied upon popular culture, notably the movies and music, to forge their romantic expectations despite the fact that these media were designed only as entertainment. The relationship between American cinema and love has been a long one, going back in fact to the late 19th century. One of the first films ever made was Thomas Edison's eighteen-second *The Kiss* from 1896, in which stage actors May Irwin and John Rice reenacted the final love scene from the musical *The Widow Jones*. (Although a mere peck, this first on-screen kiss was considered quite scandalous at the time.[15]) This kind of literally theatrical expression of love was a common feature of movies produced over the course of the first two decades of the 20th century, a byproduct of both lingering Victorian-era melodramatic sentiment and the technological limitations of the time.

The enthusiastic public reaction to *The Kiss* and other early films helped to inform producers and directors what was likely to be commercially successful in the new medium. "'Love with gestures' came into prominence as silent pictures grew longer and audiences learned that films really could tell a story," Carlisle Jones observed in the *New York Herald Tribune* in 1939, with dramatic body movements used by actors to convey that they were in love. Mary Pickford's literally throwing herself into the arms of her cinematic sweethearts did just that, as did Rudolph Valentino's amorous gazing of and reaching out for his co-stars. John Barrymore, John Gilbert, Gloria Swanson, and dozens of other now mostly forgotten movie stars of the silent era offered the public a tutorial in the ways of love, something that helped shape Americans' actual romantic lives. "The screen was a textbook of romance," Jones wrote, "and it provided a course in which nearly every one under sixty was interested." In the 1920s, a new kind of cinematic vocabulary of love was born, Jones continued, one that relied heavily on the more assertive romantic leanings of the modern woman. "Their clinches in pictures are textbooks for the jitterbug generation," she noted, with real life flappers looking to big stars like Clara Bow for cues in their own romantic pursuits.[16]

What worked in movies typically did not work in real life, however, as many would freely admit. "In fairy tales, love songs and most Hollywood

In the 1920s, many Americans picked up their romantic cues from silent film stars like Mary Pickford. "America's Sweetheart," as she was sometimes called, is widely credited for popularizing the ingénue role in film. Billy Rose Theatre Division, The New York Public Library. "In front of the fireplace." *The New York Public Library Digital Collections.* 1922. http://digitalcollections.nypl.org/items/510d47d9-40a7-a3d9-e040-e00a18064a99.

movies, any boy-meets-girl story takes the long way around to proving the predictable," wrote Caryn James, film reviewer for the *New York Times*, the standard formula prescribing some time and a few obstacles for a couple who were right for each other to get together. Actual romance was a much different story, however, as most of us who experienced it well knew. "In real life, who hasn't been an idiot in love, defying the odds to find the wrong person at the least convenient time to create an emotional mess," James continued, glad to see that a new batch of films in 1990 were challenging the conventions of fictional romance.[17] By then Hollywood had moved away from the mismatched-but-obviously-in-love pairs in films like the 1933 *Flying Down to Rio* (Fred Astaire and Ginger Rogers), 1942 *Woman of the Year* (Spencer Tracy and Katharine Hepburn), and 1944 *To Have and Have Not* (Lauren Bacall and Humphrey Bogart), thinking contemporary audiences wanted more realistic stories. "The classic film romances took our hopes about love and flashed them across the screen in exaggerated, symbolic form," she observed, suggesting that late 20th century cinema reflected "our society's deep fear and cynicism about romance." (James located the turning point of Hollywood romance as the 1987 *Fatal Attraction*.[18])

In her 2001 book *The Seven Stories of Love: And How to Choose Your Own Happy Ending*, Marcia Millman took a different tack by arguing that fictional romance had always paralleled real life relationships. Millman, who taught a popular course at the University of California at Santa Cruz called The Sociology of Love, believed that there were seven basic love stories in movies and novels, and that women drew upon them to frame their own actual romantic pursuits. These themes ("First Love," "Pygmalion," "Obsessive

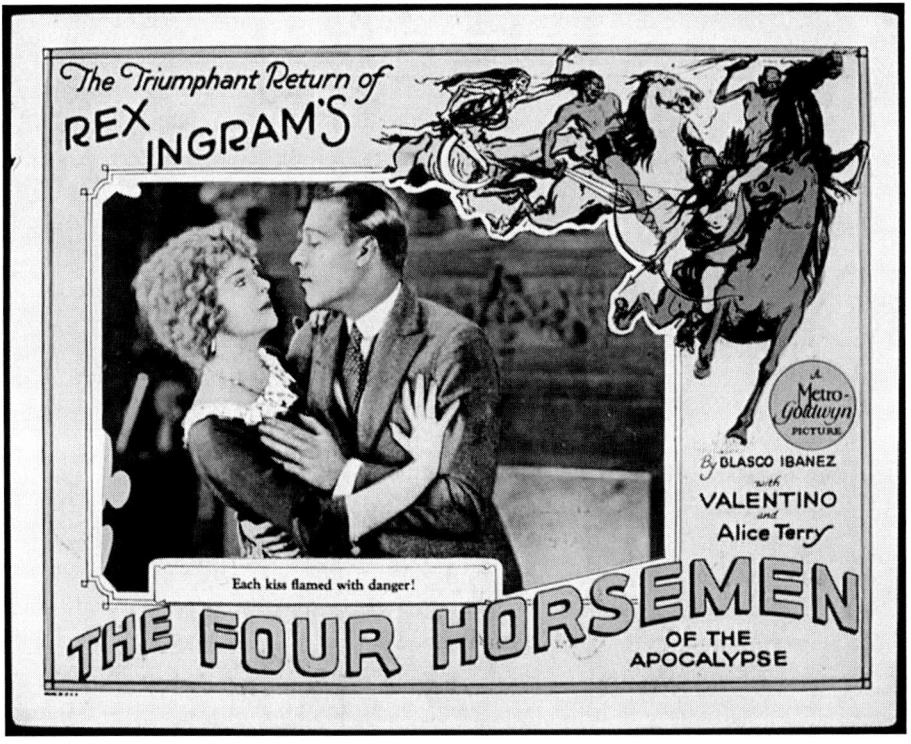

While many men found silent movie star Rudolph Valentino not masculine enough for their liking, women adored the sex symbol. Mass hysteria ensued when the "Latin Lover" died in 1926 at age 31. Billy Rose Theatre Division, The New York Public Library. "Each kiss flamed with danger!" *The New York Public Library Digital Collections*. 1921. http://digitalcollections.nypl.org/items/510d47d9-4086-a3d9-e040-e00a18064a99

Love," "The Downstairs Woman and the Upstairs Man," "Sacrifice," "Rescue," and "The Courage to Love: Postponement and Avoidance") were, like many myths, timeless and universal, according to Millman, and thus embedded in the fundamental human experience. "The Love Professor," as she was known on campus, had done considerable research to form her interesting thesis that she felt could be used by women to help them better understand their relationships and then "rewrite" them to create happy endings.[19]

In his 2003 *The Hollywood Book of Love: An Irreverent Guide to the Films That Raised Our Romantic Expectations*, however, James Robert Parish made a convincing case that romantic love as depicted in movies created unrealistic expectations about relationships. "Because of the movies, some people's perceptions about romance is that it should be magical," he explained, thinking love off the screen was typically a lot more humdrum. "We don't have the makeup man and the costume guy to help out," the expert on all things Hollywood (he had written more than a hundred books on show business) quipped, advising those waiting for fireworks to go off or perhaps waves to crash when spending time with their special someone to not hold their breath. The primary goal of Tinseltown was to make a profit, Parish reminded readers, warning anyone who viewed the product as tutorials in love that it was highly unlikely that their own story would end as happily.[20]

While Parish had a good point, the truth was that producers of most Hollywood films in recent years have acknowledged that love is a tricky business, just as James had suggested, and that the kind of romance featured in movies like *The Philadelphia Story* and *Sabrina* will not play well to contemporary audiences. "It seems as if it's never been harder to say 'I love you' and mean it—at least cinematically," observed Rachel Abramowitz in *Los Angeles Times* in 2007; she and others believed that the arrival of reality TV had a lot to do with the decline of the classic romantic comedy. It is safe to safe that it was the counterculture and more specifically the sexual revolution of a half-century ago that triggered a shift in the trajectory of love in both entertainment and real life, however. Events of the late 1960s altered the cultural DNA of America and Americans, making it impossible to take seriously the narratives of romance presented during the golden age of Hollywood.[21]

If movies have indeed offered Americans a blueprint for romantic love, whether imaginary or real, popular songs have provided its soundtrack. Pop, country music, and hip hop have served as central depositories of love, of course, but it has been the Great American Songbook—the canon of popular songs and jazz standards written primarily between the world wars—that has and continues to represent the emotion at its most romantic. The Great American Songbook has remained remarkably well liked over the years as, in terms of sheer listenability, there is little to compare with the craft of the genre's music and lyrics (that were mostly written for shows or films). "Musical fads come and go, but the classic American love song seems nearly as revered today as it was decades ago, when the Gershwin brothers, Cole Porter, Irving Berlin and others were lifting the genre to new heights," Howard Reich wrote in the *Chicago Tribune* on Valentine's Day 1999. (Jerome Kern, Harold Arlen, Johnny Mercer, and Richard Rodgers and Lorenz Hart also lead the list.) Couples of today are just as romantically inspired by these standards as their grandparents were when the songs were new, making them an essential part of how love has been expressed in America over the past century. "Step into a cabaret or jazz club anywhere from Chicago to Paris, and it probably won't be long before you'll hear someone playing or singing the Gershwins' 'Our Love Is Here to Stay,' Porter's 'I've Got You Under My Skin,' Berlin's 'What'll I Do,' Harold Arlen and Johnny Mercer's 'Come Rain or Come Shine,' or the most famous one of all, Hoagy Carmichael and Mitchell Parish's 'Star Dust,'" Reich observed.[22]

Along with his brother Ira, George Gershwin composed some of the most iconic love songs of the 20th century. George Gershwin died in 1937 at age 38, but one could still hear his music played in nightclubs around the world any night of the week. Billy Rose Theatre Division, The New York Public Library. "George Gershwin" *The New York Public Library Digital Collections.* http://digitalcollections.nypl.org/items/a59b7e97-ddee-f4ca-e040-e00a18065925

Like popular culture, consumer culture has over the years frequently appropriated love, this too helping to shape its interpretation and expression in everyday life. Recognizing the semiotic power of love, marketers have increasingly embraced the emotion in selling products and services to consumers (much like the concept of happiness). Gap, for example, has a brand of loungewear and underwear branded simply as Love, the comfortable bras

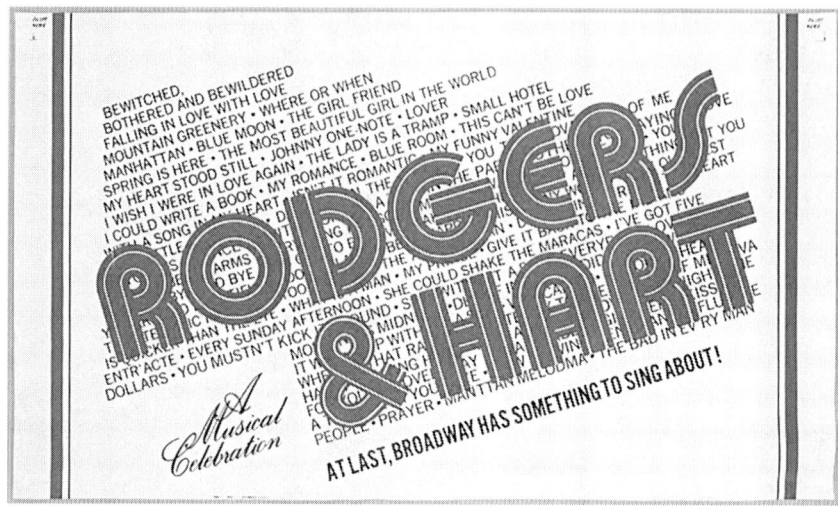

Richard Rodgers and Lorenz Hart wrote hundreds of songs for dozens of stage musicals in the 1920s and 1930s, many of them having something to do with love. This poster was for a 1975 Broadway revue celebrating their music. Billy Rose Theatre Division, The New York Public Library. "Poster for the revue Rodgers & Hart" *The New York Public Library Digital Collections*. 1975. http://digitalcollections.nypl.org/items/7f33d937-18b8-da4d-e040-e00a180604aa

and undies said to be "worn by women who inspire us."[23] Subaru has thoroughly wrapped its corporate branding around love, finding it to be a compelling point of difference in the highly competitive automobile category. The company even makes a "Love Promise" to consumers, which it defines as "our vision to show love and respect to all people at every interaction with Subaru."[24] In her 2003 *Against Love*, however, Laura Kipnis was highly critical of the employment of love as a selling tool, thinking it degraded the emotion and reduced it to just another consumable good. "In commodity culture," she wrote, "it [love] conforms to the role of a cheap commodity, spit out at the end of the assembly line in cookie-cutter forms, marketed to bored and alienated producer-consumers as an all-purpose salve to emptiness."[25] Love appears to be spreading as a brand strategy, however, as more marketers realize that it is perhaps the ultimate emotional experience one can have. It is worth going back in time to see how that came to be, with many other interesting things about love to be learned on the way.

Chapter 1

Our National Melancholia, 1920–1939

> "America appears to be the only country in the world where love is a national problem."
> —Raoul de Roussy de Sales, 1938

In July 1933, Frank Wall of 69–73 Fifty-Eighth Avenue in Long Island City received a curious letter. It was from Albert Einstein, to whom Mr. Wall, a reporter for the *Long Island Daily* Star, had recently written his own letter. Wall's letter, addressed to the renowned professor at his retreat in Le Coq-sur-Mer, Belgium, went as follows:

> I am sorry I cannot express this well enough in German. I understand the world moves so fast it, in effect, stands still, or so it appears to us. Part of the time, it seems, a person is standing right side up; part of the time on the lower side he is standing upside down, upheld by the law of gravitation; and part of the time he is sticking out on the earth at right angles and part of the time at left angles. Would it be reasonable to assume that it is while a person is standing on his head—or rather, upside down—he falls in love and does other foolish things?[1]

Apparently intrigued by Wall's unusual question, the man responsible for the theory of relativity offered a brief but informative answer:

> Very Honored Sir:
> Falling in love is by no means the most foolish thing mankind does—but gravitation cannot be held responsible for that. With highest regards,
> Albert Einstein[2]

While falling in love may not have been the most foolish thing men and women did, according to one of the smartest people in the world, many at the time believed it was an imprudent and unwise path to take in life. Between the world wars in America, romantic love was popularly viewed in cautious if not downright negative terms, a function of the "modern" values that carried major cultural currency. Rather than pursue "true" love that typically led to marriage and family—the expression of the emotion that reigned in the late 19th century and early 20th century—many Americans, especially young people, were choosing to engage in romantic endeavors that did not carry the emotional, financial, and legal costs associated with traditional domestic life. Others, however, perceived "free love" in its various forms as a genuine and serious threat to traditional love (two people embarking on a life together as a couple) and that which usually followed, with the very bedrock of society considered to be at stake in the matter. As well, popular culture, especially movies, had set too high a bar for real love, many agreed, this too contributing to disappointment in Americans' romantic lives between the world wars. Whatever the cause, love had become a national problem, the solutions to which were not at all clear.

Can the Modern Girl Love?

The formation of a much different brand of love was a function of the sea change in morality after World War I, as the "lost generation" rebelled against the strict social codes of the Victorian Age. Both in the United States and Europe, young people were engaging in behavior that more conservative types believed threatened the traditional foundation of love. Much of this was sexual in nature, and women in particular were to blame. "At present, the world is enjoying a surfeit of painted ladies," a writer for *The Living Age* posited in 1920, clearly unhappy about the more unrestricted brand of sexuality that some women, both single and married, were exhibiting. Marital infidelity was leading to a number of high profile divorce cases, all of this "free love" therefore actually coming at a high price. "One comes away with the impression of a riot of sex, a drunken orgy," the writer continued, the worst thing about all this unbridled lust being that it appeared to be just sex for the sake of sex. Practitioners of free love claimed that their behavior was based on a higher, more enlightened philosophy that celebrated the autonomy of the individual, but many critics argued that it was simply about physical pleasure. "Free love is a contradiction in terms," this writer stated, thinking that the costs associated with real love were good for both individuals and society.[3]

The different kind of behavior that many women of the early 1920s were displaying went beyond sexuality, more reason to believe that traditional love was in jeopardy. Unlike their mothers, young women were working in business, flaunting their athleticism, going to college, driving motorcars, and wearing gobs of makeup, all of these other activities possibly distracting them from what had been their primary occupation of love and marriage. "Can the modern girl love?" asked Gilbert Frankau in *Forum* in 1922, thinking that a good number of women would find the standard track of courting overly sentimental and mawkish. Culturally literate, staying busy, and, rather shockingly, not chaperoned when socializing with men, modern women could very well find falling in love an old-fashioned thing to do, many middle-aged men like Gilbert believed. "She is rather a creature of sudden and febrile attachments, easily entered into and easily broken, than of that deep enduring affection which, for all their faults, was the beau ideal of her Victorian predecessors," he wrote, finding this playing of the field "curious and almost unfeminine."[4]

It's hard to overstate how alarming the arrival of the modern woman was to those of a certain age, and how the former's determination to focus on themselves was construed as contrary to the commitment and responsibilities that came with love and marriage. Besides requiring a lot of work, running a house and taking care of a husband and children was often not much fun, making it easy to understand why many were opting out now that there were other choices. It was young women's determination to, as we now say, live in the moment that was perhaps most disquieting to those whose notions of romance were forged in a different era. "She is too selfish, too self-centered, too set on the pursuit of what she considers pleasure, to abandon herself to that self-sacrifice which is love at its best," Frankau continued, adding that this woman was also likely "too wise." What was the future for the human species if love really was heading to extinction? he and others wondered, the stakes in the matter as high as they could possibly be.[5]

As many young adults put other interests ahead of embarking on serious romantic relationships in the 1920s, authorities on love issued reminders regarding how powerful and precious the emotion was if one was lucky enough to experience it. Falling in love was "our oldest ailment," maintained George Humphrey, a professor of psychology, and a staple of the human experience that was both electric and fleeting.[6] No emotion was more primal and universal than the love for another person, he explained in *Collier's* in 1924, defining it as a form of energy that one could and should tap into:

> To fall in love is to receive through one's self the full current of the great creative urge of the world, which for the time being transforms one's whole vital mechanism. Like the lightning, this force is of tremendous strength, yet it may be turned aside by a speck of dust or a breath of wind. Chance and occasion determine where it strikes.[7]

It appeared, however, that more couples were getting married without a single spark of real love. There was greater opportunity to do this in the Roaring Twenties, at least in major American cities, as money and social status escalated in importance, especially among the well to do. In New York, notably, a fair number of society figures were marrying for financial gain and/or prestige, with love taking a backseat to such wants. Using fictitious names, Mrs. Philip Lydig wrote a tell-all for *Redbook* in 1926 that revealed how members of high society in that city had pursued such "loveless unions" and found themselves regretting their decision. "There are, of course, in fashionable life, some happy marriages of young people who fall in love naturally, in spite of their wealth, and live together as contentedly as any married couples anywhere," she wrote, "but there are few of them." The American rich were acting much like European royalty and aristocracy when seeking suitable mates, it could be said, with love between the parties often not even a consideration.[8]

Social conventions in this country were different from those in Europe, however, making it difficult or impossible for those Americans who had wed for reasons other than love to find romance outside of their marriage. Here, Lydig believed, "marriage without love is a suicide compact," with "spiritual and moral and often physical death for both husband and wife" awaiting those who chose that path. All kinds of unhealthy emotions were put in play when money or social standing was the basis for marriage, her experience showed, with divorce and sorrow the natural results. "They seem to me to be invariably haunted and unhappy," she observed of those who had never loved their ex-husband or -wife, with many a dinner party in New York and Newport filled with such troubled souls. The all-the-rage fashion of rich American girls wedding titled foreigners was also a mistake, Lydig held, another example of "marriages of ambition" that were more often than not doomed from the start.[9]

With all this social jockeying, it was easy to forget that, at its most basic level, romantic love could be seen as essentially a trick of nature to entice people to perpetuate the species. Creating a strong emotional bond between a man and a woman, along with a sexual attraction, was a clever device used by nature to induce them to reproduce, making love, more than anything else, a biological phenomenon. Why then had love assumed a position in society that went far beyond its role in mating? Why could people of the same gender fall in love just as easily given that it was not possible for them to reproduce? Did nature play this same trick on animals to get them to reproduce? Such questions made it clear that there was more to love than its biological function, and that as a human emotion it operated in ways that perhaps could never be fully understood.[10]

Just defining love was, as some of the brightest minds in history knew very well, a difficult at best challenge as its meaning mutated in the transformative 1920s. As part of its long-running series "Forum Definitions," in which the magazine targeted to and read by the educated public examined a particular term to try to get a better understanding of its meanings, *Forum* selected "love" in August 1927. The conceit of the series was to invite readers to submit their own definitions (with a prize awarded to those deemed the best), an exercise that fully illustrated how differently Americans viewed the term. "As was to be expected, 'Love' proved a magnet drawing out hundreds of poetic and analytical attempts at definition," the editor of the magazine introduced the piece, noting that several readers asserted that the word was impossible to define but one knew it when one felt it. Love was literally all over the map, with Americans from coast to coast taking the time and effort to write their definition, mail it to the magazine's offices in New York, and view the term as positive ("the mother of altruism"), negative ("one hundred per cent selfishness"), and everything in between.[11]

The winning submissions did indeed lean toward the poetic, often referencing what were believed to be heavenly qualities embedded in the emotion. For first prize winner M.T. Dunten of Olympia, Washington, love was "that dazzling garment, fashioned from ideals, which cloaks biogenic necessity and [was] so ... rare and elusive that it is counterfeited by knaves for sale to fools." For second prize winner Jocelyn Kline of Bovina, Mississippi, love was "the desire of the individual to unite his being with another and thus escape through oblivion or illusion the burden of existence." While third prize winner James Ferguson of Pasadena, California, proposed that love in its truest, purest form was "divine" and fourth prize winner Robert E. Farndon of New Rochelle, New York, conceived it as "the everlasting light," other readers recognized its darker side. "It is life's most tender emotion, yet it can be, and frequently is, its most cruel," thought fifth prize winner Stephen S. Baker of Lincoln, Nebraska, nicely capturing the dualistic and even paradoxical nature of love.[12]

Not just ordinary Americans but some of the most renowned critics of the day weighed in on the subject of love as it became clear that its defining attributes were in flux. Locating the current state of love in America within historical context was particularly helpful, as it revealed the degree to which how much had changed with regard to the emotion over the past generation. Writing for the *Atlantic Monthly* in 1928, for example, Joseph Wood Krutch made the case that love was not that long ago "the greatest and most elaborate of our creations," but that was no longer true. Like other values that had flourished in the Victorian era such as patriotism, self-sacrifice, respectability, and honor, he argued, love had lost much of its currency in the modern age. With the more rational and analytical view of life that emerged after the First

World War, love had been largely stripped of its mystical qualities, a loss that Krutch believed was regrettable. A few decades earlier, love played an even greater role in Americans' lives than religion, he held, and the erosion of the former represented an "atheism in the human soul" that was analogous to the decline of the latter. "Whatever else love may still be,—game, puerility, or wry joke played by the senses and the imagination upon the intellect,—it no longer is the ultimate self-justifying value which once it was," Krutch maintained, concluding that "a color has faded from our palette."[13]

The Wide Pastures of Free Love

That love was said to have faded from America's palette since the end of World War I had much to do with the greater sexual freedom being expressed, especially among the nation's youth. Motion pictures were both reflecting and helping to shape new attitudes toward non-marital sex, a practice that was seen by some as in clear opposition to traditional, courtship-based love. Almost a decade before the passage of the Motion Picture Production Association (MPAA) Code that was adopted by movie studios in 1930 as an attempt to "maintain social and community values," Hollywood made efforts to regulate itself in its depiction of both sex and crime. (The Code was generally not enforced until 1934, however.) In 1921, Jesse Lasky, an executive at the Famous Players studio, issued a list of fourteen "don'ts" in the making of motion pictures, with other studios setting their own similar rules regarding content. A good number of these "don'ts" related to "free love" or non-marital sex, something that was becoming increasingly seen as a direct threat to domestic life in America. "These are sad days for the scribes," the *Los Angeles Times* noted that year, as "no longer can they gallop in the wide pastures of free love or venture into the gilded hallways of crookdom." Included on Lasky's list were "No story of irregular love affairs unless to convey a moral lesson" and "No unnecessary prolonged love scenes," each of these situations deemed "insidious and demoralizing."[14]

The studios' effort at self-regulation was designed to preempt the kind of censorship that was being considered by Washington lawmakers. By including scenes of free love in (silent) films, Hollywood was in effect endorsing non-marital sexuality, more conservative politicians believed, with moviegoers more apt to engage in such behavior after going to the pictures. "Free love, dissipation, debauchery and drunkenness" were running rampant in the motion picture industry, claimed Senator Henry L. Myers, a Democrat from Montana, in 1922, urging his fellow members of the Senate to pass the bills he had proposed that would nip such cinematic depravity in the bud. Ex-Postmaster General Will Hays had recently been appointed president of the newly created Motion Picture Producers and Distributors of America, an organization whose mission was to improve the public image of the movie industry, especially after the alleged rape and murder of Virginia Rappe by film star Roscoe "Fatty" Arbuckle. Such events were inspired by "ideas of romance and crime" in motion pictures, Myers asserted, reason for Federal intervention despite the public's opposition to censorship.[15]

The arraignment of "Madame" Edith Maida Lessing that same year only added to the perception that Los Angeles was the national capital of free love. Federal authorities were holding Lessing, the "head of a local love cult," according to the *Los Angeles Times*, on the charge of sending obscene literature through the mail. Lessing was also accused of attempting to establish a "free love colony" in Los Angeles that would be based on the principles outlined in her pamphlet *Civil Marriage—Why It Should Be Abolished*. Lessing had put thousands of copies of the yellow pamphlet in the mail, some of them arriving at the homes of hundreds of public officials, bankers, businessmen, and clubwomen who were, needless to say, not pleased to read the "salacious" material. Among Lessing's proposals was the creation of a "Temple of Hymen" that would replace the institution of marriage, an idea that more religious citizens understandably found rather alarming. Lessing happened to be employed as a nurse for two small children, leading authorities to conclude that she was leading a double life.[16]

The saga of Edith Lessing continued for the next few years. In 1925, after serving eighteen months in a women's reformatory, she was again arrested on charges of sending obscene literature through the mail. This time it was a pamphlet called *The Syllabus* that, much like her previous one, set forth "radical free-love ideas in unvarnished terms," officials charged. Again, many prominent Los Angelenos were recipients of the new pamphlet, and it is safe to say that they were not persuaded by her claim that in writing and distributing the tract she was "serving God and humanity."[17] When offered probation by a federal judge in court eight months later if she agreed to cease her mission of free love, Lessing chose instead a two-year term in prison. "I have no alternative but to enlighten the world with my teachings," she told the judge, hoping that her prison time would serve as inspiration for others to join her cause. Interestingly, it was only one of many articles in *The Syllabus* that postal inspectors determined to be indecent and obscene: her support for "elastic unions" between men and women that government officials held "stripped the age-old alliance of its spiritual grandeur and suffered it to become purely physical."[18]

While Los Angeles was clearly the epicenter of free love in America, officials in other cities declared their own war on non- or extra-marital sex in order to defend the sacred institution of marriage. In Chicago in 1923, for example, Judge Timothy Hurley announced he would not hear any divorce cases involving a "triangle" of parties unless the "erring mate" came forward for prosecution. Free love, in this case defined as an extramarital affair, was responsible for 75 percent of divorces in Cook County, Hurley claimed, and he was intent on reducing that percentage by tossing the guilty party in jail on statutory grounds. "Free love never will gain my sanction as long as I sit as chancellor of this court," Hurley proclaimed, tired of seeing "Other Persons" as the principal factor for a couple seeking divorce. The judge considered the straying partner to be a "love moonshiner" (it was Prohibition), and he planned to use the full extent of the law to reduce this violation of marital vows. "Not another illicit alliance or clandestine love affair will be condoned" while he served as judge, Hurley stated, hoping that the prospect of jail time would if nothing else make cheaters flee Cook County.[19]

It was another judge, however, Ben Lindsey of Denver, who elevated the subject of free love into a national kerfuffle. In an address to that city's City Club in 1927, Lindsey claimed that what he called "bootlegging" (another Prohibition reference) in love and marriage was becoming so common in the country that the institution was being destabilized and weakened. The desire for sex was instinctive and natural, he stated, making it no surprise that individuals not interested in getting married or who were in sexually unfulfilling marriages were adopting a philosophy of free love or embarking on what was sometimes called a "trial marriage." With its rigid conventions regarding sexuality, it was American society that was at fault in the matter, Lindsey boldly asserted, pointing to the clergy as exacerbating the problem. "It is simply a struggle between convention and man-made laws and nature and God-made laws, and nature and God are winning out," he said in his address, going on to challenge local ministers to a debate on the issue.[20]

Combining the nation's two most volatile topics—sex and religion—Lindsey was not surprisingly getting a lot of attention for his thesis on "free love" and its potential consequences to traditional love and marriage. (He had already written a few magazine articles on the subject that had further spread his ideas, and his book *The Companionate Marriage* would soon be published.) Critics across the country attacked the judge and his views, mistakenly believing that he was advocating free love rather than attempting to find a solution to what he considered to be a serious problem. "Because I care so much for the sanctity and permanence of the American home, I am bitterly opposed to 'free love' and so-called 'trial marriages' as they exist under the present marriage code," he said in a statement a couple of weeks after his address in Denver. Birth control and what sociologists referred to as "companionate marriage" (in which a couple agreed not to have children and could divorce by mutual consent without financial obligation) were two ways to address Americans' obvious interest in free love, he added, ideas that likely didn't sway his many critics.[21]

Undeterred, Lindsey went on the road to speak before audiences likely to be friendly to his unconventional ideas about love and marriage. At the Los Angeles Breakfast Club, for example, he again differentiated between companionate marriage and free love, and made it clear he had not coined either term. Still, he continued to endorse what he called "voluntary parenthood" and "divorce by mutual consent," thinking both the discouraging of birth control for a married couple and our "'til-death-do-us-part" marriage vows were bad practices that should be changed.[22] Lindsey said much the same thing in his new book. In fact, such unions based on those two principles already existed in significant numbers in this country, he pointed out in *The Companionate Marriage*, and his only mission was to have them officially sanctioned.[23]

Jungle Passions

Indeed, those resistant to any kind of love other than the romantic one expressed exclusively through marital monogamy pushed back against Lindsey's kind of thinking. Just a couple of months after the Denver judge's attempt to clarify his position, Richard C. Cabot, a professor of social work and medicine at Harvard, spoke to a group of Radcliffe students that directly challenged the supposition that traditional marriage was out of date and out of sync with modern times. "Free-love is a worn-out institution," he declared, trying to turn the tables on Lindsey and those who agreed with him. In fact, Cabot argued, there was no better time and place in history than contemporary America for a couple to fall in love and get married. People could now discuss virtually anything before taking "the fatal step," he posited, something often not possible for previous generations. As well, young women of the modern age were simply more informed on the subjects of love and sex than their Victorian-era mothers or grandmothers had been, Cabot thought, and the former rarely went into a marriage thinking they could reform a less than desirable husband, as once had been common.[24]

Devout Christians, however, contended that free love was much more than "worn-out." Along with war, loveless sexuality posed the greatest danger to young adults, speakers at the 1927 International Christian Endeavor convention in Cleveland held. "The jazz age, strident with jungle music, fetid with jungle odors, sensuous with jungle motions, and inflamed with jungle passions" had created an ideal climate for contemporary substitutes for love and marriage to thrive, according to the Rev. William Hiram Foulkes, the pastor of the Old First Church of Newark, New Jersey. Happily, he thought, "trial marriage, with unchaste courtship and easy divorces" would be discarded in the dustbin of history, where it deserved to be.[25] Similar language could be heard from speakers at the annual convention of the National Council of Catholic Women in Washington, D.C., that same year. The Right Rev. Maurice F. McAuliffe, Auxiliary Bishop of Hartford, Connecticut, condemned the "naturalistic doctrinaires who glibly advocate the companionate trial marriage and free love," clearly having Judge Lindsey in mind.[26]

Although some Americans had no doubt subscribed to the tenets of companionate marriage, many religious leaders found the concept incomprehensible. There simply weren't two sides on the issue, Bishop William Manning told a group of Broadway actors in 1928 who had gathered at the Broadhurst Theatre during that year's Holy Week, meaning that any alteration of the traditional marriage contract was fundamentally incompatible with Christianity.[27] Over the next couple of years, in fact, Lindsey continued to try to find a person of the cloth with whom to debate the issue, but there were no takers. Dr. Milo Gates, dean of the Cathedral of St. John the Divine in New York, was one such notable person to decline Lindsey's challenge. "There are certain things which are not debatable," Gates stated, likening the Church's absolutist stance on the matter to "the axioms in mathematics." Moreover, he claimed, 99 percent of the 3,000 marriages at which he had officiated were "happy and successful," evidence that suggested that Lindsey's proposal was not only theologically challenged but entirely unnecessary.[28]

The attack on free love in America soon went to an entirely new level when charges were made that Communists were promoting the lifestyle through propaganda targeted to college students. Such was the claim made by Mrs. B.L. Robinson, president of the Massachusetts Public Interests League, in a talk titled "Alien Propaganda in Our Colleges and Schools" that was delivered to the Women's Political Study Club of White Plains (New York) in November 1927. Communists of the world were behind the creation of organizations such as the Fellowship of Youth for Peace and the National Federation of Students on many campuses across the United States, she alleged, as well as for the course adoption of Bertrand Russell's book *What I Believe*, which made a case for birth control for the unmarried and for open marriages. That book was reported to have been part of the curricula at almost two hundred colleges in the United States, including the freshman English course at Smith College (whose president defended its use).[29]

The idea that college students' sexual activity at the expense of love was politically motivated was echoed a few years later by Mrs. Reuben Ross Holloway, chairman of national defense for the State Daughters of the American Revolution. There was a youth movement afoot on college campuses, including those of Bryn Mawr, Yale, Vassar, Barnard, Dartmouth, and George Washington University, that was responsible for spreading the practice of free love, she told members of her organization at its annual conference in Baltimore in 1930. Holloway did not make clear exactly which youth movement (e.g., Communist, German, or American) was behind the subversive activity, but she did add that a "cult of nakedness" was part of the effort to "undermine the Government and for all it stands—the home, the foundation of the country." "Yours is the fault when your children return to you as atheists, socialists, inveigled into young political clubs and leagues and supporters of free love," she warned parents of college students who did not ask who their professors were and what they were teaching.[30]

Other ultra-patriots were very worried that the nation's youth was receiving a higher education in loveless sex and other un–American activities. "Certain professors" were offering students instruction in not just free love, companionate marriage, and atheism but the intermingling of white and Negro races, claimed Col. Edwin Marshall Hadley, former Illinois National Guardsman and an officer in the military intelligence unit of the United States Army. Hadley was also the author of *Sinister Shadows*, which argued that Communist propaganda was a menacing presence at American colleges and universities. By steering young adults away from traditional love and marriage and towards the seductive power of unrestrained sexuality, Hadley believed, the foundation of American life would be undermined, allowing what he called the "Soviet brand of internationalism" to expand its reach.[31]

Well before postwar McCarthyism, fear and paranoia about a Communist threat to the American way of life could thus be easily detected.[32] Interrupting young people's inclination to fall in love, get married, and have children was seen as one of the goals of Communists as a means to weaken our system predicated on consumer capitalism centered around family and home. "Sinister shadows" and a "red fog" (the title of another book alleging Communist propaganda had infiltrated the nation's colleges and universities) were believed to be especially prevalent at the most elite institutions, presumably because it was students of those schools who were most likely to be the leaders of tomorrow. Columbia University in New York, for example, was a hotbed of free love, according to the Women's Auxiliary of the Episcopal

Church in Chicago. In 1932, that organization sent a letter of protest to Nicholas Butler, president of the university, after hearing that a book supposedly advocating free love was being used in an undergraduate course in family relations. Ruth Reed's *The Modern Family* challenged the idea that "home and family [were] a bulwark of civilization," the letter read, and the group was shocked that "a Christian and churchman" like Dr. Butler would allow the book to be required reading. Butler responded by saying that the charge that free love was being taught at Columbia was "an absolute invention," and that the book written by the Mount Holyoke College professor was not even used in the course.[33]

The Magnificent Intruder

With the publication of a report by the Bureau of Social Hygiene of New York City in 1928, some much-needed science was injected into the contentious subject of love. In part because of the cultural inhibitions surrounding that particular dimension of life, researchers had previously not ventured into the uncharted territory of romance. As well, great strides were currently being made in sociology (the Lynd's "Middletown" study would be published the following year), and co-authors G.V. Hamilton and Kenneth Macgowan took full advantage of the cutting-edge research techniques being developed in the field. The findings of the study were published in *Harper's* magazine, and were closely examined by academics and laypeople alike, especially because they revealed insights into the typically furtive and clandestine world of love affairs among both men and women.[34]

In their study that took four years to complete, Hamilton and Macgowan probed the past and present love lives of one hundred men and one hundred women who were married (but not to each other). Most intriguing, perhaps, was the finding that the 200 subjects had had an average of seven love affairs up that point in time, certainly more than one would have thought (now and then). Also interesting was that the number of reported love affairs was the same regardless of the relative happiness of the subjects' respective marriages. Expectedly, most of the romances took place before marriage, but a relatively high number of both husbands and wives reported that they had strayed on at least one occasion (29 percent of men and 41 percent of women, surprisingly). Subjects were asked almost four hundred questions ranging from their age at each of their love affairs to whether their partner was older or younger and their physical appearance to the extent of their "spooning."[35]

The report from the Bureau of Social Hygiene (of which John D. Rockefeller, Jr., was the chairman) plainly revealed that Americans generally had much busier love lives than popularly believed in the late 1920s. Some individuals no doubt met their one true love early in life, got married, and stayed true to their spouse, but the experience of many others demonstrated that this traditional narrative of romance was by now largely a myth. Cracks in the foundation of love in America could even be seen in women's magazines at the time. One might have thought that, given their readership, those publications would have been strong supporters of traditional love and marriage, but this was often not the case. Women penning articles for *Ladies' Home Journal* and *Good Housekeeping* were just as apt to criticize domestic life as to praise it, likely in part because the writers themselves were often choosing a nontraditional path by putting their careers first. Mary Garden's 1930 article titled "Love and Marriage" in *Ladies' Home Journal* was quite typical of the rather censorious view of love taken by between-the-wars women writing for top publications (that were, need it be said, read mostly by housewives). "Love—the magnificent intruder—the erotic dictator—the divine accident of life!," she began her story, no doubt making many a reader (including myself) think that a treatise lauding the wonderful attributes of love would follow.[36]

Readers quickly learned that in her poetic introduction, however, Garden was referring to how the emotion was popularly perceived instead of how she herself interpreted it. Garden was a famous opera singer (she was often referred to as "the Sarah Bernhardt of opera") whose reputation as a diva was fully deserved. Journalists often asked the never wed Garden what her thoughts were on the subject of love and marriage (it was typically the first or last question in an interview), admittedly puzzled why she had chosen to travel the world singing for large audiences rather than have settled down and raised a family like most women of her generation. Such journalists were no doubt taken aback by her intense stance on the topic. As a young woman, Garden had made a conscious decision to "refuse to allow myself ever to be dominated or controlled by so ironic, so transient, so despotic an emotion," as the now 56-year-old star expressed it in her article, explaining her reasons for making such an uncompromising choice.[37]

Garden had actually been in love a number of times in her life, she confessed, the first time no less with a Russian prince while living in Paris. One day, however, she found herself thoroughly out of love with this "lord of creation," not precisely sure how and why this complete turnaround happened. "Every woman, at some period, has gone through this experience," she claimed, citing "the exigencies of circumstances" as entirely capable of dissolving the strongest of bonds between two people. The second time Garden fell was a prime case of love at first sight. At an afternoon tea at a friend's house, she felt "a tremendous pull on the atmosphere" and found her eyes locked on those of a man. "This man is going to be an influence in my life," she immediately said to herself, an inner thought that many have reported when experiencing the initial blush of love. The two shared a passionate romance until it was time for Garden to make her American debut after training and beginning her career in Europe. The man soon followed her to the United States but it was too late. "When next I saw him it was as though I were looking on the face of a stranger," she recalled, the magic clearly gone.[38]

As one could readily tell from these two experiences, it was the unpredictability and mercurial nature of love that made Garden permanently jettison the emotion from her life. Love "acted without laws [or] a governing principle," she held, concluding that, unlike other complex concepts like honesty or justice, "there is nothing to anchor it." Despite her obviously critical assessment of love, she still recognized its undeniable sway within the rich pageant of life. "Love is the most tremendous, the most powerful and stirring of all emotions," she acknowledged, her decision to opt out of the condition not taking anything away from it as a force of nature. As a feminist and self-described "great *artiste*," however, Garden was not about to allow her love for any man trap her into what she believed was the stacked deck of marriage. "She has made it her first credo—her worship—her religion," Garden wrote of love for most women, and "when it shipwrecks her she sits among the ruins praying for death."[39]

For Garden, it was the unreliability and unsustainability of love that contributed heavily toward her decision to choose career over marriage. (The two were considered to be generally mutually exclusive through the first half of the 20th century for women.) Love certainly existed, but keeping it going for an extended period of time was just not feasible, she believed. "It [love] is there, a part of the mightiness of a human world, but that searing, blinding emotion of ecstasy that takes two people in its grasp to be maintained and prolonged in physical completeness throughout a lifetime, I do not think possible," the opera singer wrote. In addition to what she saw as the capricious nature of love, Garden's devotion to her art made the prospect of any long term, committed relationship untenable. Women "cannot serve two masters," she held, thinking that "divided forces are what make for mediocrity."[40]

Garden's challenge to the prevailing notion that love was, at least for women, enough to ask out of life was a bold one given the standards of the time. There was more to life than love, she insisted, and allowing it (or any other emotion) to dictate what one did or didn't do was not being true to oneself. The world was a very big place filled with many fascinating things to see and do, she told readers, especially for women now that they had freedoms that largely did not exist for previous generations. "I love the consciousness of power and people possessed with a sheer passion for living, like myself," she closed, intending to continue to use her gift to explore all that there was to explore.[41]

Although she rejected the conventions of love, Mary Garden had a keen understanding of the role it was expected to play in a typical American woman's life. Because she was financially independent and genuinely loved her craft and the things that went along with it, Garden was unusually privileged to rebuff the traditional path of romance that more often than not led to marriage and family. However, too many perfectly average women were making compromises when it came to love, others argued, and in the process finding themselves unsatisfied and unhappy. While authority figures often recommended that both men and women prioritize common sense over great passion in choosing a partner for life, outliers warned of the psychological consequences that awaited those who put mind over heart. Such was the view of an anonymous writer for the *Saturday Evening Post* in 1933 who made a strong case that women should not settle for anything less than true love:

> The American girl belittles the importance of love in her life. She takes what comes to her door, and builds of the shifting sands of substitutes. And every day she develops neuroses, cults and breakdowns. No woman can live without love. Love is a woman's life.[42]

Whether undependable and limiting, as career women like Mary Garden held, or too old-fashioned and impractical given the hard times of the Depression, as this latter writer implied, love was hardly the state of bliss Americans liked to imagine it was.

This Priceless Possession

Despite all the criticism being directed to it, romantic love retained an elevated, even exalted position in modern life that transcended ordinary existence. In his 1930 article "Should We Leave Romance Out of Marriage?" for *Forum*, Robert C. Binkley made a convincing case that love was a "a cult, a creed, and a definite set of beliefs" whose principles were reinforced by popular novels, songs, and movies.[43] Binkley went on to neatly describe what he called the "magical potency" of love in Western society:

> It guarantees happiness to those who possess it. It operates as a panacea for all ills, a compensation for all misfortunes. It is inexhaustible. It burns eternally fresh and

unchanged. So precious is it that one may count the world well lost if only he acquires this priceless possession.[44]

Much of the magical potency of romantic love had to do with the idea that it came only once to each individual. The key was thus to recognize when "the real thing" came along and seize the opportunity before it was too late. The impatient married the wrong person, while others waited too long before marrying the right person; each of these unfortunate situations led to unhappiness and possibly divorce. Successful marriages were thus more than anything else a product of correct identification, Binkley held, with no shortage of imitations, counterfeits, and pretenders making the enterprise of romance much like an obstacle course that one had to cleverly negotiate. Only time would tell if a person made the right choice, as sooner or later it would become clear whether each party had found his or her own true love in life. The corollary to such thinking was, rather strangely, that love was in control of the individual rather than the other way around. "Man is its servant, not its master," as Binkley put it, with love "not something that he does, but something that happens to him." Humans were slaves to this particular emotion, this argument went, a notion to which many who found themselves making life-altering decisions because of their love for a particular person could relate.[45]

The idea that it was unlikely that one would find the person of one's dreams, and thus both women and men should instead take someone who seemed simply compatible, was a popular one. Since the odds were remote that anyone would bump into his or her "soul mate," experts advised, it was wise to choose a person who appeared to make good marriage material. "That the legitimate dream of every one of us is so seldom fulfilled is, of course, due to the fact that there are so few even quasi-perfect human beings that two of them seldom appear at the same place at the same time," wrote Jessica G. Cosgrave in *Good Housekeeping* in 1928, words of comfort perhaps to the many readers questioning their decision to have "settled" with their responsible but not very exciting husband. A mate's stability and "reasonableness" were the keys to a good and happy marriage, young women waiting for their dreamboat to come along were told, with those thinking that their white knight was right around the corner running the risk of dreaded spinsterhood.[46]

In his own examination of romance and marriage in *Forum* in 1931, W. Béran Wolfe noted the degree to which "domestic infelicity" had risen in recent years because of Americans' tendency to put practicality over passion. People used to just put up with unhappy marriages, told by men of the cloth that such things were simply a function of God's will, but now all kinds of professionals were serving as fonts of advice on the matter as the divorce rate spiraled. Sociologists, teachers, psychiatrists, and physicians (like Wolfe), and even economists had become authorities on love, often using scientific investigations to inform their opinions. Along with the greater attention being given to domestic discord was the realization that the basic model of love and marriage in the United States could very well be a flawed one. Americans' belief that the presence of romantic love would naturally lead to a happy marriage was fundamentally wrong, Wolfe and others held, as it was putting the cart before the horse. A marriage between two well-matched people led to love, not the other way around, an idea that ran completely contrary to the way that Americans typically approached the whole thing.[47]

Popular culture and even much of the guidance from authoritative sources were also doing no favors to those convinced that finding one's true love was a direct route to marital bliss. "As a nation we are subjected to a veritable barrage of romantically infantile notions," Wolfe continued, with few able to be resistant to "this enfilade of movies, magazines, pulpit texts, and Presidential messages." From an early age, Americans were immersed in what Wolfe called "romantic twaddle," making it not surprising that by the time they were ready to settle down they were wholly unprepared for the realities of married life. Americans were trained to think that they and a Prince Charming (or its female equivalent) would once wedded live happily ever after, this grand illusion not unlike a child's belief in Santa Claus. "Love is the *result* [his emphasis] of years of cooperation, of mutual enjoyment and mutual suffering," Wolfe made clear, the tendency to use it as a premise for marriage steering young adults down the wrong path.[48]

A Perfect Product

Henry Morton Robinson thought much the same way. Writing for *North American Review* a few years later, he argued that Americans had become so swept up by love that it now served as "our national melancholia." "Romantic love has become the governing fantasy of our age," he maintained, "the avowed and overt end of millions of lives." Again, it was those in the entertainment business who fueled this mass hysteria, knowing that idealized love was a very salable product. "Shrewd exploiters of the public appetite keep that vision dancing erotically before us," Robinson continued, with boundless sexual pleasure the subtext of fictitious romantic interludes. (Remember that the beginnings of the sexual revolution were still three decades away, making the prospect of readily available, socially sanctioned sex an attractive one.) Adults were acting like children when pursuing what he called the "Nirvana of love," especially when wrapped up in the magic of Hollywood, the stirring words of a good novelist, or the exaggerated promises of Madison Avenue.[49]

Other critics offered their thoughts on how the ubiquity of faux love was watering down the genuine article. "Love as we meet it in the films, in the magazines, in the press, and to a certain extent in modern fiction is a synthetic emotion," Clemence Dane wrote for *Forum* in 1935, "a sentimental delusion from which we do not appear able to escape." Part of the problem was that there was simply too much artificial love in American culture, diluting its meaning and potency. "It makes it harder for you to know true love when you see it," she thought, the appearance that it was "a pleasant and easy adventure" masking the fact that it was "the most powerful and overwhelming of human emotions." Interestingly, Dane also believed that Americans' demand for love stories was taking away their individuality, and was thus contrary to our national identity rooted in independence and a celebration of the self.[50]

Following in the footsteps of his countryman Alexis de Tocqueville and those of other visitors to the United States who had made keen observations of the national character, Raoul de Roussy de Sales wrote a piece titled "Love in America" for the *Atlantic Monthly* in 1938. Like Tocqueville, de Sales was able to perceive American attitudes and behavior in a way that no native could. While living for some time in New York, the French journalist and historian was particularly struck by how problematic the subject of love was in this country. "Nowhere else can one find a people devoting so much time and so much study to the question of the relationship between men and women," he stated, and "nowhere else is there such concern about the fact that this relationship does not make for perfect happiness." For de Sales, love was a lot like democracy, each great in theory but each also something that did not work too well in actual practice. Because they were both complex concepts and necessarily involved more than one person, love and democracy were difficult to manage and coordinate, he felt, making it highly likely that neither would function especially well even with considerable effort.[51]

While many American critics had observed that the ways in which love were depicted by Hollywood gave the romantically involved too high or simply wrong expectations, de Sales remarked how the movies had created a false impression to foreigners like himself. Based on the American movies he had seen in France before coming to the United States, he had been led to believe that the only reason for men and women to get married here was for love. Furthermore, love was wholesome and genuine in America, he had assumed, with real life couples living happily ever after much like the characters in the pictures did following whatever obstacles the screenwriter had put in their way to make the story interesting. Not just American cinema but radio was positively love-struck, he concluded after listening to local New York stations. "No country in the world consumes such a fabulous amount of love songs," he thought, the music and advertisements on the radio melding together to create a seamless blend of romantic commercialism. "In America the idea seems to be that love, like much else, should be sold to the public, because it is a good thing," de Sales wrote, our idealized view of the emotion just another part of the nation's "optimistic outlook on life."[52]

Although most observers of the national scene considered the advent of modernity to be the catalyst for Americans' love problems, de Sales argued that it was specifically the arrival of psychoanalysis on our shores. Before Freud, "America lived in a blissful state of puritanical repression," he wrote, with "love, as a sentiment, glorified and sanctified by marriage." The popularization of Freud's theories made love appear to be real and attainable as long as one made some mental adjustments, however, this the source of the problem. The standardization of consumer culture in the 1920s also contributed heavily to Americans' high expectations regarding love, according to de Sales, with shoppers of romance seeking "a perfect product." "They want to get out of love as much enjoyment, comfort, safety, and general sense of satisfaction as one gets out of a well-balanced diet or a good plumbing installation," he wrote, the emotion viewed much like any other commodity.[53]

Finally, de Sales used another analogy to paint the not very pretty picture of love in America. In this country, he had observed, those using a cookbook to prepare a meal tended to follow the recipe as precisely as possible, believing this would result in the best tasting food. In France, however, cooks typically used recipes just as a general guide, knowing the meal would come out just fine (and better, perhaps) if one didn't follow the instructions to the letter. Americans approached love much like their cooking, a formula de Sales described as "proper ingredients properly measured," something that explained a lot about the dissatisfaction many couples felt in their relationship. The French, on the other hand, knew that love, like eating, did not operate along the lines of an automatic formula, so no attempt was made on their part to strive for perfection in either pursuit. In Europe, love was treated as an art while in the States it was considered as a science, one could say, an important distinction that revealed why Americans found much about romance to be wholly unappetizing.[54]

De Sales's and other critics' observations about the impact of cinematic love on Americans' love lives appeared to be as acute as ever. Through the 1930s, what was sometimes referred to as "screwball love" was featured in the flippant comedies of that genre. Following the wild success of Frank Capra's 1934 *It Happened One Night* (one of the last movies to be made before the MPAA began enforcing the 1930 production code), screwball love could be seen in movies such as *Mr. Deeds Goes to Town* (1936) and *Yes, My Darling Daughter* (1939). Also popular in the thirties was what Carlisle Jones of the *New York Herald Tribune* called the "'treat 'em rough' school of romance" that had virtually been invented by James Cagney in *The Public Enemy* (1931). By the end of the decade, however, it was more what Jones referred to as the "if you would kiss me now it would save a lot of time" school of romance that could be seen on the silver screen. John Garfield and Priscilla Lane were Hollywood's go-to actors for this genre, with the pair co-starring in the recent films *Four Daughters* (1938), *Daughters Courageous* (1939), and *Dust Be My Destiny* (1939). "Consciously or unconsciously, we ape our screen favorites, and their manners in love," Jones believed, thinking that "'if you would kiss me now it would save a lot of time' may be a cue line in half a million romances before summer [of 1939] is officially ended."[55] World events were about to make that remark more than an amusing quip, as another era of love in America began.

Chapter 2

America's No. 1 Problem?, 1940–1959

"The miracle of human love lies in the fact that upon a very simple instinct, desire, are built edifices of the most complex and delicate feelings."
—Andres Maurois, 1940

In October 1940, readers of *Good Housekeeping* were likely surprised to come across an article with the unlikely title "Never Marry for Love." Many and likely most Americans did indeed get married after falling in love at the time, making the very questioning of what was one of the staple experiences of life in this country odd and perhaps a little disturbing. According to the author of the article, however, love and marriage were polarized and often incompatible forces; the former was an almost entirely irrational state of being, while the latter was a legally-binding institution that demanded considerable reasonable and sensible thought if it was going to work out.[1] "The main trouble with marrying for love is that you run the risk of staying in love," Arthur Gordon wrote, thinking that managing a relationship while under the full effects of the emotion was a difficult if not impossible task to ask of people. "It's high time that somebody passed a law making it a misdemeanor to marry for love," he only half-joked, concluding that it was no wonder that many couples who had wed while under such an unsound mental condition confronted problems somewhere along the way.[2]

As in the 1920s and 1930s, love in America during the war and postwar years was viewed suspiciously, its unpredictability and volatility making it something best avoided if at all possible. We tend to remember the World War II years as romantic ones, with wives and girlfriends happy to not sit under the apple tree with anyone but their respective man fighting bravely overseas. Love on the homefront was hardly such a sweet affair, however, as the between-the-wars disenchantment with cupid continued in the early

1940s. Love may have been "America's no. 1 problem," according to *Science Digest* in 1943, a sentiment that accelerated in the 1950s when logic and rationalism ruled the day.[3] Love emerged as an area of serious study in the postwar years, as social scientists devoted considerable time and energy to gaining a better understanding of that and other human emotions. While some affirmed the unique ability of love to connect us to other people, others argued that this particular emotion was a deleterious force that threatened the very American way of life. Either way, love in America could not be ignored at midcentury, as the strong feelings that surrounded the subject increased in intensity.

A Mere Cream Puff

As always, Hollywood was considered much to blame for contributing heavily to Americans' love problems, now because of movie stars' habit of taking marriage (and divorce) very lightly. For decades, movies had shaped Americans' views regarding love, principally by creating expectations that far exceeded the possibilities in real life. This was of course not Hollywood's fault as it was, after all, in the myth making business. But what could explain why the loves lives of movie stars themselves were an equivocal train wreck? A look at the world of Hollywood romance circa 1940 was indeed a frantic coming and going of characters not unlike what could be seen in a Marx Brothers movie. While shooting a film, it was not unusual for the male and female leads to get involved in a way that mimicked their fictitious one, although more often than not they did not live happily ever after as their characters did. Working long days closely together and often sharing love scenes with passionate kisses, stars frequently extended their cinematic relationship to their personal lives, at least until the next picture came along when they would do it all over again with someone else.[4]

The list of stars who had begun an affair while working together was a long one. Carole Lombard had met both of her future husbands on movie sets (William Powell in *Ladies' Man* and the still-married Clark Gable in *No Man of Her Own*), as did Joan Crawford (Douglas Fairbanks, Jr., in *Our Modern Maidens* and Franchot Tone in *Dancing Lady*). Other non-real and real cinematic pairings included Robert Taylor and Barbara Stanwyck (*His Brother's Wife*), Tyrone Power and Annabella (*Suez*), Vivien Leigh and Laurence Olivier (*Twenty-One Days*), Ronald Reagan and Jane Wyman (*Brother Rat*), and Lana Turner and Artie Shaw (*Dancing Co-Ed*). None of these marriages lasted long. The undisputed champion of serial Hollywood romance was George Brent, however, whose string of relationships involving his lead-

2. America's No. 1 Problem?, 1940–1959

Franchot Tone and Joan Crawford

Joan Crawford and Franchot Tone met while filming the 1933 *Today We Live*, married two years later, and divorced in 1939. Hollywood actors were (and remain) famous for falling in love on movie sets, but their real life romances were often not as successful as those of their cinematic characters. George Arents Collection, The New York Public Library. "Franchot Tone and Joan Crawford." *The New York Public Library Digital Collections*. http://digitalcollections.nypl.org/items/510d47e3-07e6-a3d9-e040-e00a18064a99

ing ladies included Ann Sheridan, Ruth Chatterton, Greta Garbo, and Bette Davis. Love was as illusory as that depicted in the movies, Americans could reasonably conclude when reading about the romantic doings of their favorites stars in fan magazines, a light-hearted affair in which someone else and seemingly better was always waiting in the wings.[5]

With America's entry in the war, however, Hollywood had the opportunity to at least in part redeem itself by making more serious films that affirmed the power of love. Stars still may have stayed on the merry-go-round of marriage and divorce in their personal lives, but wartime movies sent a clear message about what Americans were fighting and dying for. "Gone are the days when the movie makers could give us the saccharine pap that once substituted on the screen for the grand passion," Hedda Hopper wrote in her popular syndicated column "Looking at Hollywood" in 1943, thinking, "life is too real these days." The love scenes between Joel McCrea and Jean Arthur in *The More the Merrier* and Glenn Ford and Marguerite Chapman in *Destroyer* were indeed not bits of action one likely would have seen in the 1930s, when escapist films offered moviegoers a much needed break from the hard times of the Depression. "Love is something I have to hold on to," Ford's character (a Navy officer) says to Chapman's, telling her, "I may never have another chance." Similar expressions of love could be seen and heard in other wartime films including *So Proudly We Hail, Private Hargrove, What a Woman, Pin Up Girl*, and even Alfred Hitchcock's *Lifeboat*, which was set entirely in less than romantic circumstances.⁶

With millions of men and women involved in some kind of war effort, real love on the homefront was also a more earnest and complicated affair than it had been. In a piece called "How to Woo and Win a Strong Woman" published in *Tomorrow* magazine, David L. Cohn captured some of the complexities associated with romances between female war workers and men who were not serving overseas. "A woman who has spent months or years welding the plates of a destroyer or catching hot rivets on the wing and driving them into the steel sides of a tank isn't likely to swoon into a man's arms," he wrote, thinking that these real life Rosie the Riveters were "far more complex creatures than their grandmothers." Cohn advised men interested in attracting the attention of a war worker to avoid their standard virile persona in romantic situations now that things had been turned upside down. "In a world of strong women it is pointless to for him to pose as a strong man," he explained, suggesting that such wooers play the role of "the hurt and wounded boy for whom the world is too much to bear."⁷

Vivien Leigh and Laurence Olivier, seen here in the 1937 film *Fire Over England*. The two had begun an affair the previous year (each was married), providing an abundance of on-screen chemistry. They would marry in 1940 and divorce in 1960. George Arents Collection, The New York Public Library. "Fire Over England. Laurence Olivier as Michael Ingleby. Vivien Leigh as Cynthia Burleigh." *The New York Public Library Digital Collections.* http://digitalcollections.nypl.org/items/510d47e2-e8d4-a3d9-e040-e00a18064a99

Although he hailed from Mississippi, David Cohn was spending most of his time during the war as an advisor to the British Ministry of Information in Washington, D.C., where he was getting a lot of attention because of his frank thoughts about love in America. In fact, Cohn had just written a book titled *Love in America*, in which the unmarried man pulled no punches on the sensitive subject. "Americans are emotionally adolescent," went one of his observations, adding that in this country, sex was "a three-letter word meaning love." Both husbands and wives were typically dissatisfied with their respective mates, according to Cohn, with much of popular and consumer culture designed to capitalize on this vast sea of marital discontent. Newspaper columnists liberally doled out advice for the lovelorn (thousands of letters to them were reportedly received a day nationwide) but rarely provided any really useful information, as the problem of love in America ran too deep. Even Dorothy Dix, the queen of love columnists, conceded that most middle-aged couples found their spouses less than desirable, to put it mildly, and offered few solutions except to grin and bear it.[8]

With its title and image of a darting cupid on the book's cover, a browser may have thought that *Love in America* was a celebration of one of our favorite national pastimes. That was not the case. "Few peoples talk about love as much as Americans and few people write and sing about love as much as Americans," Cohn wrote, but "the final accolade which we can bestow upon anything is to give it the status of a problem." With chapter titles such as "My Wife's a Mystery to Me," "He's Just a Great Big Boy," and "Do American Men Like Women?," it was clear that the author perceived the country's landscape of love as a rocky terrain.[9] (The answer to the latter chapter's title was "No.") Interestingly, in their Middletown studies, the Lynds put forth a similar if less acerbic observation. Husbands found their wives "largely incapable of facing facts or doing hard thinking," hardly a sentiment that reflected the kind of love that one might expect between partners for life. Spouses rarely talked to each other except about practical matters, Cohn also noted, another sign that love was a rare commodity in the typical American marriage.[10]

While accounts of the less savory side of marital life was a common feature of novels, it was unusual at the time to see such criticism in nonfiction. Husbands felt comfortable and acted confidently at work but, knowing little about women, behaved childishly at home. Wives, meanwhile, fell victim to the beauty industry and other marketers, not knowing how to use their abilities and or employ their potential power. As others had done, Cohn contrasted love in America with the way it was expressed in Europe, a comparison that one reviewer of the book nicely captured. In the Old World, "love is something to be cultivated, cherished and striven for after every moment," Albert Lernard of the *Washington Post* wrote, "not a mere cream puff to be gulped at the end of a day's business and 18 holes of golf."[11]

The Most Potent Force in the World

Cohn's rather scathing analysis of love in America was especially pointed given the patriotic sentiment that so defined everyday life on the homefront during the war. Any kind of condemnation of the American way of life, especially something as sacred as marriage, could be seen as an attack on the nation itself. Soon after the war, however, it was open season on Americans' problems with love, with popular culture as usual heavily to blame. Magazines, comic strips, and radio serials all depicted love in unrealistic ways, but it was Hollywood that was most responsible for giving young people a wrong impression of what romance was really like. "True love, according to the Hollywood formula for romance, is an instantaneous and overwhelming affair in which two persons are irresistibly drawn to each other across a wide barrier of obstacles which, in real life, would put the kibosh on any ideas that most normal young persons might have about trying to make a go of romance," wrote an editor for the *Baltimore Sun* in 1947.[12]

The recipe was indeed a predictable one. Both the leading man and woman typically had some kind of major problem—alcoholism, sickness, poverty, a criminal past, or an abusive marriage were popular choices—but instantly fall in love, and proceed to overcome whatever hurdles stand in their way. While such a scenario might prove entertaining, the damage occurred after viewers left the theater, according to this editor. "Young people who attend the movies regularly are bound to feel that 'love' must be something akin to the emotional magnetism which works such wonders for film couples," the editor believed, "and, feeling this way, have a tendency to rush into love affairs and marriages with persons for whom they feel only a superficial and fleeting physical attraction."[13]

Were the movies really responsible for what most agreed were too many rocky marriages, extramarital affairs, and divorces? Or was Hollywood simply a reflection of reality, with the hard truth—that Americans were clueless when it came to love—just difficult to accept? The answers were not clear, but there was no doubt that many Americans had little understanding about love, something not surprising given that there was little formal education in it.[14] While marriage and family courses were frequently offered to college women after the war, especially for those planning to get hitched, the subject of love remained largely cloaked in mystery. "Love is the most popular topic of fiction, the inspiration for most music, poetry, drama and art," noted Judith Chase Churchill in *Woman's Home Companion* in 1947, "yet if you start searching for its why and wherefore you'll find little or nothing in the encyclopedia, even less in the dictionary."[15]

Surprised by this, Churchill decided to interview experts in the field to learn more about what she described as "love's rhyme and reason." Myth busting composed a big part of her exercise. Common beliefs about or related to the subject, i.e., that a lack of money quashed the flourishing of a romance, that people most often fell in love in springtime, that the heart served as the wellspring of love, that sex was both the strongest of human drives and the strongest emotional experience, and that a woman who wore red clothing had a better than average chance of making a man fall in love—were false, she found after speaking with some of the nation's leading psychologists, sociologists, and endocrinologists and immersing herself in the field's literature.[16] One woman, at least, was doing something about young people's lack of education in love. Mrs. Herbert T. Hatch, the dean of girls and assistant principal of Hanover High School in Hanover, Massachusetts, had decided to teach courses called "The Philosophy of Love" and "The Psychological Side of Romance" after determining that "high schools teach everything but what concerns us most—choosing a mate." The widowed mother of three was a trailblazer in the emerging field of human emotions, with the parents of students who took her classes entirely pleased with her approach to what must have been a difficult subject to teach.[17]

More education about love certainly seemed in order after World War II. Divorces had doubled in the United States between 1940 and 1947, and one out of every three marriages was ending. Some critics pointed directly to how love was expressed in this country as the source of the problem. "We are submerged from birth in a bath of the most nauseating sentiment about love," thought Waverly Root in *American Mercury* in 1947, the emotion considered "the be-all and the end-all, the seventh heaven, the achievement of Nirvana, the ultimate goal." Given the "absurd saccharine promises" made in the world of entertainment, it was not surprising that young people were lured into marriages that turned out to be little like what they had been led to believe. "The fact is that love is one of the major causes of unhappiness in America," Root bluntly stated, an observation that could be said to run completely contrary to our core cultural value grounded in domestic felicity.[18]

While Root had an unusually negative take on romantic love in America, more scrutiny was being paid to the emotion after the war because of the alarming numbers regarding divorce. Correctly assuming that most Americans did not possess any systematic knowledge of love (John E. Gibson believed that most people in this country viewed it as "a strange and nebulous thing which can be *felt* but not understood"), more sociologists, psychologists, and psychiatrists began to take a close look at the emotion as it was expressed in courtship and marriage. In 1943, Abraham Maslow had placed love (along with belonging) right in the middle of his five-level hierarchy of needs, but other social scientists were now arguing that it was at or near the top of human urges.[19]

Research by organizations such as the Institute of Marital Relations (IMR) shed new light on love as it related to marriage. One study conducted by that organization found that the popular belief that Americans got married almost exclusively because of the love for a person was untrue, at least among the 18,000 women sampled. Just 56 percent of women married for love, that study showed, with the balance considering financial security, the fear of becoming an "old maid," or the desire to have children more important. As Judith Chase Churchill had found, myths surrounding love were pervasive. People were generally not attracted to their "opposite" when choosing a partner, for example, as it was more similarities in likes, dislikes, and values that drew them together. Most interesting, however, were revelations regarding the rarity of "perfect" marriages. Just one out of 20 couples described themselves as being in an "ideally happy" marriage, according to the IMR, although most reported that they were "reasonably happy" in their relationships.[20]

In his 1948 book *Love and Marriage*, MIT professor Alexander Magoun made it clear that Americans simply did not want to understand what he called "the most potent force in the world." Both religious leaders and now scientists were saying how humans needed love not just to thrive but often survive, but such words of wisdom were largely not being heard. Instead, it was "Hollywood myth, physical beauty and poetic passion" that were ruling the day when it came to love, the idea of "two hearts in star dust beating as one" too compelling to resist. Marriages suffered from such an illusion, Magoun suggested, as the thrill and ecstasy of an initial romantic attraction was not sustainable. Rather, he proposed, love between two people is "the passionate and abiding desire to produce conditions under which each can be, and spontaneously express, his or her real self," with such a relationship the basis by which to "produce together an intellectual soil and an emotional climate in which each can flourish." Too many people viewed marriage in individualistic terms when, ironically, it was only as a partnership that each party's best interests could be served.[21]

Roald Dahl, the British author who would go on to write classic children's books such as *James and the Giant Peach* and *Charlie and the Chocolate Factory*, certainly had interesting thoughts on love at midcentury. Everyone knew that familial love was very different from romantic love, of course, but few were able express that distinction so compellingly. The former was "an exceedingly strong affection, usually constant, and invariably powerful," he posited in *Ladies' Home Journal* in 1949, while the latter was "an alarming and uncontrollable state of mind which causes those afflicted to be lifted suddenly to the most astonishing pinnacles of happiness and to be dropped with equal suddenness deep down into the darkest wells of despair and misery." Dahl went further by breaking down romantic love into what he believed were its two essential ingredients: profound affection/respect and intense sexually attraction. Ideally, he proposed, the "love ratio" of newly married couples should be about 60 percent profound affection/respect and 40 percent intense sexually attraction, although over time the second percentage would naturally fall while the first one rose (but still add up to 100 percent). Bad marriages were those in which the ratio was in the vicinity of 30/70 percent, he added, with divorce almost certain if the ratios were 0/100 percent or the other way around.[22]

Others had a mathematical view of love had but broke its components down differently. Murray Campbell argued that there were "five faces of love," and it was important that couples understand that with the good came some bad. "All real love, as you may have discovered, is sometimes mixed with pretty ugly emotions," he wrote in *Woman's Home Companion* in 1949, thinking many divorces were the result of a husband or wife being surprised when anything but affection was showed towards them by their spouse. Besides affection, four other, less pleasant emotions—hostility, jealousy, hate, and submissiveness—made up the whole of love, Campbell posited. While affection comprised 90 percent of love and the four darker ones just 10 percent collectively, all married people should expect hostility, jealousy, hate, or submissiveness to rear its ugly head once in a while. Many were apt to bail out of a marriage at the first sign of some unpleasantness or disagreeability, a mistake given that it was entirely normal for any one of these faces of love to appear on occasion.[23]

A Mysterious Visitation

While such theories were certainly useful, it was only through science that the full power of love could be appreciated, something that was fortunately being achieved in midcentury America. "Science finally has discovered love," claimed Howard Whitman in *This Week Magazine* in 1950, the remarkable discovery the result of considerable research by psychologists, psychiatrists, sociologists, and criminologists. All roads led to love or, more accurately, the lack of it, a fair number of experts were concluding, with mental and social illness often due to our misunderstanding of the emotion. It was true that many used the word too liberally, not distinguishing between their love for another person and, say, baseball or bananas. Physicians too were claiming they had at last solved the mystery of love, and were using it to patients' advantage. "We doctors are learning how to prescribe human love," stated Abraham Stone, a New York physician who also served as president of the American Association of Marriage Counselors, thinking that "it is the greatest medicine."[24]

Like other medicine, however, it was up to professionals to decide when and how to use love. Even seemingly happily married people didn't truly understand love, Stone believed, with many mistaking it for possessiveness, dependency, or even self-sacrifice. Americans in particular were inclined to think that in some way they "owned" their respective spouse, part of our acquisitional, materialistic ethos. Love was possible only by giving up our promise "to have and to hold," as wedding vows often stated, as attempting to control another person was completely opposite from its true meaning. (The phrase was the title of a 1899 novel by American author Mary Johnston; it was the bestselling novel in the United States the following year.) Love was gladly granting another person "the full right to his [or her] unique humanhood," according to Harry A. Overstreet, who had taught for many years at City College in New York and whose recently published book *The Mature Mind* had become a bestseller. Genuine love was more about giving than taking, experts agreed, something that required much effort and time as it went against our innate instincts.[25]

Experts continued to warn of the dangers of romantic and erotic love, and advised couples thinking about marriage to put practicality first. Successful marriages were not predicated on what Paul Popenoe, director of the American Institute on Family Relations, called "a mysterious visitation not subject to human control," thinking "modern writers" had vastly exaggerated the importance of both romance and sex in relationships.[26] Marynia Farnham, a psychiatrist, called for "more love, less sex" in marriage, an about-face of her profession's proud achievement of making sexuality less taboo in the Victorian era. For the record, she pointed out, psychiatrists did not "make love an outcast," as it was only later with the popularization of Freud's ideas that sexual satisfaction began to trump love as a measure of a happy marriage.[27] Whether the motivation was romantic love or sexual attraction, too many Americans were entering marriage in a reckless fashion, it was agreed, with not enough attention paid to companionship, common interests, and firm plans for their future.[28]

Members of the clergy certainly didn't see romantic love and/or sex appeal as a good basis for marriage. The Rev. Myrus L. Knutson made that clear in an April 1951 sermon at Our Savior's Lutheran Church in Los Angeles, reminding his flock that "we don't fall in love as we fall in a ditch." Rather, the love in a marriage should be allowed to grow over time, he maintained, as a relationship built on infatuation was likely to fizzle out once the thrill was gone.[29] Celebrities such as Barbara Hutton might have befitted from the Reverend's preaching. The 38-year old Woolworth heiress and socialite was awarded her fourth divorce in 1951 after things with her latest husband, Prince Igor Troubetzkoy, didn't work out. "There is very little romantic love left," the "Poor Little Rich Girl" sadly told reporters after her Mexican divorce was granted, although the Prince announced he would legally contest the judge's decision. Hutton recovered quickly from her latest ill-fated foray in romance, however, as she was to marry three more times in her relatively short life.[30]

Rather than putting romance first when choosing her various husbands (which ultimately included three princes, a count, a baron, a jet-setting playboy, and Cary Grant), Hutton might have heeded some of the abundance of marital advice in the early 1950s if she truly wanted a lasting relationship. "Romantic love is a great and noble emotion but I am simply stating a fact when I say it is not an emotion which is self-sustaining," David R. Mace stated in 1952, thinking modernity had fundamentally altered the concept of marriage. Marriage had traditionally been what Mace, a professor at Drew University, called "a mutual exchange of services," with the husband providing economic security and the wife managing the home. Women in the workplace, more sexual freedom, and advancements in contraception broke down that model, however, opening the door for what Mace referred to as "the cult of love" to permeate marriage. People now married "because a blessed state of ecstasy mysteriously pervades two beings as a result of their proximity towards one another," he said in a talk at Oxford University in England, wondering if things were better for both husband and wife in the old days.[31]

One journalist felt the need to distinguish between love and romance, as the two terms were often equated and lumped together. "Love is a matter of giving," he wrote in *McCall's* in 1953, while "romance is mostly a matter of getting." Wives often complained that their husbands didn't love them enough, when it was really that they did not romance them enough by giving them attention, admiration, and flattery. Women's preoccupation with romance, fed by advertising and the media, was giving both men and love a bad name, he believed, and turning America into "a nation of emotional adolescents." Because they refused to fall into the trap of romanticized love, American men were accused of being immune to any kind of passion, something this writer felt was untrue and unfair.[32]

Officials in East Germany had no attention to allow any of its citizens to be seduced by juvenile Western-style romance. Just a month after the

McCall's article was published, editors for *Life* reported on what they called "Love Among the Commies," contrasting that country's official version of love with that in the United States. Editors for *Neues Deutschland*, the "East German *Pravda*," reminded its readers that "our love already is different from that of the declining bourgeois world," and warned writers in the Communized country about over-romanticizing their fiction. "A true love story of today must reflect the changes in our social and moral, physical and intellectual life," the item read, classic Communist rhetoric grounded in the fear of the state losing control of its people to some other, even more powerful force. Similar instructions were given in the Soviet Union to that country's writers who might otherwise fool Russian citizens into believing in the sentimentalized and commercialized expression of love that was so popular in the morally corrupt West.[33]

A Loaded Word

While love was turned into a political football during the Cold War, Americans continued to struggle with gaining a firm grasp of the parameters of the emotion and even defining the term. "What is this thing called love?" Zelda Popkin asked in *Coronet* in 1953, quite certain that "the response will be vague, since this is a loaded word, freighted with misconceptions." It was admittedly difficult to put into words what she considered to be "life's deepest emotion," not sure that Havelock Ellis's definition—"a synthesis of sex and friendship"—was entirely accurate. Contemporary psychologists were also saying that sex was an essential element of love, but there was clearly much more to the emotion than physical intimacy. While individuals' range of emotions varied greatly, everyone was capable of loving and, presumably, being loved, psychologists also believed. As well, one didn't have to give up any part of oneself to love another person, experts pointed out, and those who had somehow lost the "love of their life" need not worry that they had used up their innately assigned quota of the emotion.[34]

Above all, however, those with a deeper understanding of love in America recognized that the romantic kind was virtually a complete fabrication. In her 1953 book *The Mature Woman*, Anna K. Daniels, an obstetrician and gynecologist, considered romantic love to be a "story-book fairy-tale" that had "little or no relation to reality." The standard narrative, reinforced by popular culture, began with a man and woman meeting, typically under unlikely circumstances, with love immediately in the air. After overcoming a prescribed set of obstacles, the couple weds and lives happily ever after, fulfilling their destiny as soul mates. The nuts and bolts of a real relationship—in which a couple gets to know each another over a period of time—was not part of the story, deemed too prosaic and tedious a detail. Many Americans actually believed this fairytale, Daniels insisted, and lost interest in a relationship once they learned that genuine love involved hard work. While undeniably beautiful, such romanticism was "unsound and dangerous precisely because it is so beautiful," she wrote, with those who tried to be a character in that fable ironically "doomed to a loveless, lonely life."[35]

No less of an expert than Margaret Mead offered thoughts on romantic love as what she described as "the American marriage dilemma" showed no signs of disappearing in the mid-fifties. The famous anthropologist agreed that misconceptions about love and sex were widespread and potentially hazardous to individuals and society in general. Once smitten, flaws in the personality of one's beloved were often overlooked, as were fundamental philosophical differences that would at some point serve as a wrecking ball to a marriage built on romantic love. Parents and friends often pointed out such warning signs but to no avail; the conviction that love would ultimately triumph was woven too tightly in our cultural fabric to deter lovebirds from moving ahead with their plans. "They know from the movies and from stories and ads that love will solve all," Mead stated in a 1954 article in *Cosmopolitan* tellingly titled "Romance Can Ruin Your Marriage."[36]

Even in the so-called staid 1950s, the ubiquity of sex in America was deemed a major obstacle to the realization of genuine love. The sexual revolution, cable television, and the Internet were all years away, but sex was already considered a mainstay of the media and advertising, diverting Americans' attention from the less physical aspects of relationships. Sex was a symbol of the love between two people, explained Paul H. Landis, a professor of sociology and author of a number of books on marriage, but many couples felt pressure about it because of the ways in which it was presented in popular and consumer culture. Thinking they had a sexual problem because their experience was falling short of what they assumed it should be, many Americans were reading manuals, going to counseling, and talking to their doctors in search of potential solutions. "Don't expect too much of sex in marriage," Landis plainly put it in *Reader's Digest* in 1954, advising that the physical part of a relationship was just one dimension of enduring love.[37] "Love-making is simply one expression of love," agreed Hannah Lees in that same publication a few years later, thinking "there is room in a lifetime of marriage for the whole spectrum of emotions."[38]

With the divorce rate still rising in the mid–1950s, many social scientists were alarmed at what they concluded were some of the negative consequences of failed marriages. Divorce typically was not only a difficult experience for each spouse, at least temporarily, but also their children, if there were any, as they often exhibited some level of psychological and emotional distress. Juvenile crime was running parallel with the escalating divorce rate in the United States, leading some to believe that there was a direct link between the two. Angry youths upset about the breakup of their parents were taking out their frustrations on society, experts surmised, making divorce not just a domestic issue but a national problem. That all this was taking place during the Cold War only made matters worse, as it could be easily imagined that the Soviets could point to the high incidence of both domestic discord and juvenile crime as telling failures of our keep-up-with-the-Joneses society.

How did all this relate to love, one might ask? Common sense dictated that the underlying cause for divorce was some kind of failure in the dynamics of love between two people, reason enough to try to find solutions to the apparent problem. The postwar years were a golden age of problem solving, it's fair to say, with experts of diverse backgrounds spending their careers examining difficult situations that were vexing society in some way. A greater understanding of love would naturally lead to ways to sustain the emotion between spouses, it was believed, making this effort an important one within the sociological and psychological communities of the 1950s. In short, fixing love could fix the juvenile crime problem, something that would be greatly beneficial to the country not just socially but politically and perhaps economically as well. Mending the cracks in the foundation of American life—family and home—would serve a variety of national interests, in other words, a valid basis for a dedicated scientific inquiry into the nature of love.

To that point, the first place authorities tended to look were the two recently published Kinsey reports. It was surprising if not shocking to learn of how many married Americans had had extramarital affairs, although most adults had some personal familiarity with the practice, and trysts of one sort or another occasionally served as a plot point in movies. Infidelity was probably just as common in Europe but the divorce rate there was lower, suggesting that there was a fundamental difference in the way that Europeans approached both love and marriage. While Americans typically considered an affair grounds for divorce, Europeans were generally less rigid on the matter, a function of their historical view of marriage as a social institution that went far beyond an expression of love. As well, love and sex were closely aligned in the United States while in Europe that was not necessary so, explaining why Americans were more apt to seek a divorce upon learning their that partner had strayed. Finally, and more simply, Europeans were more realistic and practical when it came to matters of the heart, and a husband's having an affair (or even a mistress) was not immediate cause to end an otherwise good marriage.[39]

An Exchange of Energy

There was ample evidence to suggest that many American couples were not putting in the work that most experts believed was required to create loving relationships. While the honey-I'm-home sitcoms of the 1950s often depicted married life as a perfect (or nearly so) pairing of soul mates, one didn't have to look far to see that in the real world there was plenty of trouble in paradise. "What became of the man I married?" a 1952 article in *Better Homes & Gardens* inquired, a question many wives were asking themselves a few years into their rather hastily arranged postwar marriages.[40] Not finding it at home, some of these women were seeking affection from alternative sources. "You can't get away with marital infidelity!," *Coronet* cautioned that same year, the rising divorce rate another sign that postwar domestic life was more problematic than we might think.[41] Quizzes to determine one's love quotient were a popular feature in women's magazines of the era. "How much do you love each other?," *McCall's* asked its readers in 1954, some of them no doubt disappointed to learn that their score was lower than they wanted to believe.[42]

Because it was perceived as a problem, love in America was a hot literary topic in the mid-1950s, with various authors offering their take on the subject and suggesting ways that it could potentially be solved. Few books about love made as big a splash as Smiley Blanton's 1956 *Love or Perish*, in which the notable psychiatrist (who had co-authored two bestsellers with Norman Vincent Peale) argued that the emotion was in all its forms essential to human survival. Blanton took a holistic view of love, seeing it ideally as something that, in his words, "pervaded one's entire personality and infused every action with its creative beneficence." True love between two people had nothing to do with the mythical romantic version trafficked by those in the entertainment business. "It is, above all, an exchange of energy," he wrote of love, describing it as a "dynamic force that nourishes the spirit as powerfully as bread and water sustain the body." For Blanton, love was nothing less than a spiritual experience, not surprising given his unusual belief that psychiatry and religion were entirely compatible.[43]

With his book *The Art of Loving* published that same year, Erich Fromm also made a case that at its best the love between two people can be transcendent and divine. The fundamental problem of human existence, according to the eminent psychoanalyst, was that each of us was alone in the world, separate from each other. Love connected us with another person and, by implication, humanity itself, he believed, something that belonging to a group could not do. Fromm also flipped the usual conditions of love around, seeing that only in the giving of it can our own individuality be affirmed. It only was by loving another human being that an individual could become a complete person, he argued, a counterintuitive concept that challenged standard thinking. Loving (he saw it in active versus passive terms, and thus more as a verb than a noun) was thus an art that could and should be nurtured, Fromm maintained, certainly not an approach that many Americans were taking given the number of failed relationships.[44]

With the likes of Blanton and Fromm taking a close look at love, the subject was enjoying a new kind and higher level of intellectual thought that further exposed the mythologies that surrounded it. Professionals were increasingly challenging the popular notion of love as an inexplicable feeling in which the mind played a very small part. The workings of the mind were much underrated when it came to love, experts agreed, shifting control of the emotion towards the individual and away from some enigmatic, supernatural source. If there was any consensus among these psychologists, psychiatrists, marriage counselors, and clergymen, it was that romantic love was part of something bigger than an attraction or attachment between two people. Love was a universal emotion that connected all people, this theory went, and a force that brought out the best in each of us.[45]

Sadly, the waiting offices of many such professionals were filled with people whose love lives were by all measures bringing out the worst in them. In his *The American Sexual Tragedy*, Albert Ellis described in painful detail the type of patients he saw in a typical week and why they had come to see him. Nine out of every ten patients had love on their minds, he explained, or more accurately the angst they were experiencing because of some romantic trouble. The problems varied, of course, but all seemed to be ultimately about dissatisfaction with the person they were currently with or frustration with not finding the kind of person they wanted to be with. Why did so many Americans, even those who were highly successful in other avenues of life, have such difficulty with love? The answer appeared to relate to our determination to interpret love in mysterious and miraculous terms, thinking perhaps that to analyze it too much in an objective way would take its magic away or make it never want to come one's way.[46]

The interest in love among specialists in human relations continued to rise in the late 1950s. "Not since the last song writers' convention has there been so much serious—and businesslike—discussion of love as went on at the annual meeting of the American Psychological Association," noted Dorothy Barclay in the *New York Times Magazine* in the fall of 1958, with the same level of attention given to the subject at the recently held Tri-State Council on Family Relations conference. While such specialists had mused on the nature of love for decades, "the painstaking study and experimental analysis of love by psychologists is a much newer development," she reported. That love was an active process, versus an entity unto itself, was the principal finding of scientific research in the field, implying that couples should endeavor to make it evolve and grow over time. Again, however, the nurturing of love was beneficial not only to a relationship but to individuals. Love was "that relationship between one person and another which is most conducive to the optimal development of both," according to the sociologist Nelson Foote, the reward residing more in the expression of the emotion versus its reception.[47]

Efforts to solve the problem of love in America in order to help remedy some of the nation's social ills continued through the late fifties. Since 1949, with funding from the Lilly Foundation, world-renowned sociologist Pitirim A. Sorokin was leading the Harvard Center in Creative Altruism, whose task was to investigate love as a means to promote positive cultural change. There were seven forms of love—religious, ethical, ontological, physical, biological, psychological, and social—according to Sorokin, the underlying theory being that all human relationships could benefit from having more of it. One could conclude from Sorokin's work that by being more altruistic, i.e., selfless or acting for the good of others, couples would have a much greater chance of having successful marriages, precisely what relationship experts were saying. On a much grander level, more love around the world would go a long way towards preventing it from being blown up, Sorokin (a Russian immigrant) no doubt reckoned, this the subtext of his work during the peak years of the Cold War.[48]

While some of the brightest minds pondered how love really could make the world go round, Americans continued to struggle with the emotion, especially with regard to their marriages. Advice from experts was in high demand as, despite what Frank Sinatra had sung in his 1955 hit song "Love and Marriage," the two were often not going together like a horse and carriage. In the United States, unlike in Europe, marriage was typically seen as the end product of love, i.e., its logical result, so it was no surprise that so many couples here were getting divorced. Rather, marriage ideally served as the means for a couple to express the emotion to each other, authorities pointed out, with the "I dos" just the beginning of what could be a long, ever evolving journey of love. Women in particular tended to view getting hitched as having officially achieved the search for love which had dominated their lives up to that point, Jessamyn West argued in *Ladies' Home Journal* in 1959, not at all a good way to begin a marriage. "Love is not what you think," she told readers, thinking a major overhaul of our concept of the emotion was much needed.[49]

The Elixir of the Good Life

Begging to differ was Mrs. Ruth E. Dillon of Bellville, New Jersey, who was getting awfully tired of all the recent badmouthing of both love and marriage by so-called experts. The tipping point for Dillon was a series of newspaper columns written by Phyllis Battelle, a New York based journalist who had consulted with notables such as Pearl Buck, Margaret Mead, author Marynia Farnham, and historian Arthur Schlesinger, Jr. The group was highly critical of married life in America and the narrowly defined gender roles of the middle class in which husbands worked hard to be able to afford creature comforts for their pampered wives. Dillon was proud to be a suburban housewife, and did not appreciate elitist intellectuals professing there was little opportunity for real love to thrive in such a bourgeois setting. "When evening comes and my husband folds me tenderly in his arms, I am still a wife and thank God a woman in love with my husband!" she told a reporter, wishing all the social scientists probing the lives of married couples, especially their sexual habits, would turn their attention elsewhere.[50]

There did indeed appear to be a brewing backlash against the turning of love into an extensive clinical experiment as the 1950s wound down. The more research that was done, the more that romantic love was attacked, it fully appeared, particularly at American universities and colleges. Courses in courtship, marriage, and the family were popular at hundreds of schools across the country, but the professors teaching these classes were apt to warn students of the hazards that lay ahead for those planning to settle down. Such instructors were "almost to a man, hostile to romantic love," wrote Morton Hunt in the *New York Times Magazine* in 1959, "holding it to be a deception, a danger, and even a disease." Professors of sociology and family life occasionally referred to romantic passion as "cardiac-respiratory love" because of the accelerating effect it often had on the respective hearts and lungs of the besotted. Statistics and case histories of this kind of love gone bad were presented in abundance with the purpose of steering young people away from what was described as a fantasy of disturbed minds. Rather, it was "mature" or "conjugal" love that students should seek out, they insisted, a much more pragmatic and practical emotion that would serve them well as they sought out potential life partners.[51]

There was no shortage of sources that those presenting love in such terms could use to make their case. Assigned books might include F. Alexander Magoun's *Love and Marriage* ("Only those people who do not know each other intimately can feel romantic"); Robert Francis Winch's *The Modern Family* ("Romantic love is a relationship of remoteness and adoration [and] attuned to persons who are emotionally adolescent and insecure"); and Ray Erwin Baber's *Marriage and the Family* ("[Romantic love] is like a drug [although] time and common sense frequently restore even the violently afflicted to sanity"). While there had always been critics of romantic love, these observations were put forth under the banner of science, making it difficult to refute such charges. Above all, American society was singled out for its psychological abnormalities regarding romantic love. "All societies recognize that there are occasional violent attachments between persons of the opposite sex, but our present American culture is practically the only one which has attempted to capitalize on these and make them the basis for marriage," anthropologist Ralph Linton had written in 1936, a view that had only gained in acceptance among social scientists of a generation later.[52]

Hunt, author of *The Natural History of Love*, was quick to come to the defense of romantic love. His first problem with the likes of Magoun, Winch, and Baber was that these scientists could not even define romantic love with any precision. Sociologists accepted "a kind of love characterized by idealization of the love-object and by its accessibility" as a working definition of the term, but this was hardly consistent with the academic rigor they professed in their research of the subject. A stream of descriptors often followed—intense, poetic, inexplicable, erotic—but these too were vague and immeasurable. Even worse, Hunt pointed out, these "anti-romantics" had no definition for the "mature" or "conjugal" form of love that they were recommending to young people. It had something to do with "adjustment," "accommodation," and "companionship," from what he could discern from the literature, but outside of that conjugal love "sounds unpleasantly like basic military training," he only half-joked.[53]

Surely intelligent college students did not take the standard narrative of romantic love as presented by novelists, Hollywood, and Madison Avenue as seriously as these critics seemed to believe, Hunt continued. Those smitten in fictitious tales of romantic love often somehow spotted their special someone across a crowded room, knowing instantly that he or she was *the one*. Differences in age, ethnicity, and education of the principal players mattered little, as these were only technical details that served to prove their love was real. The determination to overcome the series of obstacles that always popped up also demonstrated that this was no fleeting affair, and that life for these two people was only worth living if they could be together for eternity. No housework, whining children, or money problems were in this couple's future, according to the story, with marriage to consist largely of nightly candle-lit dinners and continual tender expressions of affection. Was an entire generation really incapable of distinguishing this fairytale from reality? one had to ask, if so the country in much more trouble than having a high divorce rate.[54]

Beyond their discounting of young people's acumen, anti-romantics appeared to be overly concerned with the factor of social divisions within failed marriages. Each and every difference in cultural identifiers such as social status and religion decreased the chances of a happy marriage, they argued, using mounds of statistics to prove their point. It was thus in the best interests of those looking for a partner to try to find someone as much like him or her as possible, leading Hunt to quip that the ideal mate for a man would be his sister and a woman her brother. Many psychoanalytically inclined marriage counselors viewed relationships between people of diverse backgrounds as a conscious or unconscious expression of revenge against their parents, an indication of the antipathy that most of Freud's descendants felt towards romantic love. "Being in love is an obsessional state which, like all obsessions, is in part driven by unconscious anger," stated Lawrence Kubie, for example, with Theodor Reik considering love to be "a reaction-formation to envy, possessiveness, and hostility."[55]

What was it about love that attracted so much hate among the intellectual elite? one had to ask; certainly there were other subjects that were more deserving of such disparagement and condemnation. For that matter, what was the real motive of anti-romantics? Hunt wondered, hinting that their actual interest in the field was to make a mark within their academic circle. Was it really to help mate seekers choose someone better suited for them, or to let them know that marriage would be something quite different than what they likely believed? Perhaps, but such critics were taking some of the joy out of life, and offering little in return. "Clearly, the opponents of romantic love would like to rid us of a disease most of us have found enjoyable and important," he wrote, "offering us instead a condition of health that will be good for us, and no pleasure whatever." How could something as banal as "adjustment" compete with the undeniable power of passionate love? he asked, and why question the latter's validity even if it was a trick of nature to get two people together so they could then really get to know each other? "What has been passed off as a theory based on scientific method is, therefore, so tangled in its own contradictions that one may suspect the method has been used wrongly," Hunt concluded, thinking plucking romantic values out of marriage could "weaken its structural ties and render it unrewarding."[56]

Having the final say on love in America in the 1950s was, I think fittingly, *Life* magazine. In a photo essay published just a few days before the beginning of a new decade, the magazine's editors featured images of couples clearly in the throes of the controversial emotion. One black-and-white picture taken by Henri Cartier-Bresson showed a young man and young woman on a beach holding each other, while another by George Silk was of a pair of college students waiting for the school year to end so they could get married. Other photographs by Howell Conant, Mark Shaw, Bert Stern, Nina Leen, and Philippe Halsman also depicted young people who, judging by their body language, had by all accounts not listened to a word of any professorial lecturing on the perils of romantic love. Love was "the elixir of the good life," *Life* told its millions of readers, a claim that was difficult to contest based on its collection of images.[57] Love in America was about to take a major turn, however, and in a direction that no one could have predicted.

Chapter 3

Revolt Against Love, 1960–1979

> *"The sexual revolution has so redefined love that many of us are no longer sure what it is."*
> —Anatole Broyard, 1974

In the fall of 1960, a war of words was waging in China over the subject of love. A number of writers were publishing articles that made the radical argument that love, as well as beauty and truth, were universal concepts that transcended political ends. One popular writer, Pa Jen (the pen name for Wang Jen-Shu, Communist China's Ambassador to Indonesia), had maintained that the search for romantic love, in addition to the pursuit of happiness and the aversion to death, were "all things common to mankind," an idea that caught the attention of the country's officials. Editors of *China Youth*, a magazine published by the state-run Peking University, quickly responded to Pa Jen's article, stating that such a claim was absurd, especially the notion that "bourgeois love" was in any way superior to the love that the people had for the Communist party. It was not even possible for those of different social and economic classes to fall in love, the editors made clear, evidence that the "lofty Communist morality" surpassed any and all romantic feelings. Western-style romantic love was "fundamentally different from the love of the proletariat," the article in *China Youth* read, with anyone challenging that basic assumption "reactionary through and through."[1]

On the other side of the world, a different but equally prickly kind of war was taking place over the idea of "bourgeois" love. A contentious site now for decades, love in America emerged as a divisive battleground in the tumultuous 1960s and 1970s, when the country experienced its own cultural revolution. Love intersected with the feminist and gay rights movements over the course of these years, with the sexual revolution adding a complex dimension to the subject. Self-help and pop psychology came into full bloom in the seventies, these too serving to make love a hot topic among scholars and laypeople alike. The still rising divorce rate alone justified more research in the field, with many theories proposed by social scientists regarding why so many marriages were failing. As always, however, the idea of love retained an exalted position in American society, while its realities functioned as a lighting rod among critics. The beating that love continued to take was reason enough for *Harper's* to declare in 1975 that there was a full-fledged "revolt against love" in America, a reasonable conclusion to make given the controversy surrounding the subject.[2]

Love Is an Art

The country may have been embarking on a New Frontier as the Kennedys moved into the White House, but Americans' contentious relationship with love showed no signs of letting up. "What ever became of romantic love?" asked *Look* magazine in 1960, a question that had been asked when Calvin Coolidge was president.[3] As well, despite the greater degree of attention being given to the subject, defining love remained as challenging as ever. There was no doubt that recently published books about love authored by great minds such as Smiley Blanton, Eric Fromm, Ashley Montagu, Andre Maurois, Theodore Reik, and Denis de Rougemont offered considerable insight into the subject, but even these were ambiguous and abstruse. Most were somehow critical of love, much like how writers of earlier centuries were apt to warn readers of its various dangers. There were, of course, exceptions, but pro-love authors tended to lean too far the other way, speaking of the emotion as a magical force that put people in some kind of spell. ("When Love is Love it sees first and foremost and clearly the highest need of the beloved, and its whole effort is to minister to that need utterly regardless of return or reward," Russell Maguire mused in the *American Mercury* in 1960, a good example of the language that was often employed by writers when describing the majesty of the emotion.[4]) "Most current books on the subject get so bogged down with words that they blunt the meaning of the elusive subject," thought John G. Fuller of *Saturday Review*, wondering if love simply went beyond the capacity of literature.[5]

If deep knowledge about love was beyond the scope of the humanities, perhaps science could provide some answers. Psychologists and sociologists were continuing to pursue research in the field, and uncovering some interesting findings. Previous studies had shown little correlation between intelligence and education and how "lucky" one was in love, but sociologist Paul

C. Glick did believe there was a link. People with higher IQs and greater levels of education had more successful relationships than others, Glick had found after analyzing census data, suggesting that general "smartness" could be an asset when addressing the problems that typically came with love and marriage. Those with longer marriages tended to live longer than those who were divorced, separated, or remained single, life insurance company studies showed, backed up by research done by Harvard University sociologists. Love was good for one's physical health, one might thus conclude, compensation perhaps for critics' claims that it wreaked havoc on one's emotional state of being.[6]

Other studies added to the growing scientific literature of love. Prior research had shown that people were generally not attracted to their "opposite" when choosing a partner, but sociologists at Stanford University found differently. Extroverts were attracted to introverts and vice versa, the latest studies revealed, with the same kind of inverse relationship between more emotional types and more analytical sorts. (People were drawn to those who shared physical characteristics, however, according to research by sociologists Ernest Burgess and Paul Wallin.) As well, there was more evidence to show that "love at first sight" was a myth; an instant attraction and infatuation could very well take place the first time two people met, sociologist Judson T. Landis reported, but true love required some time to develop. Finally, there was some research showing that not all people loved equally. Some could receive love but were incapable of giving it, while for others the emotion was considered completely inaccessible due to some kind of "mental block."[7]

Social and cultural forces also played a role in shaping the contours of love. According to Hans J. Morgenthau, a key figure in international politics at the time, love was really about loneliness, or, more accurately, our compulsion to try to avoid it. As others had argued, the fundamental problem that all humans faced was being alone in the world, making falling in love with another person (and often vowing to spend the rest of one's life with him or her) a logical way to attempt to skirt this existential predicament. "Through love," he wrote in *Commentary* in 1962, "man seeks another human being like himself, the Platonic other half of his soul, to form a union which will make him whole." Ultimately, however, there was no escape from loneliness, as even a great love for and by another individual was not able to overcome the basic fact that we each entered and would leave this world alone. It was this (rather depressing) philosophical truth that explained why so many relationships failed, Morgenthau explained, a much different theory than the more commonly heard ones put forth by psychologists and sociologists steeped in individuals' deficiencies of some sort.[8]

3. Revolt Against Love, 1960–1979

Whatever the explanation for the active pursuit of love, more cracks in the marital firmament were appearing, causing some to speculate whether the emotion was simply unsustainable between two adults. "Can husbands and wives stay in love?" Morton Hunt asked in *Redbook* in 1962, casting some doubt on the long-term viability of the very institution of marriage.[9] Hunt's *The Natural History of Love*, a sweeping survey of love in Western society from ancient times, had been published a few years earlier, so his rather negative thoughts on the matter were taken seriously.[10] In such a cultural climate, it was not surprising that professional advice from psychologists and psychiatrists was eagerly sought by and liberally doled out to love-challenged Americans. "Cupid [was] on the couch," quipped *Seventeen* magazine in 1963, meaning that love problems had become a hot topic in all the rage psychoanalysis.[11]

Many psychologists and psychiatrists did indeed have love on their minds in the early sixties. The late 1950s backlash against "mature love" led by defenders of romance was still in play, with some arguing that mystique, for the lack of a better word, was an essential dimension of the emotion. Allan Fromme, for example, was not a proponent of reducing marriage to a working partnership, thinking such an analytical perspective took all the creativity out of love. "Love is an art, and art is larger than life," the director and chief psychologist of the Mental Hygiene Clinic at the University Settlement House in New York said in 1962, of the persuasion that "music, poetry and some irresponsibility" were necessary for the emotion to thrive. While love could not solve all of one's problems, as those on the opposite end of the spectrum were apt to believe, Fromme contended, viewing the emotion through a rational, scientific lens turned marriage into more of an organization than a human relationship.[12]

Other psychologists felt the need to point out that, given the nation's current values, the chances of love or marriage prospering were not particularly good. Walter J. Coville, chief of clinical psychological services at St. Vincent's Hospital in New York, felt that "loving with one's total personality seems to be a relatively rare phenomenon today since partners in love and marriage experience so many difficulties in their adjustments." Coville had much experience as a practicing psychologist, and found that the young couples he counseled were vastly ill equipped to establish healthy long-term relationships. Both husbands and wives frequently entered marriages based on reasons other than love and, even worse, appeared to have little understanding of the meaning of the word. Each party was quick to abandon a marriage at the first sign of trouble, not too surprising given that spouses had little faith in or respect for their respective partner. Much attention was given to what

Coville described as "the insignificant and superficial problems of daily living," with men and women more interested in things like success, status, and sensual pleasures than the nurturing of love.[13]

It was true that not only were more Americans divorcing but they were splitting up at an earlier age. While there could be many reasons for a couple to call it quits, the common assumption was that there was just one motive for two people to marry: they were in love. And while the reasons to get divorced were typically concrete and rational, the motive to get married was grounded in the vagaries of an emotion, an interesting distinction given the vow to commit to each other for life. Sociologist Ernest van den Haag wondered why so many people still got married when being single in the latter part of the 20th century did not carry the social stigma it used to, especially for women. Women could now go to college, have a career, and enjoy sex with whomever they chose if they liked, but many continued to marry (at an earlier age, in fact). Why was this so? Van den Haag believed that modernity had brought with it a widespread feeling of isolation, the impetus for most young people to marry despite the far greater opportunities to now be had. In short, love was typically perceived as making life meaningful, and there was no better way to recognize that idea than through the "normalized" institution of marriage.[14]

For J. B. Priestley, the renowned British author and playwright, it was Westerners' habit of confusing love with sex and eroticism that was causing so many relationship problems. Eroticism was primarily a marketing strategy, he pointed out, an artificial and impersonal device used to connote the idea of sexuality in order to attract consumers' attention. (He cited the movie stars Brigitte Bardot and the recently deceased Marilyn Monroe as symbolic of contemporary eroticism.) Sex, on the other hand, was "a natural hunger and need" but also had a strong psychological component, Priestley argued, making it much more than superficial eroticism but still lacking the power of love. Love was "supremely personal," he believed, and rooted in the simple concept of two people sharing "an immense amount of liking" for each other. Should that be present, a man and woman had the opportunity to turn their relationship into "a glorious work of art" over the course of many years, a nice way of describing marriage at its best.[15]

Semantics too seemed to be in play regarding the often-linked words "romantic" and "love." The latter term was undoubtedly linguistically convoluted, a function of the complexity of the emotion, but the former also elicited considerable confusion. "'Romantic,' in its modern sense, conjures up sentimental visions of a bare-headed knight doing homage to a long-haired damsel beside a hedge of damask roses, while his horse paws the turf in a verdurous background," observed the historian Robert Graves in *Life* in 1965. Previously, however, the term simply meant "of Roman origin," he pointed out, making its modern interpretation ironic given that the people of the ancient empire were notoriously pragmatic and brutal. "Love of women meant little to them," Graves observed, with wives, mistresses, and slave girls all in service to Roman men who would find the modern expression of "romantic" odd indeed.[16]

The One Universal Human Involvement

The parsing of love in the 1960s went far beyond the musings of the intellectual elite; the mainstream media also considered the subject a worthy one to examine given its central role in everyday life. On the last day of 1966, *Saturday Evening Post* devoted its entire issue to love, an interesting and perhaps courageous choice by the magazine's editors given the tremendous change that was taking place in the country at the time. America was on the brink of a cultural revolution as the seminal year of 1967 approached, but editors for the decidedly square magazine recognized the central role that love still played in everyday life. In the introduction to the series of articles (which included poems, short stories, and cartoons), the editors described love in truly remarkable terms, recognizing its value in a way that rivaled that of the foremost authorities on the subject, past or present:

> Nothing matters more to more people. No other interest cuts so broadly across all the ages and stations in life to touch every human being so powerfully. No other endeavor consumes more of our energies than the quest for love, the nourishing and enjoyment of it, the mourning for it if it dies. Love is the one universal human involvement, and the most personal.[17]

Kicking off the magazine's love issue was Russell Baker, who had occasionally opined on the subject in his popular syndicated newspaper column. "Love, your magic spell is everywhere, dammit," his piece began, making it clear that he had strong but mixed feelings about the emotion. Americans were pressured to be in love, or at least act like they were, Baker felt, with popular and consumer culture loudly and continually hammering home the message that only that could lead to happiness. "What a depressing thing has happened to love in America!" he exclaimed, considering the emotion to have been turned into "the snake oil of the 20th century." Not just those in the entertainment business and marketers were at fault, however, citing the clergy, physicians, educators, and authors as conspirators in the aggressive selling of love to Americans. Love could solve any and all problems, we heard from a plethora of trusted sources from an early age, with a more perfect society waiting in the wings if each of us could find that special someone. Psychologists were especially to blame, Baker believed, as it was they who were responsible for probing the minds of citizens to learn who was in love, who was not, and, if the latter, why not. A seemingly successful love life afforded certain professional advantages, not unlike having a college degree. Not being in love, however, most obviously displayed by remaining single, was generally deemed a suspicious and almost subversive activity, with some sort of penalization, such as not being promoted at work, entirely possible.[18]

Baker obviously saw many problems with what he called the "burdensome command" of love. The biggest one was the impossibility of most people being in love all or even much of the time, a fact that the burgeoning self-help industry was eager to exploit. The message that love took work was an essential part of recently published books like *The Technique of Loving*, *The Chemistry of Loving*, and *The Physics of Loving*, and something that Americans, with their can-do spirit, embraced with gusto. That research was being used to uncover the secrets of love was also comforting to those trying to find it, Baker believed, as Americans liked science, or the veneer of it, nearly as much as work. Most of us began our cultural immersion in love as teenagers, with "going steady" seen as the normal state of affairs for any respectable young person. The lyrics to pop songs reinforced the convention of love among teenagers, with stolen glances at a *Playboy* or *Cosmopolitan* magazine fortifying gender stereotypes and adding sex to the equation.[19]

Young people's education in love was not yet complete, however. "By college," Baker continued, "he [or she] is a well-conditioned student of love," with readings of Freud now augmenting the young adult's view of romance and sexuality. As suggested by the protest slogan "Make Love, Not War" and the lyrics of songs by popular folkies like Bob Dylan, counterculture-era students believed in the healing power of love in its broader sense, something that clearly illustrated the flexibility and adaptability of the emotion. Best be careful what you wish for, Baker warned such idealist youth, as the usual pressures of romantic love were likely in their future. "In America, a married man and woman are expected to be in love day after day, week after week, year after year, for as long as they live," he wrote, thinking this to be "the cruelest imposition of all." Rather than love growing in a marriage, as some believed it did, Baker was convinced it typically diminished within a matter of months after the wedding day. This was not only entirely normal but a good thing, he felt, as being in love was "a terribly difficult and even an agonizing state for most people." A little love and a lot of patience was the best recipe for a happy marriage, according to Baker, challenging prevailing pop psychology thought prescribing the same ingredients but in reverse order.[20]

In his caustic thesis of love, Baker even disputed the generally accepted view that being in possession of the emotion was a good thing. He certainly did not think so, citing the common physical symptoms of being in love— loss of appetite, weight, and sleep and high blood pressure—as evidence that the state of mind was harmful to one's health. Wide swings in one's mental health also frequently came with the onset of love, more reason to conclude that one should try to avoid it like the plague. Large quantities of love also wreaked havoc on one's social life, Baker pointed out, with the smitten individual no longer interested in spending time with other people or doing other things. Likewise, work no longer seemed that important to the man or woman with a bad case of love, as it was difficult to concentrate on anything when one was in the full throes of the emotion. In the worst cases, marriages were ruined, families torn apart, and even lives were taken (sometimes one's own) in the name of love. Fortunately, "love leaves us alone most of the time," Baker maintained, leaving us in peace and able to do what had to get done.[21]

Given all these downsides to love, why would anybody in his or her right mind decide to plunge into it? "Even in the worst onsets it compensates with pleasures so mysterious, so irrational, so inexplicable and yet so rare and exalting that the finest poets have never succeeded in expressing their joy," Baker admitted, nicely capturing the baffling nature of the emotion. Something akin to Morgenthau's theory of love, i.e., that it was employed as a means to escape our inherent loneliness, could also help explain why so many us were eager to get romantically involved despite the heavy price to be paid. Along similar lines, we were flesh and blood but love was a spiritual force, allowing us to transcend the limitations of our corporeal selves. Whatever the reason, the magic spell of love remained everywhere in America, to Baker's chagrin, and there was no basis to believe that would change in the foreseeable future.[22]

What Does Love Mean to You?

Researchers were partly to blame for Americans' unhealthy relationship with love, Baker believed, but that did not stop the editors of *Saturday Evening Post* from including the findings from such a study in its 1966 issue wholly dedicated to the subject. Highly respected researcher Elmo Roper asked a nationally representative sample of 1,000 Americans no less than 75 questions about love, making the study one of the most thorough completed on the subject to date. "How many times have you been deeply in love?" "Do you think it is realistic to expect a husband and wife to love each other all of their lives?" "What does love mean to you?" If nothing else, the answers to such questions would add some science to Baker's strong opinions, and perhaps make the magazine's readers feel not so ashamed or guilty about being in love or wanting to be after digesting his scathing critique.[23]

Indeed, contrary to one of Baker's assertions, most Americans believed it was "completely realistic" for a husband and wife to love each other throughout their lives, good news for the pro-love camp. Interestingly, when asked to choose from a list of words that best described their feelings when they first fell in love, more respondents picked non-romantic terms such as "closeness" and "companionship" than romantic ones like "excitement" and "passion." Respondents' interpretation of love became even less romantic as they got older, suggesting Americans had a more practical view of the emotion than generally believed. Still, more than twice as many married people reported that their love for their spouse had grown over time than those who said it had faded, directly contradicting Baker's contention that the emotion was unsustainable in marriage. What was the big takeaway of this investigation of love in America in the mid-1960s? "Viewed as a whole, the survey indicates that American men and women pass through very definite and contrasting cycles of love," Sandford Brown wrote for the magazine, seeing the Roper study as adding another piece to what all agreed was a highly complex puzzle.[24]

Going door to door to ask ordinary Americans about their love lives, which is exactly what Roper's field interviewers did, was at the time considered the best way to learn more about the sensitive topic. (The interviewers actually waited in respondents' homes until the questionnaires were finished to maximize the completion rate.) The editors of the *Saturday Evening Post* went into their ambitious "Love in America" project thinking that citizens of this country approached love in a unique way, consistent with the popular Cold War–era belief that the United States was different from (and superior to) all other nations. "If we, as a people, are different from all others," the editors noted, "so too [is] our way of loving one another." While there were some interesting insights to be gleaned from what was one of the largest studies of love to date, the editors admitted that the emotion was simply beyond full comprehension. "Love remains free, a wild beast, seen but uncaptured," they wrote, unsure if they had contributed anything of real value despite commissioning experts like Elmo Roper.[25]

It did not take a researcher like Elmo Roper to know that love was big business in America. As the final piece of the same *Saturday Evening Post*

3. Revolt Against Love, 1960–1979

issue, Max Gunther examined the close relationship between love and business, or what he cleverly called "the merchants of Venus."[26] Love, and its romantic kin of beauty and sex, drove many businesses, a fact of which Gunther was keenly aware:

> There are few sounder businesses on earth, in fact, than those built on love. Markets may crash, great financial towers may crumble away. Yet the pale romantic moon is always there, and the stars and the soft summer breezes and the whisperings of the heart. Love—and the Love Industry—goes on. Every year millions of Americans spend billions of dollars to find love, to catch it, to keep it.[27]

To prove his point, Gunther visited a handful of marketers in the "love industry" who were selling some aspect of the emotion. With its advertising slogans "Does she ... or doesn't she?" and "Is it true blondes have more fun?," Clairol was dangling the juicy carrots of beauty and sex to pitch its hair coloring products to women wanting to spice up their love lives. The cosmetic surgery business in the United States had tripled between 1955 and 1965, with many of the customers women who had yet to find their special someone presumably because of some facial flaw. Perma-Lift was doing quite the business selling "form accenting" brassieres and girdles, and "finishing schools" were helping women improve the way they walked and talked in hopes to attract a good man or, should that fail, a good job. Single bars and greeting cards were also part of the love industry, Gunther believed, with plenty more marketers offering consumers ways to give the laws of nature a little push.[28]

The money to be made from Americans' keen interest in improving the odds of being loved and loving others was of course grounded in the cultural value we placed on the emotion. *Commonweal* drama critic and book review editor Wilfrid Sheed believed that Americans "overrated" love, so much so that other important pursuits, especially those creative and aesthetic in nature, did not receive the attention they deserved. "The obsession with love has slighted many other forms and gradations of affection," he wrote in 1967, thinking, "a fully developed taste for art and beauty can be casualties of the monomaniacal concentration on love and marriage (and on the income to support same)." Teenagers particularly were missing out on meaningful life experiences, he believed, their inclination to go boy or girl crazy closing off other more productive opportunities. Even preadolescents often engaged in a kind of dating that laid the foundation for falling in love, Sheed observed, something that was unique to Americans.[29]

Despite Americans' penchant to go overboard with love, a proclivity that limited their full potential, the emotion remained clearly adored in the United States, and wildly celebrated in popular and consumer culture. If love was so bad for us, as many critics claimed it was, why did we, well, love it so much?

"It's difficult to get mad at love, because love is whatever anybody wants it to be," Sheed argued, suggesting that the emotion was "thus, by definition, absolutely perfect." Because of the power it wielded in the human mind and in society as a whole, in other words, love was essentially resilient to all the attacks it had endured for generations and still suffered. Observers of the scene could say whatever they liked about love in America, and even back up their claims with hard evidence, but love would ultimately triumph, it appeared, the emotion immune to the most virulent criticism.[30]

Love Story

The Teflon-like quality of love did not stop the more determined from getting mad at the emotion. Indeed, if serious doubts about the prospects of love had been raised during the postwar era, critics of the counterculture years were frequently downright hostile to the emotion. Love was sometimes treated by women as an enemy as the feminism movement intensified in the late 1960s and early 1970s. Even mainstream women's magazines were often down on love, advising readers to tread lightly in the romantic waters. In 1968, for example, *Mademoiselle* informed readers "how to fall madly out of love,"[31] for example, while that same year *Redbook* opined on "how little love means."[32] As in the 1920s, questions about the effect of a more liberated woman upon love were being considered. "Will liberalized sex kill romantic love?" celebrity psychologist Dr. Joyce Brothers inquired in *Good Housekeeping* in 1971, raising a legitimate concern given the unknown consequences of the sexual revolution.[33]

Love was still alive in America, Rollo May argued in his 1969 book *Love and Will*, but it was only by having an awareness of one's own mortality that an individual could experience the emotion. Eternal life—something so many dreamed of—would likely crush any chances of being in a truly loving relationship, the existential psychologist believed (echoing the thoughts of Abraham Maslow), as it was the reality that both the lover's and lovee's time was finite that allowed the emotion to thrive. May also had interesting theories related to the interplay between love and sex as the sexual revolution reached full swing. Rather than see casual sex as reflective of the looser moral codes of the counterculture, he considered it as part of a "new puritanism" that defined contemporary society. "We cling to each other and try to persuade ourselves that what we feel is love," May wrote, with sex serving as a safe surrogate for deeper emotions of which many individuals were incapable.[34]

The awareness of death played a central role in one of the most popular

3. Revolt Against Love, 1960–1979

books about love ever written. An associate professor of classics at Yale, Erich Segal began drifting into the popular realm in the 1960s, writing pop songs, screenplays, and books for musicals. On Valentine's Day 1970, Segal's weepy *Love Story* was published, and the novel was a monster hit (it was the best-selling work of fiction that year). The wild success of the book was all the more amazing given that contemporary novelists had all but ignored that kind of melodramatic romantic weepie. In terms of story and sentiment, the novel could be said to have been more 1870s than 1970s, tapping into readers' heartstrings with its tragic tale of true love interrupted by cruel fate. Everyone seemed to be reading *Love Story* in the early seventies, with many a sniffle to be heard from men and women of all ages and occupations in life as they turned the pages of the book. Considered by most to be an unhip anachronism that had little relevance in the midst of the feminist movement and sexual revolution, romantic love was showing definite signs of life.

Not surprisingly, *Love Story* was immediately green lit for a movie that was released in December that same year, and the film became the highest grossing film of 1970.[35] One particular line in the novel and film—"Love means never having to say you're sorry"—entered the national lexicon, much to the dismay of *Love Story*'s many critics. (The five-member jury of the National Book Committee threatened to resign if the novel was nominated as a candidate for best fictional work.[36]) Interestingly, Segal did not quit his day job at Yale, claiming that pursuing serious work by teaching the classics remained important to him. While he became somewhat of a laughing stock among intellectuals after innumerable interviews to shamelessly promote *Love Story* and the movie version ("the first printing of *Love Story* in paperback was the largest single printing of any book since the invention of movable type," he claimed in one of them), Segal no doubt laughed even harder all the way to the bank.[37]

With love in the air and apparently much money to be made from it, more marketers were not so subtly appropriating the emotion as a device to package their own stories. One of them was Southwest Airlines, which was shaking up the airlines industry with its marketing campaign steeped in love (and sex). The new Texas-based commuter airline had chosen "The Somebody Else Up There Who Loves You" as its slogan, backing up that promise by hiring "shapely," especially friendly "hostesses" and ticket agents to attract the attention of its passengers (primarily businessmen). "Other airlines may meet our price but remember, you can't buy love," the airline said in its advertising, not something consumers were used to hearing. Seeing a drop in its business, Southwest's main competitor, Braniff, responded by offering its passengers a host of perks, including free beer on its flights. But Southwest was pulling out all the stops in making consumers feel like they were loved, such as by calling their ticket kiosks "love machines" and having its flight attendants deliver safety information in an unusually intimate way. "Hi, I'm Suzanne, and we're so glad to have you on our love flight," passengers traveling from Dallas to Houston heard, who were then told to put on their seat belts as "we don't want anything happening to you because we love you." Right after takeoff, a complimentary beverage called "love punch" was offered to passengers by the attendants who had shed their uniforms to reveal, as the *New York Times* described it, "tanned legs in tangerine hot pants." Dispensing of a bourbon—or scotch-based "love potion" came next, with most passengers not surprisingly finding their short flight to be highly enjoyable. "We loved having you," the stewardesses (who wore necklaces featuring a heart) told passengers as they deboarded, with many a businessmen looking forward to their return trip.[38]

While Southwest's marketing campaign was obviously over the top, love did seem to be seeping into the nation's more pedestrian landscape of consumer culture in the early 1970s. One would not think of the federal government as a particularly sophisticated marketer, but one of its agencies cleverly adopted love as the centerpiece of its campaign in 1972. Fastening seat belts was "A Nice Way to Say 'I Love You,'" Americans were told by the National Safety Council in its attempt to get more drivers to buckle up in order to reduce the startlingly high number of fatalities resulting from automobile accidents. The new public service advertising campaign, which was delivered via television, radio, newspapers, and magazines, reflected a change in strategy after recent efforts to get more motorists to wear seat belts had failed. Previous campaigns had focused on fear and logic to try to persuade drivers to buckle up but had little or no effect, reason for the council to try a more positive and emotional approach. One newspaper ad was presented in the form of a love note hand-written in script and complemented by the image of a rose. "My dearest, you are the one," the ad read, "your eyes are like stars, your lips are cherries." "Let us never part," the ad continued, the writer's sweetheart then told to "fasten your seat belt."[39]

The Emotional Equivalent of Wealth

While marketers looked to love as a powerful means by which to get consumers to do something, academics continued to ponder how the emotion actually worked. Theories regarding such had become by the early 1970s a legitimate part of the social sciences, with the study of love neatly dovetailing with the long established field of marriage and family within sociology and psychology departments. Rather elaborate, scientific-sounding theories were being put forward as research studies focused on love became more sophisticated. "The visceral response can be expected not only if the primary stimulus is physically present but also if such a remotely associated stimulus as the street on which the loved one lives is mentioned," wrote Marek-Marsel Mesulam and Jon Perry in *Psychophysiology* in 1972, a fancy way of describing the effects of love on a human body.[40]

Thankfully, not all scholarly excursions into love were that esoteric. That same year, Bernard I. Murstein, a professor of psychology at Connecticut College, suggested that romantic love went through three distinct stages, with the choice of a spouse involving a wide variety of factors, some conscious and others not. The first stage of Murstein's "stimulus-value-role" (or SVR) theory was a kind of screening process, in which individuals judged marital candidates according to their respective physical, mental, and social attributes. If each candidate passed this stimulus stage, it was on to the value stage, where the person in question was evaluated based on his or her attitudes regarding such things as politics, religion, and sex. If making it through this second stage, it was on to the third and final one, in which the candidate's views on each partner's prospective role in marriage were closely considered. With his theory, Murstein joined the chorus of dismissing the popular idea of "love at first sight," agreeing with previous researchers positing that the genuine version of the emotion could only result after individuals went through this multi-level regime over a period of time.[41]

Others viewed the state of love in the nation through an economic lens. Russell Baker revisited the subject in 1974 by comparing love in America in the early seventies to that in the 1930s, as each era was heavily defined by hard economic times. Baker remembered the Depression years as a very good time to fall or be in love, as Americans' primary ambition—the making and spending of money—had for many been put on hold. "This variety of love that was then called 'romance,' in which one fell in love, married, went on a honeymoon and, of course, raised a family ... strengthened the only social survival unit that seemed to work," he observed, recalling that the words to many songs affirmed this narrative. "Love was the emotional equivalent of wealth when a man could find 'a million-dollar baby' selling dishes in a five-and-ten-cent store or be 'rich as Rockefeller' simply by having the woman of his dreams show him to 'the sunny side of the street,'" Baker wrote, combining some of the lyrics of a few well-known Depression-era tunes. Now, however, amidst the deep recession and energy crisis of the early 1970s, Americans had no such faith in romantic love, believing that the postwar economic boom and the sexual revolution that followed had made it seem irrelevant and silly. "On our present excursion into hard times we are traveling without our love to keep us warm," Baker concluded, paraphrasing the words to another song from the 1930s that, quite apropos, referenced the high cost of heating a home.[42]

Of course, not everyone agreed with Baker's thesis that romantic love had become extinct. Even die-hard feminists like Barbara Grizzuti Harrison recently had their hearts pierced by Cupid's arrows, something that was for her totally unexpected and contrary to her commitment to what was called at the time "consciousness raising." Declaring independence from the patriarchy required a distancing from romantic love, she and many other feminists believed, making it all the more surprising when she became smitten with a man. "Many of us, having newly discovered who we were, were damned if we were going to endanger our tentative self-awareness and newly found strength by 'falling in love,'" she recalled in *Ms.* in 1974, thinking that it was a "'cultural con,' a male-designed rip-off, a form of self-destructive lunacy, a taking leave of one's senses." Women like herself were getting divorced, focusing on their careers, and/or choosing to be celibate, Harrison explained, remembering a colleague using the terms "pathological," "virus," and "plague" as descriptors of romantic love. "We had come to understand that our love for men was often obsessive and tyrannical," she wrote, adding that it also "made you look ridiculous."[43]

But then, Harrison continued, "a strange thing happened on the way to autonomy." Some women in her circle had begun to confess they had fallen in love with a man, making her wonder if this was a form of backsliding or rather a kind of post-feminist thing to do. Either way, the burial of romance was premature, she began to conclude, gradually coming to the re-realization that love could be an ecstatic experience. "In love, we are propelled into an intensity of consciousness that transforms the world and our perceptions of it," Harrison observed, thinking Carole King's lyric "I feel the earth move under my feet" (from her song of that name) did justice to the emotion. Although her recent love affair did not end well, she was now convinced that the emotion was worth investing in should the occasion arise, regardless of one's gender politics. "Love was—is—a form of perception and a way of learning the world anew," Harrison declared, describing the emotion as "a state of grace."[44]

Alongside the feminist movement, the drug culture of the 1970s was informing contemporary interpretations of love in America. "Love can be an addiction," claimed Stanton Peele and Archie Brodsky in *Psychology Today* in 1974, describing the emotion not as a state of grace but as "interpersonal heroin." The two social psychologists were not using the term "addicted" metaphorically but quite literally, with those hooked on love sometimes displaying many of the symptoms of dependent drug use such as tolerance and withdrawal. Psychologists had come to apply the concept of addiction to activities other than drug use, including work and religion, making it a relatively easy leap to conclude that some people appeared to be overly fixated with love. "Addicted lovers become less able to cope with anyone or anything else," the pair wrote, with "users" putting aside all other interests and activities. Peele and Brodsky were careful to make a distinction between addicted love and what they called "mature love," the latter allowing each party to grow and develop both within and outside of the relationship. Love addicts, on the other hand, were on a "trajectory of self-destruction," they believed, the emotional equivalent to the physical damage that habitual users of heroin were likely to ultimately experience.[45]

The dependence-like qualities of love dovetailed nicely with the more woo-woo brand of psychology that was popular in the seventies. Writing for the same publication a couple of months later, John Alan Lee argued that the primary reason why the "failure rate" of love was so high was that people tended to define and express the word in very different ways. Relationship problems stemmed not from varying levels of love but from different styles of love, he contended, a reasonable enough theory. From there, however, Lee, who taught sociology at the University of Toronto, launched into his concept of "the colors of love" and his splitting of the emotion into six archetypes: Eros (beauty), Ludus (playful), Storge (companionate), Mania (obsessive), Pragma (realistic), and Agape (altruistic).[46] The magazine then invited readers to graph their own "style of loving" by describing themselves along a spectrum of thirty-five characteristics, an exercise entirely consistent with the keen interest in self-analysis of the times.[47]

Even worse than an addiction to love was when an individual used the emotion to exercise power over someone else. In his practice, Michael Vincent Miller, a Boston-based psychotherapist, had come across such situations, calling this dark side of love "intimate terrorism." As in political terrorism, intimate terrorism preyed on vulnerability in certain kinds of unhealthy relationships, with a quest for power and control at the root of such nefarious tactics. The maneuvers, which included invasion and sabotage, varied, but they were all designed to instill anxiety in the intended target. Power struggles were typically benign at first but escalated over time to the point where the relationship was simply an excuse for an individual to exert his or her power over someone else. All really was fair in war and love, one might conclude after digesting some of Miller's accounts of intimate terrorism, with no end to how some people employed the emotion to satisfy their own insecurities.[48]

The Love-Racket

Given the new, less conventional thinking on the subject, it was not surprising that not everyone was happy to learn that love had become a respected area of scientific inquiry. Upon hearing the news that the National Science Foundation was spending $83,000 a year to discover why people fell in love, Senator William Proxmire made his position on the matter quite clear. "Biggest boondoggle of the year," the fiscally minded Democrat from Wisconsin described the study in 1975, thinking that not even that esteemed organization could make the argument that "falling in love is a science." (Even if a scientist did solve the riddle why people fell in love, "I don't want the answer," he added.) Funding for the study was predicated on trying to find out why so many couples were getting divorced, a social trend many believed to pose a real threat to the sustainability of the American family, but Proxmire would have none of it. Any and all attempts to solve the mystery of romantic love was a waste of taxpayer money, he felt, using his position as chairman of the Senate Appropriations subcommittee (which was in charge of the National Science Foundation's budget) to urge that the project led by Ellen Berscheid, a psychology professor at the University of Minnesota, be killed. "Get out of the love-racket," he told the foundation, seeing no value to the research.[49]

Editors for the *New York Times* thought otherwise, however. While the reasons why people fell in and out of love would always remain largely a mystery, they conceded, the stakes of the study were extremely high, making the project a worthy one. "If the sociologists and psychologists can get even a suggestion of the answer to our pattern of romantic love, marriage, disillusion, divorce—and the children left behind," the editors wrote in reporting Proxmire's action, "it could be the best investment of Federal money since Mr. Jefferson made the Louisiana Purchase." More reason to support Berscheid's work was that she already had some idea regarding why so many marriages were breaking up. (There were 970,000 divorces in the United States in 1974 versus 913,000 in 1973 and 479,000 in 1965.) As some had previously argued, there was a big difference between the kind of love that stemmed from infatuation and enduring love, and it was this that disparity that served as the principal cause of divorce among young couples, she postulated. More was needed to know about the illusions that were often embedded in romantic

3. Revolt Against Love, 1960–1979

love, Berscheid felt, agreeing that even modest learnings could benefit the social health of the country in many ways.[50]

While the worthiness of love as a scientific line of inquiry was debated, the subject retained considerable currency in the literary world. Just as *Love Story* served as a vivid reminder that romantic love, as least its fictional version, was alive and well in the 1970s, so did *Love Stories*. The book, which was published in 1975 and edited by Martin Levin, was a collection of twenty-eight short stories that were about love. No overt sexuality or four-letter words could be found in the stories penned by such writers as H.G. Wells, Willa Cather, John O'Hara, William Saroyan, Joyce Carol Oates, and F. Scott Fitzgerald, making the book a throwback to an earlier, more innocent time. Why publish such a book in the less than virtuous mid-seventies? "Love is an idea whose time has come back," Levin explained in his introduction to the book, thinking the stories would resonate with readers weary of contemporary fiction and its focus on the darker side of life. At least one reader believed *Love Stories* was, ironically, *au courant*. "I trust Mr. Levin is right that love as a natural phenomenon is coming into fashion again," Helen Bevington wrote in her review of the book in the *New York Times*, the emotion now charged with a kind of retro coolness.[51]

In his *Friends and Lovers* published the following year, Robert Brain also recognized the high value of love in Western society, but made the case that it came at the expense of friendship. While romantic love was revered, in part because of its association with the sacred institution of marriage and sexuality, friendship was relegated to secondary status, or what Anatole Broyard called in his review of the book "a consolation prize for the lonely." "Romantic love is regarded as a feast and friendship mere bread and butter," Broyard continued, thinking Brain was making a valid point. Love was exciting and glamorous, even dangerous at times, Brain posited, while friendship was something we did when there was nothing more interesting to do. In short, friendship had no chance to be taken seriously in a society that put love on such a high pedestal, a state of affairs that the author felt was regrettable.[52]

Brain's argument that friendship was getting the short end of the stick because of the cultural splendor of love reflected the wide range of views on the subject that were now in circulation. The fragmentation of American culture could be detected in the disintegration of love as a concept, with countless perspectives of the emotion being disseminated. "Love—the spiritual essence of love—has always been a mystery, but we live in an age when it is extremely difficult to write about love even from a superficial point of view," Erica Jong maintained in *Newsweek* in 1977, knowing of which she spoke. There were so many divergent opinions on the subject that someone was bound to strongly disagree and quite possibly be offended by what she had written, even if the work was fiction. This was unfortunate, given the richness of love as a literary device. "The truth is that there is not much of consequence to write about *except* love," she added, doing just that in her brand new novel *How to Save Your Own Life* that featured her fictional doppelganger, Isadora Wing.[53]

While love would likely always be fertile territory to explore in fiction, the real McCoy could be perceived as a relic of the past. The ever-cynical Russell Baker, writing again on the subject in 1978, believed that love had become an anachronism in a time that so celebrated the individual. Baker was surprised to hear of a couple who had fallen "hopelessly in love," thinking that the practice had gone extinct a couple of decades ago. "Falling in love is archaic, like cookouts and tail fins on your Plymouth," he wrote in his "Sunday Observer" column in the *New York Times Magazine*, the activity replaced by an adoration of oneself that left little opportunity to share the emotion with another human being. "Nowadays the fashion is to fall in love with yourself," Baker added, with feeling that level of affection for someone else considered "bad form." Americans might have been falling in love with people other than themselves but they were reluctant to confess such a thing, he explained, with much more public conversation about one's marital infidelity. Loving someone else would be seen as cheating on oneself, Baker half-joked, suggesting that this reluctance to fall in love was grounded in the current desire to avoid any and all kinds of commitment. It was also clear that self-help thinking and language had reshaped the way that Americans described love. Terms such as "relate" and "communicate" had replaced the much more emotional language of the past, with "fulfilling therapeutic experiences" and "positive mental sets" now the objective of what used to be romance.[54]

A Kind of Strange Commitment

Given his effort to stop taxpayer money going towards finding some answers to the question "What is this thing called love?," one only has to wonder what Senator Proxmire would have thought to hear the emotion expressed in such therapy-speak. Even a man in his position couldn't stop all the research delving into the dynamics of love, however. A handful of social scientists were pursuing work in the field in the late 1970s, determined to unlock what were still considered hidden secrets of the mind. One of them was Elaine Walster, a psychology and sociology professor at the University of Wisconsin, who had been researching different aspects of love since the early 1960s. One of Walster's lines of inquiry was comparing romantic (or passionate) love and companionate love, an area of interest for more than half a century. She believed the former lasted anywhere between six and thirty months at which point the latter kicked in, a finding that many a couple could have benefited from before getting hitched. Interestingly, obstacles to pursuing passionate love (such as parental disapproval or, say, one of the partners already being married) only made the desire to do so that much stronger, Walster had found after talking to thousands of people. She and her husband, William Walster, whom she had met and had fallen in love with while colleagues at Stanford, had included such findings in a recently published book, *A New Look at Love*.[55]

Additional findings from Walster's research indicated that, despite what Proxmire believed, science could reveal some of the machinations of love. About half of the subjects she had interviewed believed falling in love was wonderful, while the other half thought it was a terrible thing because of the loss of control and common sense the emotion brought with it. Contrary to popular belief, men were often more romantic than women, Walster had also discovered, and typically fell in love more quickly than women. As well, men were not more likely to go after the "hard to get" type, and in fact preferred women who they had a better chance of "getting" than did other men. And again, as previous research had shown, opposites did not attract; the longest and happiest relationships tended to be those in which two people had much in common, both physically and mentally. "It's a kind of strange commitment to the unknown," Walster described an individual's falling in love, conceding that there would always be a mysterious component to the process.[56]

While they struggled with the real thing, Americans continued to enjoy watching actors make their "strange commitment to the unknown" on the silver screen. The more that romantic love was viewed as something from an earlier generation, in fact, the more that viewers seemed to want to experience it vicariously. "If there's anything in this cynical age more than a fine romance," observed Joy Gould Boyum in the *Wall Street Journal* in 1979, "it just may be a fine romantic movie." Boyum felt there was something to the idea of there being an inverse relationship in romantic love, i.e., that the apparent lack of it in everyday life was driving what was perhaps a primal need for it that was conveniently found within the fictional universe of entertainment. "In recent months," she continued, "we've been inundated with love stories, all of which implicitly take [into] account our waning faith in romantic love." To appeal to contemporary audiences, however, such movies had to have some kind of twist, citing the involvements in *Ice Castles* (blind ice skaters), *Voices* (deaf singers), *A Perfect Couple* (older man and younger woman), *A Different Story* (lesbian and homosexual), *A Little Romance* (13-year olds), and *An Almost Perfect Affair* (filmmakers) as examples of the trend.[57]

For all those claiming that love had become stylish and fashionable at the end of the seventies, Richard Stengel had a firm retort. "Love's out," he wrote in a rather remarkable piece for the *New York Times* in 1979, stating that the romantic version of the emotion was "a supreme fiction" and a "delusion." With the Census Bureau estimating that one out of every three marriages in the United States led to divorce, he believed it was due time to take a serious look at the cause of the trouble. Rather than being a natural instinct or a feeling based on human biology, love was a behavior that we learned, Stengel (who was unmarried) held, labeling it "an artificial ritual." As many before had argued, popular culture served as our primary tutorial in love, with Americans in particular likely to imitate the characters we read about in books and magazines and saw on television and in the movies. "We learn to adore love, to idolize love, to fall in love with love," he wrote, most of us unable to resist this "drive or state of tension induced by our prevailing romantic myths."[58]

Considering the current state of marriage in the United States to be an utter failure, Stengel placed the blame squarely on Americans' fantasy of romantic love. The draw of love was indeed powerful, he admitted, promising a state of bliss and an opportunity to compete with others to win over a particular partner. Those who had not married were deemed the losers in the game of love, according to Stengel, with choosing to be single dismissed as a cover-up for just that. Because of our love for love, our expectations for spouses were absurdly high, and it was this that posed the real problem. A husband or wife had to be a lover, friend, colleague, and therapist, Stengel argued, and excel at all those jobs or run the distinct risk of being fired. Consistent monogamy and continual passion were assumed, an ideal that had no scientific basis in the makeup of the human organism or, for that matter, for most of the history of the species. Perhaps taking a cue from Christopher Lasch's *The Culture of Narcissism*, which had recently been published, love was "fundamentally narcissistic," Stengel concluded, calling for, believe it or not, a return to the pre-romantic love practice of arranged marriages.[59]

In her 1979 book *The Name of Love*, Jill Tweedie wasn't nearly as hard on love as Stengel, but she too felt that falling into its trap was a foolish thing for people to do. Women got shortchanged when it came to love, she believed, a function of the significant gender disparity that remained despite the feminist movement. Much of the book dealt with Tweedie's personal experience with love, and she concluded that what she considered to be the "most powerful of human forces" was something much different than the many-splendored thing celebrated by romanticists. Things were changing for the better, however, with the British journalist of the mind that love was in a period of transition. "Another kind of love is slowly becoming an evolutionary necessity," Tweedie wrote, this new, more gender-neutral interpretation of the emotion presenting an opportunity for "women [to] come onto center stage."[60] As the decade drew to a close, there were growing signs of a backlash to the war on love that had been waged for more than a half century. Was there hope for love in America after all?

Chapter 4

Are You Lovable?, 1980–1999

"Cyrano de Bergerac would have loved the Internet."
—Laurent Belsie, 1997

On January 31, 1984, the United States Postal Service (USPS) issued a stamp in which the word "LOVE" appeared over "USA 20c." (The "V" in "LOVE" was replaced by various colors of a heart.) By mid–March of that year, 237 million "Love" stamps had been distributed, a number sizable enough for the USPS to decide to print larger quantities of it than with most stamps and to keep it in circulation longer than usual. This was actually the third Love stamp distributed by the USPS; the first one, designed by pop artist Robert Indiana, was issued in January 1973 after the postmaster general received a letter from an Oklahoman suggesting there be a stamp dedicated to love, and the second, designed by New York artist Mary Faulconer, was issued in February 1982. The USPS was not surprised by the immediate popularity of its latest Love stamp, which was designed by Bradbury Thompson, a graphics and design instructor at Yale University. One either loved or hated Indiana's "hippyish" design, and men hesitated using Faulconer's stamp that featured a floral design and pastel colors. Everyone could love the new Love stamp, USPS officials believed, thinking it was perfect not just for weddings and birthdays but for everyday use.[1]

The popularity of the 1984 "Love" stamp was perhaps related to a shift in cultural values that was being expressed in various ways. A palpable change in the nation's mood could be felt as the 1980s began, making many believe it really was, as the new president had promised during his campaign, a new morning in America. A celebration of traditional and conservative values could be easily detected, ushering in an appreciation for romantic love that had been conspicuously absent from the country's social scene since Johnny came marching home after the First World War. In 1980, *Harper's Bazaar* pronounced "the return of love and marriage," a declaration with which other women's magazines and mainstream media concurred.[2] "Are you lovable?" *Mademoiselle* asked its readers that same year, a question that women a decade earlier would have found either offensive or absurd.[3] Was love finally achieving the respect it deserved? one could ask, if so something that marked a major turning point in the history of the emotion.

Aflame with Desire

A big part of the new status being awarded to love had to do with its growing recognition as a legitimate area of scientific inquiry. As in the postwar years, when psychologists sought a deeper understanding of human emotions as a means to improve the nation's mental health, a new generation of scientists was putting love, as it was said at the time, "under the microscope." Strong feelings toward another person produced and/or resulted from certain chemical goings-on in the brain, neuroscientists were discovering, leading to the conclusion that love was essentially a biological phenomenon. Chocolate, of all things, contained a fairly high amount of these elements, it was learned, explaining why it was said that some women craved the food when their love life went south. *Glamour* used such findings to shed light on "why love makes us feel fat," a silly but telling example of the increasing attention being given to the direct connection between the mind and the body.[4]

Despite William Proxmire's efforts to keep the secrets of love hidden, a small but growing number of scientists were now devoting research to the subject. About a dozen such researchers, most of them psychologists, were examining various dimensions of love such as physical attraction, and concluding that human biology and chemistry had a lot to do with why one person felt so strongly towards another. Pituitary secretions and phenylethylamine were two physiological reactions associated with what we generally called "love," although there continued to be much confusion around the term itself. In fact, experts could not even agree whether love was an emotion (like fear or anger) or something all its own, in part because of the enduring nature of many relationships. Emotions came and went but love often lingered for decades, reason enough for researchers to concede that they were pioneering work in what was a little understood field. Some people with brain damage were capable of experiencing many emotions but not romantic feelings, evidence that love was indeed somehow unique and special. Psychologist Dorothy Tennov of the University of Bridgeport was one such researcher contending that love stood apart from all other human experiences, so much so that she decided to coin a new term for it: "limerence."[5]

Whatever love was, Americans were keen on having more of it in their lives, even if was mostly imaginary. If the real thing was in short supply, there were plenty of surrogate versions to be had, one of them the ever popular literary category of "romance fiction." Harlequin Books was the world's largest publisher of such books, with some sixteen million readers (the overwhelming majority women) avid consumers of the genre. Steamy best-selling novels by authors like Judith Krantz and Harold Robbins had recently pushed Harlequin to up the ante of sex in their books, but the publisher was remaining largely true to its successful formula of unconsummated passion (until the wedding night).[6] Carol Wallace of the *Boston Globe* nicely described the Harlequin literary blueprint:

> A handsome, strong, sexually experienced and often moody man encounters a sweet, fragile, sexually inexperienced and often moody young girl who has yet to be set aflame with desire. (OK, a few simmers, maybe, but not a fire.) They detest each other immediately. Somewhere, usually around page 180, the plot thickens and the two fall madly in love. By page 188 (nearly every book ends on page 188) the two are married, have a child and are packing for a journey into the happily ever after.[7]

An evening out in a Manhattan nightclub could very well prove to be another rich source of fabricated love found only in the world of entertainment. Tunes from the Great American Songbook by composers and lyricists like Irving Berlin, Cole Porter, Jerome Kern, Richard Rodgers and Lorenz Hart, and Jimmy Van Heusen that praised the ecstasy of being in love were staples at such clubs that offered guests full immersion in romance at its zenith. (Reservations recommended, especially on Valentine's Day, despite the absurdly high cover and two-drink minimum.) An evening spent at the Hideaway (in the Waldorf-Astoria), Bemelmans Bar (in the Carlyle Hotel), the Upstairs Room of the Copacabana, and the Oak Room at the Algonquin Hotel was like going back in time to the golden age of romance, which musicologists placed as the 1920s to 1950s. Everything changed with the British Invasion in the 1960s, they agreed, when a new, less starry-eyed kind of love song entered the cultural vernacular.[8]

Such creative narratives of love had little to do with real life, of course, but it was exactly that which Americans and foreigners alike found so compelling about them. In the real world, pursuing love often came at the cost of more practical matters, something many Americans were learning firsthand. Romantic endeavors demanded a careful balancing act with work, for one thing, especially as careers became a top priority in the money- and success-oriented 1980s. "Love and work are the cornerstones of our humanness," Sigmund Freud had famously written decades ago, unable to anticipate the degree to which the latter would take precedence over the former. In his book *Work and Love: The Crucial Balance*, psychiatrist Jay B. Rohrlich made it clear how the scale of life was tipped in favor of future-focused work over present-focused love for a good number of Americans. Love was complicated and not goal-based like work, he explained, with the security and self-respect that a good job offered too seductive for workaholics to find time for romance.[9]

Love was getting only more complicated with the growing number of "dual-career couples" as more women entered the workforce and got high-paying jobs. Prenuptial (and postnuptial) contracts stipulating the division of assets should a marriage end were becoming quite common as money and love became increasingly entwined. Lawyers and bankers were actively offering advice in the area, all of them emphasizing the need for such couples to "get it in writing." While they preferred the term "relationship planning" to pre-nup, divorce lawyers were getting plenty of business as more states passed laws stating that, unless otherwise indicated, a couple's assets would be divided "equitably" (often 50/50).[10] Given that the divorce rate in the United States had increased 96 percent between 1971 and 1981, attorneys specializing in that area of law could hardly go wrong. Breakups after just a year or two were filling the courts across the country, with lack of communication and partners going different directions in life the typical reasons to call it quits. One economist was predicting that in a few years the number of divorces in the country would exceed that of first-time marriages, quite a statistic if so.[11]

Marital disharmony could certainly be seen in the films being produced in Hollywood. The kind of romantic comedy that had served the movie business very well for half a century could now be hardly found in theaters, as writers, directors, and producers embraced the new normal of love in America. In place of the contentious but ultimately live-happily-after films populated by the likes of Fred Astaire and Ginger Rogers, Spencer Tracy and Katherine Hepburn or Joan Crawford, and Rock Hudson and Doris Day, movies such as *Annie Hall, Kramer vs. Kramer*, and *Ordinary People* reflected the harsh reality of many relationships in the late 20th century. Couples had always experienced conflict and gone separate ways, of course, but Hollywood had long appealed to previous generations' preference for a fantasized version of love. Now, however, after the new forms of moviemaking in the sixties and seventies, not to mention the cultural turmoil experienced those decades, that formula steeped in innocence was no longer commercially viable.[12]

Residing somewhere between the darker side of love in contemporary cinema and the literary and musical throwbacks of romance was *The Love Boat*, one of the most popular television shows since its debut in 1977. (Heading into its sixth season, the show had never dipped below the top twenty in the United States and aired in 82 countries.)[13] Most Saturday nights (date night) until the series' end in 1987, millions of viewers tuned in to watch a few individuals or couples sailing on a cruise ship confront whatever issue that was blocking their respective path to true love. By hour's end, however, often with the help of the chipper crew, love or a reasonable facsimile was usually realized by each passenger of the *Pacific Princess*, adding to the idealized version of the emotion found almost exclusively in popular culture. Guest stars well past their prime—Ann Miller, Ethel Merman, Carol Channing, Della Reese, Van Johnson, and Cab Calloway all appeared in a 1982 special—further contributed to the anachronistic nature of *The Love Boat*, which was actually one of the show's strongest selling points.[14] Because of its overt detachment from reality, viewers (including myself) found the show quite comforting, and a welcome weekend escape from the pressures of everyday life (much like its televisual sibling that immediately followed on ABC, *Fantasy Island*).

Spencer Tracy and Joan Crawford in a love scene from the 1937 film *Mannequin*. The movie was described by one reviewer as "a present day romance that concerns two people in search of happiness with the world against them." By film's end, in true Hollywood fashion, "they follow the dictates of their hearts." George Arents Collection, The New York Public Library. "Mannequin. Joan Crawford as Jessie Cassidy. Spencer Tracy as John L. Hennessey." *The New York Public Library Digital Collections*. http://digitalcollections.nypl.org/items/510d47e2-e8e2-a3d9-e040-e00a18064a99

The Chemistry of Love

While love as a theme in entertainment straddled the line between fantasy and reality, scientists and others continued to try to figure out what it actually was. (Isaac Michael Rubin, a professor at Brandeis University, argued that there were twenty-six criteria of love, the key ones being "affiliate and dependent need, predisposition to help, exclusiveness, and absorption.")[15] Although most researchers believed it was a myth, the notion of "love at first sight" remained an area of interest, especially among those who swore they had experienced it. (Erica Jong, who knew a good deal about love, claimed she fell at first sight with a driver who had come to pick her up at the Beverly Hills Hotel in 1974.) Given that love appeared to be a product of some form of brain chemistry, however, the idea of a person being smitten with another upon their initial confrontation was not entirely unreasonable. A rush of phenylethylamine resulting from an intense physical attraction to someone was likely what we called love at first sight, and something many of us experienced to some degree one time or another.[16]

Some of those who had not had the experience of being instantly drawn to a person like a moth to a flame were taking more proactive measures to fall in love. Classified ads or "personals" had long been a rather scandalous means for the lovelorn to find a partner, but now in the early 1980s they were becoming a staple of many mainstream publications. Even *Harvard* magazine had gotten into the personals act, with unattached alumni of the elite university hoping to connect with someone with equivalent brainpower. Nationwide, about half such ads were placed by men and half by women, with seekers usually in their 30s. It was not unusual to receive a handful of replies to each ad placed, with SWMs, DBFs, or a plethora of other acronymic identifiers often making dates with about half of those that came in. "Outdoorsy middle-aged woman seeking sensitive man with sense of humor for long term relationship," an ad might read, with "romantic dinners" and "long walks on the beach" almost obligatory "likes." Exaggerating or downright lying about age, appearance, and occupation (as well as marital status) was common. But compared with the other popular way of meeting someone in these pre-Internet days—the dreaded singles' bar—personal ads offered those looking for love a reasonable chance of finding someone suitable, if only because totally incompatible people were usually screened out.[17]

Having things in common was all well and good to create some sparks but there was a growing recognition that it was indeed brain chemistry that determined who we would fall in love with. "Someone becomes important to us because of the ways he or she affects our brain chemistry," Michael Leibowitz stated in his 1983 book *The Chemistry of Love*, like others comparing love to narcotics in terms of bodily reaction. Because it was "some sort of amphetamine-like chemical" that was responsible for stirring up the emotion that we called love, he continued, we were not pursuing relationships the way we should. "A futuristic dating service, where potential partners would be matched for biological compatibility," made much more sense given the chemical basis of love, Leibowitz argued, an interesting idea that could very well become reality given recent advances in DNA decoding and bioengineering.[18]

Leibowitz, who taught clinical psychiatry at Columbia University, wasn't sure if it was dopamine, norepinephrine, serotonin, or one of thirty-plus other neurotransmitters that made a human brain, in his less than scientific words, "go bonkers," but he felt confident that love was overwhelmingly a chemical reaction to romantic attraction. The heart raced, breath became faster, and there was a general feeling of excitement, anticipation, and happiness, Leibowitz explained, things one didn't need a Ph.D. to know what love did to one's emotional and physical state. It was specifically the brain's pleasure center in the limbic system that became activated with the chemical bath that kicked in upon meeting that special someone. From an evolutionary perspective, love was a survival mechanism, he added, with both attraction and attachment tricks of nature designed to perpetuate the species. What nature did not account for was the letdown that often occurred once the chemistry of love ebbed, with many a partner ready to abandon a relationship once the thrill was gone.[19]

Love could also be located at the intersection of the acute therapeutic culture and accelerated use of addictive drugs in the early 1980s. A connection between love and drugs, specifically heroin, had been established in the mid-1970s, but now it was the rush from cocaine to which psychologists were comparing the thrill associated with the emotion. "Are you in love with love?" *Mademoiselle* asked its readers in 1982, labeling such people the following year as "passion junkies."[20] Likewise, biochemistry explained why some folks were "hooked on love," according to *Omni* magazine in 1984, with *Glamour* making note of the presence of "career lovers" that same year.[21] It was thus not surprising that Robin Norwood's 1985 *Women Who Love Too Much* became a number one bestseller; the self-help book struck a chord among those who could identify with its premise that there was an addictive quality to the repeated pattern of pursuing intense but unhealthy relationships.[22]

Now that many more women were working right alongside men in Corporate America, the workplace was fast becoming a place for chemically induced brains to go bonkers. In a 1983 article in *Harvard Business Review* titled "Managers and Love," Eliza Collins warned about the personal and professional risks that came with love affairs between colleagues, namely ruined careers, organizational disorder, and employee troubles. "Love between managers is dangerous because it challenges—and can break down—the organizational structure," she wrote, her conclusion based on what ensued at four different companies in which affairs took place.[23] Interoffice gossip and bad-mouthing was common when two co-workers began a romance, disrupting business as usual within the company. It wasn't unusual for one of the workers, usually the woman, to leave the company once news of the relationship spread, as office politics came into play. Things got especially dicey if one or both of the co-workers were married; company get-togethers in which spouses were invited suddenly became much more interesting because of the potential fireworks. More companies were issuing policy statements banning interoffice romances, framing them as conflicts of interest predicated on the assumption that love and work was simply too volatile a mix.[24]

With love now getting more attention within the scientific and business communities, it was not surprising that the subject was gaining greater status among psychologists. Love, much like happiness, was historically ignored within the fields of psychology and psychiatry, as it was problems like anxiety and depression that were considered more fertile territory to explore. That was fast changing as the relevance of love to everyday life was increasingly recognized, however, and as it became clear that the subject carried its own heavy emotional freight. New, very interesting findings about love were coming forth, some challenging standard assumptions about the topic. One study, for example, showed that the relative health of a relationship was not based on the degree of love but rather its distribution between the parties, with the more equal the better. Another study revealed that women loved their best friends as much as their respective partners (but in a different way) and, as a kicker, liked the former more than the latter. Robert Sternberg, a psychologist at Yale University, had published each of these studies, and was building on previous work dedicated to measuring love and evaluating its fundamental qualities.[25]

Fully aware that exposing some of the mysteries of love made good copy, the mainstream media reported the progress that academics were making in the field. "Researchers charting the course of love are beginning to put some order into an area that has long been regarded as chaotic and undefinable," Daniel Goleman wrote in the *New York Times* in 1985, informing readers what Sternberg and a few others in the growing field were up to. Sternberg argued that it was intimacy, passion, and commitment that served as the building blocks of love, with the more of each in a relationship the better. Each grew or faded at its own pace, however, meaning every relationship was literally a work in progress. The idea of marriage being a haven for stability was more myth than reality, his research suggested, a rude surprise for those thinking that getting hitched would be a steady ride until, well, death do us part. The related notion that one no longer had to put work into a relationship once one tied the knot was also wrong, according to Sternberg, confirming what most therapists had been telling their unhappily married clients and patients for years.[26]

As love further developed as a legitimate field of scientific inquiry in the mid-eighties, it was not surprising that rifts were beginning to form among researchers based on different points of view. The study of love had so far been approached from an analytical and logical perspective, something entirely understandable given the perceived need to add some much needed scientific method to the nascent field. But now a new group of researchers was making the case that understanding the subject required an approach steeped in emotion due to the fact that it was within the nonverbal parts of the brain where feelings of love sprang. Measuring love via questionnaires and surveys and then tabulating the results as if it was a tangible asset was the wrong way to go about it, this other contingent argued, as it was the irrational aspects of the emotion that mattered the most in the real world. The standard problems of research based on asking respondents questions were another issue; it was typically difficult for people to objectively assess their relationships, and there was a tendency to put a positive spin on negative experiences of the past. Since love was not a rational experience, why was it being studied as such?[27]

No Longer a Four-Letter Word

As researchers of love struggled with how to best approach the subject, Americans continued to be avid consumers of products and services that were avenues to greater romance. Romance was "back," some in the media were claiming in the late 1980s, a byproduct of the neoconservative values that had guided the nation over the course of the Reagan era. Old-fashioned expressions of romance such as sending flowers and having candlelit dinners at home had become *au courant* with the smart set, evidence that the country was further distancing itself from the wild days of the counterculture and the sexual revolution. More importantly, perhaps, the rate of divorce had appeared to finally level off, suggesting that the country was turning a corner in its social history as a new century and new millennium drew near.[28]

Signs that a new narrative of love in America may have been emerging could certainly be found in the literary marketplace. Books having to do with some aspect of romance were more popular than ever, with sales of both fiction and non-fiction in that genre up. The sunnier side of love was literally embodied by the ebullient Leo Buscaglia (aka "Dr. Hug" aka "Professor of Love"), who held that the physical embrace of another human being was healthy for each party's mind, body, and soul. His collected lectures *Living, Loving & Learning* was having an extended run on the bestseller list, largely a result of his relentless touring and frequent television appearances.[29] Another affirmation of the power of committed love was George Leonard's 1988 *Adventures in Monogamy*, in which the author argued that, in an age of trivialized sex, the emotion could serve as a nourishing source for individuals.[30]

Nothing in the literary marketplace having something to do with love compared with the ever-popular romance novel, however. Harlequin Books sold more than 200 million copies of its hot and heavy novels in 1987, with its books found in stores in over a hundred countries and printed in nineteen languages. After finding considerable success in Japan, Harlequin had its eyes on China, where sales could potentially pass those in the United States. Seeing where the action was, Crown, a large publisher, had recently introduced its own line of romance novel under the Pageant imprint. In non-fiction, Margaret Kent's *How to Marry the Man of Your Choice* had recently proved to be a bestseller, much in part because of the unique promotion its publisher offered consumers: a money-back guarantee if buyers of the book did not get married within two years. Kent's follow-up was *Love at Work*, which was described as a guide to "using your job to find a mate." Despite the initial warnings put forth, office romances had only increased over the past few years, with much of the taboo that had surrounded them now gone.[31] "Now, as more women are in the work force, particularly in the managerial ranks, and people spend more hours in the office, the workplace becomes one of the likeliest places to make a match," wrote Sandra Salmans for the *New York Times* in 1988, noting that employers were becoming more tolerant of—and in some cases even encouraging—co-workers to date or get married.[32]

Others agreed that love, after being "out" for decades, had come into favor in the late 1980s. "It looks as if narratives of relationship are being revived and 'love' is on the rebound," wrote Kenneth Gergen and Mary Gergen in *Psychology Today* in 1988, citing women's desire to have children within a family circle (even those enjoying successful professional careers) and the AIDS epidemic (which was commonly believed to significantly lessen the practice of casual sex) as key factors for the apparent shift. "Love is no longer a four-letter word," the two social psychologists continued, thinking the country was indeed embarking on a different trajectory of love that was reminiscent of the one in place from the late 19th century through the early decades of the 20th century. After decades of being out of sync with prevailing cultural values, in other words, it appeared that romantic love was now in the right place at the right time.[33]

The fact that romantic love had become an area of interest among anthropologists was more evidence that the subject was gaining cultural currency. Still covering the "love beat" for the *New York Times* in 1992, Daniel

Goleman reported the news that "romantic love is a new focus for anthropologists," with the first scientific session dedicated to it soon to be held at the annual meeting of the American Anthropological Association. An intense attraction between two people was a universal experience, anthropologists had recently concluded, something obvious to many but apparently not to those who studied humankind for a living. Bonding between a man and a woman went back millions of years, anthropologist Helen Fisher explained in her new book *Anatomy of Love*, a survival mechanism that became rooted in humans' biochemistry. Different cultures expressed romantic love in different ways (arranged marriages or polygamy, for example), but the idea that its essence could be found in the four corners of the world was considered a breakthrough in the field.[34]

Not everyone, however, subscribed to the idea that love in America had turned a major corner in its history. "If love in America is not dead, it is ailing," thought Kay S. Hymowitz in 1995, arguing that displaying any intense emotion in this country was currently considered "uncool." Writing for the *Wall Street Journal* and drawing on work by historian Peter Stearns, Hymowitz posited that love, along with other intense emotions like grief and jealousy, was in opposition to the kind of personal detachment that was in favor among Americans, particularly young people. Any and all strong feelings went against the grain of society, a byproduct of a broader dulling of the sensibilities that had accelerated in the early 1970s, in part because of the feminist movement. College students and twentysomethings appeared to be most anti-love, she observed, apt to describe relationships as friendships with little or no reference to romance or commitment. *Mademoiselle*, the magazine read by many young women, had recently suggested that we were living in a "post-idealist, neo-pragmatic era of relationships" in which the terms "dating," "boyfriend," and "girlfriend" were not seen as relevant. Freedom and pleasure had effectively trumped love, it appeared, for Hymowitz not at all a good thing. "In the past, love has had the virtue not only of satisfying our longing for profound connection but of lifting us out of mundane life into enchantment," she concluded, thinking many young adults were missing out on an essential dimension of the human experience.[35]

For Thomas Sowell, an economist at the Stanford, California–based Hoover Institution, it was simply that most Americans were embarrassed to talk about and/or take on the usual challenges of romantic love, again a function of our reluctance to engage in deep-seated emotions. Like Hymowitz, Sowell felt that our aversion to love was unfortunate, as it limited the potential of individuals and society as a whole. "Love is one of those bonds which enable people to function and societies to flourish," he wrote for *Forbes* in

1996, one of the best things about it being that large institutions like governments, corporations, and organized religions did not and could not control it. From his interesting perspective, the ability for someone to love another was an expression of personal autonomy and power, with those foregoing the opportunity because the emotion made them uncomfortable or self-conscious relinquishing one of our fundamental rights.[36]

Given how love was now being presented in the movies, it was understandable how some were reluctant to dive in headfirst. Compared to the romantic comedies made during the Golden Age of Hollywood (such as *My Man Godfrey*, *His Girl Friday*, *It Happened One Night*, *Bringing Up Baby*, and *Mr. and Mrs. Smith*), recent films like *Jerry McGuire*, *Michael*, *One Fine Day*, *While You Were Sleeping*, and *Fools Rush In* suggested that, as M.S. Mason put it in the *Christian Science Monitor* on Valentine's Day 1997, "romance is hard to come by and difficult to keep." The United States was a much different place in the 1990s than it was in the 1930s, of course, so it was not surprising that filmmakers approached sex, marriage, and family from alternative angles. Despite the more complicated plotlines that reflected romance in *fin de siècle* America, however, the power of love and often marriage and family was reaffirmed in these and many other movies being produced in Hollywood. Marriage was "still the safest harbor for romantic love, the most fertile valley, and the highest pinnacle of its fulfillment," Mason wrote, with the best interests of children especially used as a cinematic device to win over the hearts of viewers.[37]

While the sacred institution of marriage was affirmed in movies past and present, one essential part of cinematic romance had definitely changed: the on-screen kiss. "Long before sex went mainstream on screen, the kiss was the thing," remarked Devra Maza in the *Los Angeles Times* in 1998, citing the first smooch between Rhett Butler and Scarlett O'Hara in *Gone with the Wind* ("Kiss me, Scarlett, kiss me...") as a prime example of never-to-return-again romance. Other great kisses in film history include those between Audrey Hepburn's and Peter O'Toole's respective characters in the 1966 *How to Steal a Million*, (real life lovers) Humphrey Bogart and Lauren Bacall in the 1944 *To Have and to Have Not*, Gregory Peck's and Ingrid Bergman's characters in the 1945 *Spellbound*, Montgomery Clift's and Elizabeth Taylor's characters in the 1951 *A Place in the Sun*, and John Wayne's and Maureen O'Hara's characters in the 1952 *The Quiet Man*. Now, however, a kiss was used almost exclusively as a prelude to the obligatory middle-of-the-movie consummation scene, mirroring our more sexual times. Cinematic kisses used to "matter," Maza reminded younger moviegoers, thinking a rather wonderful aspect of romance had been lost over the years.[38]

You've Got Mail

One couldn't kiss online, but by the late 1990s it was becoming increasingly clear that the Internet presented a new and powerful means of finding many people to literally connect with. As with many arenas of everyday life, the Internet was revolutionizing love, sex, and everything else within the universe of romance by offering entirely new ways of meeting potential partners. "Courtship is going on-line in the 1990s," Laurent Belsie observed in the *Christian Science Monitor* in 1997, with the growing time spent on personal computers encouraging "new twists on the rituals of dating." The Internet had by then reached a certain critical mass, but no one yet was able to determine the role it would play in interpersonal relationships or, for that matter, anything else. "Can you really fall in love in cyberspace?" Belsie asked, with most experts, including Daniel Barrett, author of *Bandits on the Information Superhighway*, believing so. Early users of the "World Wide Web" or "Net" would typically find each other in a "chat room" and begin to exchange "electronic messages," with telephone conversations usually following next to hear the voice behind the typist. (Skype was years away, and even posting photos of oneself was rare because of the technological constraints and very narrow bandwidth.) If those went well, users would likely met in person, with a long drive or plane ride frequently involved. Reports of marriages between people who had met online were becoming more numerous, real evidence that love could indeed blossom in cyberspace.[39]

It was also rapidly becoming apparent that those looking for love on the Internet were not as a rule desperately lonely people suffering from some social malady rendering then incapable of "real world" romance. Those frequenting Love@AOL or CompuServe's romance chat room were, overwhelmingly, just regular folks using the Internet to complement their existing love lives, a surprising finding at the time. Anonymity and safety accounted for much of the popularity of online dating, early research in the field was showing, and women especially liked it because no effort was required to get dressed or do their hair. As well, many users felt comfortable disclosing highly personal information to someone they felt close to on the Internet, things they would never reveal to another in the early stages of a real world relationship. Even though many of those involved in an Internet relationship had never met in person, a fair percentage of them considered their online friend to be their "significant other" and were not seeing any other people, either digitally or offline. Sexually coarse language was already creeping into love chat rooms, however, and there was little doubt that some cyber daters were married. Was engaging in intimate online relationships cheating on one's spouse? researchers were wondering, the answer still not clear twenty years later.[40]

Those with considerable foresight in the late nineties were recognizing that the Internet would very likely revolutionize the ways in which people met and fell in love. Some experts in the area were making the interesting case that the digital world was in some ways superior to the analog world in terms of the formation and development of relationships. "Relationships developed on shared values, experiences and life goals, the type of information commonly exchanged online, stand a better chance of lasting than those based on hair color or height," thought Trish McDermott, advice columnist for Match.com, in a nice counter to critics of the phenomenon. This "inside-out" aspect of online dating that focused on personality versus appearance was also a retort to the popular belief that computers were making us more alienated people. The impressive numbers that Match.com, the leader of online matchmaking, were citing definitely suggested otherwise. As of June 1998, some 600,000 people had registered on Match, with 300 marriages reportedly resulting from a couple's meeting on its site. Fifteen thousand more of whom the website called "upscale, professional singles" searching for "meaningful friendships and romantic relationships" were signing up every week to find that special (or perhaps not so special) someone, an astounding statistic by any measure.[41]

Because it took place on a new medium and exponentially expanded the geographic playing field, online dating possessed a coolness that newspaper and magazine personal ads never did or could. Nora Ephron's movie *You've Got Mail*, which opened during the holiday season of 1998 and was based around an Internet romance, encouraged millions of more people to sign up with America Online and with other sites offering romance chat rooms. (That film could be seen as a next generation version of Ephron's *Sleepless in Seattle*, which relied on the conceit of a radio show to attract two people meant for each other.) Thirty thousand people were now registering on Match each week, and academics had begun to study the phenomenon and pose theories explaining the popularity of online dating. "The written word tends to promote frank conversation in cyberspace," Andrea Baker, an assistant professor of sociology at Ohio University, told a reporter in 1999, thinking the technology (paradoxically) allowed people to get to know each other quickly because they were more honest when typing on a computer screen versus talking face to face. The efficiency of the Internet alone was enough reason for people to sign up in droves; it was not unusual for users to receive hundreds of responses to a single post, making online dating like shooting fish in a barrel.[42]

As more venture capital flowed into the Internet and company valuations ballooned in the technology sector (despite a lack of revenues), consumers had an ever-increasing number of online dating sites from which to choose. Besides Match.com, Love@AOL, and American Singles (which also claimed to be the world's largest Internet dating site), MSN.com had its Love Café chat room while Yahoo! hosted Yahoo! Personals. Startups like Swoon.com (funded by Condé Nast) and niche-oriented sites such as Christian Singles Online were growing as well, with many more "cyber-matchmakers" to be found on the web. Many such sites went beyond their respective matchmaking service by offering peripheral love-oriented initiatives in order to differentiate themselves from the competition and to attract additional users. MSN.com offered a "Romance-O-Meter" for users to determine if they were gifted or challenged in the love department, for example, while relationship experts could be found giving out advice on iVillage.com, a site for women.[43]

With more than 1.3 million members paying $12.95 a month to Match, it could be seen why more online dating sites were popping up. Theknot.com, a wedding site that like Match came online in 1996, was also proving that love was a good fit for the Internet. One thousand new members were signing up to The Knot every day in order to register for gifts, find a wedding gown, and put together a honeymoon package. As well, Valentine's Day 1999 was proving to be a good one for marketers that were using the Internet to sell flowers, chocolates, and greeting cards. Another industry that was thriving online was adult entertainment; the Internet was proving to be an ideal match, so to speak, for pornography, with that business earning an additional $185 million from users in 1998, according to Forrester Research. All aspects of the mating instinct appeared to be advancing from this new technology. "Love always sells," observed Pam Stubing, a retail analyst at Ernst & Young, telling her clients that the Internet presented "a wonderful way to make money."[44]

As the scale and scope of the online universe expanded, some were making the case that such a leap in technology boded well for social relationships, including those involving love. Web sites and email allowed people around the world to connect in ways never before possible, they pointed out, theoretically increasing the chances of two people who were right for each other to find each other. The fact that the Internet was coming into its own at the dawn of a new century and new millennium made technology enthusiasts that much more excited about what possibly lay ahead. The Third Millennium would be a good one for love, veteran romance novelist Elizabeth Bevarly told the *Detroit Free Press*, a much different story than for most people who had lived during the First and Second when there were typically far fewer possibilities for whom to choose (or have chosen) for a mate.[45]

Outside of the efficiencies to now be had due to technological progress, there was additional reason to think that love was, as the saying goes, on the right side of history. Over the course of the 20th century, love had been increasingly corporatized and institutionalized, arming citizens with new sets of tools intended to better their romantic lives. "For centuries, Romance struggled along without receiving professional attention from the best business minds," Judith Martin observed in the *Wall Street Journal*, arguing that "love's progress was maddeningly slow and haphazard." Singles bars and personal ads helped to speed up and systematize love in the 1970s and 1980s, she posited, with the Internet now serving as a powerful agent of romantic acceleration and organization. Professional matchmakers represented another recent development that helped to progress love, Martin added, and offered a much higher success rate than the arranged marriages of the past.[46]

It's safe to say that there was little or no formal education in the ways of love for the general public before the turn of the 20th century. Now, however, many continuing education classes, seminars, and workshops in the subject were being offered across the country, this too considered by some to be a step forward in the evolution of love. "The baffling world of romance, once considered largely instinctual and intuitive, now is being touted as something that can be broken apart and taught in a classroom," Julie Deardorff wrote in the *Chicago Tribune*, citing courses such as "How to Flirt," "The Secrets of Charisma," and "How to Seduce a Man/Woman" as examples of pedagogical love. The San Francisco Learning Annex was offering a course called "Practical Intuition in Love: How to Find or Rediscover the Love of Your Life," with experts saying there was a real need for such classes. Spending more time working, traveling, and yes, on computers, made it difficult for people to meet someone with whom to fall in love, they pointed out, challenging the idea that we were embarking on an era of romantic ascent because of technological progress.[47]

Inevitably, a backlash to online dating was escalating even as more members signed up to one or more of the dozens of sites to be found on the Internet. Experts had warned of the potential dangers of cyberdating and recommended using an assumed name, but now a growing number of those who had tried it wished they hadn't. Married people were falling in love with people they had met online—a source of angst for all parties involved in the triangle—and reports of stalking stemming from some kind of contact on the Internet were increasing. Some men in the online world were turning out to be women in the virtual world and vice versa, creating its own special set of problems. What those in the business and a few academics had argued was one of the key benefits of online dating—a fast-track to intimacy because of its anonymity—was also turning out to be one of its biggest problems. "Freed from the conventions of face-to-face meetings, they [online daters] are using the Internet to act out their fantasies, work out their demons and expose their hang-ups," wrote Pamela Gerhardt in the *Washington Post*, with some aspect of sexuality more often than not involved in such inappropriate chat.[48]

Brazen Women

As the dot-com bubble grew bigger and bigger at the back end of the 1990s, marketers in all categories, including those selling some form of love-oriented product or service, launched their own websites to connect with consumers. Harlequin was still doing quite the business (one of its books was sold somewhere in the world every second), and was pleased to see that its website was getting 26,000 hits everyday. Having an online presence made much sense given the passion, so to speak, of readers of romantic novels. The literary category was bigger than ever, a backlash it seemed to the overt sex and violence found in much of the world of entertainment. Old-fashioned love appeared to be in short supply in people's actual lives as the 21st century beckoned, making the kind of escapist fantasy found in romance novels that much more compelling. Nora Robert's books were routinely on the *New York Times* best seller list, and, while not romantic novels per se, fiction such as Robert James Waller's *The Bridges of Madison County* and Nicholas Sparks's *The Notebook* were filled to the gills with (over)sentimentalized love.[49]

The numbers associated with romance novels were truly staggering. Half of all paperbacks sold in the United States were romances, according to the Romance Writers of America, and 150 new titles in the genre were published every month. (K-Mart was at the time the biggest seller of paperbacks, with romances accounting for 40 percent of its total book sales.) The category was broken down into 17 sub-genres, including medieval, paranormal, and inspirational. (A new sub-genre featuring zaftig heroines and targeted to plus-size women had just emerged.) What was most surprising even to industry insiders was that business executives and other professionals represented a sizable portion of the 45 million women in North America who read romance novels. Such career women read an average of fourteen romance novels per month—almost one every two days—explaining why it was so difficult for supply to keep up with demand. Smaller publishers like Thorndike were dipping their into their backlists to issue new titles as a cost-effective means of satisfying reader's seemingly insatiable thirst for what had once been rather disparagingly labeled as "bodice rippers."[50]

Even librarians, who had long dismissed romance novels as not worthy of being on their literary shelves, were coming around to the genre. Recognizing the demand for the books among women of all social and economic stripes, buyers of fiction for libraries were now adding them to their catalogs. *Library Review* now included reviews of some of the new titles being published, another sign that the genre was now considered legitimate from a literary perspective. What was it about romance novels that made them so popular? Was it their narrative of love, in which a troubled hero with a mysterious past cannot keep away from the meek heroine, something readers actually wished for? Or was the appeal merely escapist entertainment? No one could really say, but the fact that the love story in each and every book had a happy ending was certainly a prime reason for the genre to be selling like hotcakes.[51]

Whatever the secret was to the amazing popularity of romance novels, more people wanted to get in the game. In 1999, nearly 2,000 aspiring authors—almost all female—gathered in Chicago for the annual conference of the Romance Writers of America; each of them was there to pick up valuable tips and to meet editors and publishers. The industry generated more than $1 billion in the United States alone, making it easy to see why so many were trying to get a piece of the action. With workshops like "Brazen Women: Creating the Adventurous Heroine," "Arsenic and Lace: Crafting Female Villains," and "Tight Fittin' Jeans: How to Create Sexual Tension in Your Writing," the conference was certainly delivering on its promise to help turn writers into the next Susan Elizabeth Phillips or Ruth Wind (each a winner of that year's RITA award, the industry's "OSCARS™"). "All the expected kinds of discussions were taking place," reported Kirsten Schamberg of the *Chicago Tribune* who was on the scene, specifically "how love endures, how emotions rule, and how Shakespeare botched Romeo and Juliet by having it end unhappily."[52]

That year's Romance Writers of America conference (they are still held) was indeed packed with useful information. When writing sex scenes, for example, attendees were encouraged to use such phrases as "quivering bosom," "pouty lips," and "luscious hips," and locate them not just in the bedroom but in the bathroom or kitchen or, even better, on the beach. Sex had come a long way in the genre over the last few decades, although adultery was strictly forbidden in the books. As well, more leeway was now permitted in plots and characters, with the appearance of divorced women, single mothers, and bi-racial couples not raising any eyebrows. The paranormal had recently become a common theme in romance novels (and American pop culture as a whole), with heroines enjoying relationships with a ghost or an angel more often than one might expect. One new title in this sub-genre published by Silhouette Books was *Doctor Dad to the Rescue*, which was described as "a steamy romance about a hero falling in love with a heroine who is the reincarnated spirit of his dead dog." "The opening just makes me cry," the book's editor told Schamberg, thinking many readers would find the premise equally compelling.[53]

The undeniable allure of a romance between a man and his reincarnated dog notwithstanding, the more important question was whether these novels, and popular culture in general, was helping or hurting Americans' chances of having loving relationships in real life. Fictional stories were not just enjoyable to consume but served a more important role, it could be argued, by functioning as a central repository of a society's values and myths. While romance novels were incredibly popular, at least among a particular segment of the population, it was the movies where many Americans' concept of love was forged. "For most of us, our earliest images of romantic love flickered across a movie screen, and we've been trying to re-create them ever since," wrote Renee Graham in the *Boston Globe* in 1998, citing Fred Astaire and Ginger Rogers films and *West Side Story* as examples that set the bar of love overly high. More recently, it was the relationship between Kate Winslet's and Leonardo DiCaprio's characters in *Titanic* that gave viewers an idealized, thoroughly unrealistic impression of love. "Hollywood did not invent romance, but it surely perfected it," she noted, adding that "movies make love look so easy."[54]

It was true that when set to a beautiful score, the gorgeous, sanitized version of love in the movies created by directors, cinematographers, art and set decorators, lighting people, costume designers, and makeup departments (and sometimes special effects people) had little to do with what people actually experienced in their lives. Did the movies really shape people's expectations regarding love even though we all knew it was actors up on the screen reading words written by someone who did that for a living? Graham certainly thought so, arguing that not just the visual language of love in films but lines spoken by actors heavily informed viewers' conversations with significant others. "Celluloid love creates expectations unattainable for those who aren't lucky enough to have a screenwriter and director to map out their romantic lives," she observed, the illusion having a direct impact on reality.[55]

Judging by the flood of romantic self-help books published in time for Valentine's Day of 1999, it did indeed appear that many Americans were having trouble in their love lives. Online dating had made it much easier to meet someone (or at least his or her avatar) than in the past, but finding a mate with whom to settle down or even have great sex seemed as elusive as ever based on the quantity of practical advice being doled out. Recently published books included, for example, *The Kissing Companion: Secret Technique of Over 500 Kisses*, *10,000 Ways to Say I Love You*, *Recruiting Love: Using the Business Skills You Have to Find the Love You Want*, *The Art of Spooning: A Cuddler's Handbook*, *101 Nights of Great Sex*, and *Sex Tips for Straight Women from a Gay Man*. More tellingly, perhaps, updated versions of two classics—*Everything You Always Wanted to Know About Sex (but Were Afraid to Ask)* (originally published in 1969) and *The Technique of the Love Affair* (originally published in 1928)—had just been released, suggesting that many readers still had not mastered their love and sex lives. Also new on the bookshelves was *The Breakup Book*. "It's for people who could use all the advice they could get after the bitter reminder that it doesn't always work out," explained John Aherne of Warner Books, which published the work, thinking it was the perfect "anti–Valentine's Day book."[56]

While such self-help books offered potential ways for readers to draw more or "better" love into their lives, fiction served as an avenue to a kind of romance not to be found in the real world. Nicholas Sparks followed up his wildly popular *The Notebook* with *Message in a Bottle*, another bestseller that combined all the elements of a great love story. "He [Sparks] renews our faith in destiny, in the ability of lovers to find each other no matter where, no matter when...," the jacket copy read, the sheer implausibility of the book its greatest appeal. Many a husband would notice his wife reading the book in bed, knowing they could not compete with "Garrett," the romantic lead in the book. "Nicholas Sparks is ruining romance for the rest of us," half-joked Chris Erskine, a columnist for the *Los Angeles Times* in 1999, who had observed his own wife lost somewhere in the 400 pages of what one reviewer called at the time "a three-hanky love story." Making matters worse for Erskine was that a movie based on the book had just come out, with Garrett played by the hunkish Kevin Costner. (The very easy-on-the-eyes Paul Newman also appeared in the film, no consolation at all for the journalist.[57])

Many Americans had bigger problems regarding love than feeling inferior to good-looking fictitious characters in bestselling novels and Hollywood movies. There was no shortage of advice to be had from the plethora of romantic self-help continually being published, which now included titles such as *How to Make Anyone Fall in Love with You*, *How to Attract Anyone Anytime Anyplace*, *The Seduction Mystique*, and a seemingly endless series of sequels to John Gray's *Men Are from Mars, Women Are from Venus*. As well, new twists on online dating could be found for those who for some reason or another had not had success with Match, AOL, or the other big sites. Great Expectations, for example, provided videos of members so those prospecting could see and hear potential mates, and presumably filter out definite mismatches. Despite all the additional information and new tools, however, finding the (or just a) right person to share one's life with seemed as difficult as ever. "The search has been a source of golden moments and seemingly infinite repetitive misery," thought Florence Shinkle of the *St. Louis Post-Dispatch*, describing Americans' pursuit of love as "a psychological puzzle, a matter of luck or fate, a test of skills, or a libido-induced sham."[58] Love in America would continue to be a complex and often polarized experience in the new century, but many remained prepared to take on the challenge.

Chapter 5

Your Brain on Love, 2000–2009

"Down with love? Just eat some chocolate, forget the man, and take control of your own life."
—From the 2003 movie *Down with Love*

In the year 2000, a new poll revealed Americans' widespread belief that romantic love was in shorter supply than it once had been. Sixty one percent of those surveyed said that love was less readily available in years past, an interesting finding that Dave Eggers could not resist satirizing. "Like you, I am unhappy, outraged even, with the decline of True Love in society," the author and editor of *McSweeney's* wrote in the *New York Times Magazine*, mocking our common conviction that our values had gone steadily downhill through the 20th century. "Since 1930, when scientists started accurately measuring true-love levels, we have been losing it at a rate of 4 percent a year," he joked, with even the "True Love Protection Act of 1977" doing nothing to slow the erosion. True love once "roamed the prairies, filled the forests, and stocked the lakes," Eggers funnily observed, his way of critiquing Americans' genuine habit of looking back at the past through rose-colored glasses.[1]

While Eggers's analysis of the state of love in America was obviously over the top, there was some truth in his observation that the emotion was in a kind of rut at the dawn of the 21st century. What might be considered an "anti-love" movement was percolating, a reaction against the ubiquity of the emotion in everyday life, especially popular culture. Significant numbers of young women in particular were rejecting the idea and practice of love, seeing it as a sign of weakness and an annoying disruption. Alongside this societal dismissal of love, however, was a celebration of it within the scientific community. The very contours of the subject were reshaped over the course of the first decade of the new century, as a handful of neuroscientists and psychologists dedicated their careers to solving the mysteries associated with the emotion. Brain research made great strides these years, adding much to our understanding of the scientific underpinnings of love. Self-help books like Stan Tatkin's *Your Brain on Love* and *Wired for Love* showed readers how they could use their own neurobiology (and that of their partner) to help form healthy relationships, a fascinating development in the history of love.

Looking for Love

"Researchers went looking for love," reported Antonio Regaldo in the *Wall Street Journal* in November 2000, the big news being that the search was located "in the human brain." Neuroscientists at the University College in London had examined the brain activity of seventeen students "truly and madly in love" using functional magnetic resonance imaging (fMRI), which revealed increased blood flow. Blood rushed to certain areas of the brains of those students who viewed photos of their respective sweeties, the scientists observed, an important finding. There really was a drug-like effect of love on the brain, the team concluded, with the scans revealing that the limbic systems of those in a romantic state of mind lit up like a pinball machine due to the release of a chemical cocktail of dopamine and neurotrophins. This would "open up the whole field of studying the neural correlates of interpersonal relationships," said one of the researchers, fancy talk for the knowledge to be gained regarding what happened to brains on love. Historically, neuroscientists had largely ignored emotions in general, adding to the significance of this study.[2]

The discovery of love in parts of the brain was considered quite newsworthy beyond the scientific community. "Mother Nature casts her strong shadow over much of that initial activity that sparks the cascade of events leading to love," Josh Fischman wrote for *U.S. News & World Report* a month into the new century in that magazine's report of how many of the rituals and routines of romance were rooted in biology and genetics. Flirting, for example, apparently had its basis in evolution, according to some social scientists, used as a means of attracting and being attracted to suitable mates. The biological purpose of love was to propel one's genes into the next generation, after all, something not addressed by Hollywood filmmakers or in the Great American Songbook in their much more glamorous expressions of the emotion. The relative healthiness of another person's hormonal and immune systems were difficult or impossible to determine, but there were outside clues to fertility that served as attention grabbers for those seeking a partner.[3]

While scientists reminded those interested that at its core love was essentially a matter of reproduction, others viewed the subject in much more personal terms. Highly respected scholars in a variety of fields were in fact taking a close look at love at the dawn of the new century, trying to figure out what it was, why a good number people had trouble finding it, and the reasons behind many 20somethings' admitted lack of interest in it. bell hooks, for example, had just published a book called *All About Love: New Visions* in which the African American feminist theorist attempted to define love and identified the obstacles that prevented people from realizing it in their life. For hooks, career ambition had gotten in the way of a long-term relationship, making her conclude that, at least for herself, love and professional success were largely mutually exclusive. As a teenager, hooks had read Erich Fromm's *The Art of Loving*, stirring her lifelong interest in the subject. In her own book, hooks criticized our habit of equating love with romance or sexual desire, and located the problem as our general difficulty or reluctance of engaging with others on a deep emotional level. While the book could never fulfill the promise of its title, *All About Love* was spot-on with its thesis that there was no real model of love for Americans to follow except the illusory one generously doled out in popular culture.[4]

While hooks couldn't find love despite her perceptive insights on the subject, many claimed they had found it within an hour of meeting someone. Some research was showing that love at first sight (or LAFS) was real, with a surprising number of Americans saying it had happened to them. One study of 1,500 adults found that almost two-thirds of Americans believed in LAFS, and that more than half of that number had experienced it personally. "His eyes almost put me in a trance, my heart fluttered and I got tingly," said one 32-year old woman in the study, the even more remarkable thing being that it happened to her when she was fifteen. Experts were careful to distinguish LAFS from lust, as the former was much more than physical attraction or sexual desire. Love at first sight was "magical and sacred for those lucky enough to have the experience," noted Howard Markman, a psychologist at the Center for Marital and Family Studies at the University of Denver and co-editor of *Why Do Fools Fall in Love?*, seeing it as an ideal basis for marriage. Anthropologists, meanwhile, believed the phenomenon was rooted in physiology and evolution, although the conditions had to be right for it to happen.[5] (Timing, mystery, and the presence of some kind of barrier[s] all played a part.) The Internet version of LAFS was LAFB—love at first byte—in which two people somehow instantly fell head over heels with each other after a simple exchange of text.[6]

While Markman and others believed love at first sight was a wonderful thing, others held that any form of the emotion was a kind of oppression. Writing for the *New York Times Magazine* in 2001, Laura Kipnis made it clear that she was "against love," as the title of her self-described "polemic" was called. Love was "the tyranny of two," according to Kipnis, a professor at Northwestern University whose book sharing the same title would be published a couple of years later. Conceding that love was "a mysterious and controlling force [with] vast power over our thoughts and life decisions," Kipnis went on to argue that the emotion served as a primary source of anxiety among many Americans. We rarely had enough of it or had it long enough, she correctly pointed out, and the expectation for people to love their chosen mate for decades was unrealistic. While the book had what could be considered major flaws—the conflating of love with things that often came with it, i.e., sex, marriage, and living together, an overemphasis on adultery, and an absence of solutions (except staying single)—Kipnis's scathing critique of the nation's obsession with idealized romance was an important contribution to the field.[7]

As the title of his 2001 article for the *New York Times Magazine*—"The Love Bloat"—made quite clear, Andrew Sullivan's antipathy towards romantic love rivaled that of Kipnis. "Can we please ease up on our secular cult of romantic love?" he pleaded, informing unaware readers that the concept was just a couple hundred years old. In terms of emotional heft, romantic love paled in comparison to many other sentiments (including friendship, patriotism, and parental love), he felt, but Americans considered it the primary path to happiness. Sullivan believed that there had been a dip in love as a cultural force in the 1990s, but now it was back and, sadly, bigger and badder than ever. Kindergarteners were dating, gays were fighting for equal marriage rights, Ronald Reagan's collection of love letters had become a bestselling book, and the banal movie *The Wedding Planner* was a recent hit, all evidence suggesting that love in America was serving as nothing short of a civic religion. Love was a false idol, however, as it could rarely deliver what it promised, according to Sullivan. Americans liked to pursue love but, once finding it, quickly lost interest, our expectations more often than not exceeding the reality.[8]

It would be easy to view Americans' obsession with romantic love as a harmless exercise in narcissism or a good excuse to engage in socially sanctioned sex, but Sullivan believed the problem ran much deeper. Love was a "curse," he felt, and something that was harmful to individuals and society as a whole. Sullivan subscribed to Rousseau's argument that bourgeois love functioned as a safe substitute for the taking on of more important philosophical and moral issues, enervating the potential power of the people. Love was "a salve for the empty emotional center of restrained, law-bound societies," as Sullivan translated Rousseau's thesis, a comforting diversion that prevented us from having to consider "what to believe in or strive for." The (undeserved) power of love effectively forced many to succumb to its demands, as the alternative was worse; those not in love were deemed lonely or social misfits, making it not surprising that so many signed up despite its obvious flaws.[9]

After 9/11, however, it was hard for anyone to make a serious case of being against love. A clear shift in the cultural dynamics of the emotion could be detected immediately following the tragic event. Matchmaking services reportedly doubled virtually overnight, and people with long-time platonic relationships began wondering if they could turn into romantic ones. "Since the attacks, the clock seems to tick faster for rituals of romance," Frances Parnes wrote for the *Times* a couple of months after 9/11, with evidence suggesting that many Americans were fortifying healthy relationships and ending unhealthy ones. Engagements were being shortened to fast-track weddings, and those on the fence about getting married were getting their licenses. Business on theknot.com was up, seemingly in part because of stories of those who had lost their fiancés in the towers. "At a time when everything feels unmoored, the desire to anchor one life to another is stronger than ever," observed Matthew Klam in a special issue for the same publication dedicated to couplehood.[10] Some bad choices in the romantic arena were also being made in the months following the attacks, however. In pursuit of companionship, people were dating and sleeping with partners they otherwise would not have, and were regretting doing so.[11]

A different tone could certainly be heard on *Delilah*, the syndicated radio show in which callers shared personal life stories, most of them having something to do with love, with the host and millions of listeners. Debuting on four stations in 1996, *Delilah* soon became a national phenomenon, with the titular host's on-air persona a compelling combination of therapeutic self-help, New Agey spirituality, and, if warranted, tough love. Every weeknight, callers—almost all women—conversed with whom the *Washington Post* called "the leading lady of love" to reveal their "pains and passions" and receive inspirational wisdom to guide their relationships. By early 2002, the show was airing on 200 stations across the country, with dedications and love songs by the likes of Michael Bublé and Celine Dion essential parts of the mix. While some joy could be heard in the confession-like mini-stories, much of *Delilah* was (and remains) filled with loneliness, regret, and remorse, reflecting the sad state of love for many Americans. This was especially true in the months following 9/11, when the nation as a whole felt a shared sense of loss.[12]

Stephen Mitchell's (posthumously published) *Can Love Last?: The Fate of Romance Over Time* helped shed light on why so many had not found happiness in their relationships, particularly (and ironically) if they had been with their respective partners for a considerable amount of time. Mitchell, one of the founders of relational psychoanalysis, dismissed the popular notion that breakups were mostly due to couples growing bored with each other over the years. With the initial thrill (and dopamine) gone, this "familiarity breeds contempt" (or at least ennui) idea went, it was understandable why someone would consider looking elsewhere for excitement. Mitchell believed something very different was in play, however, arguing instead that partners distanced themselves from one another because they feared the dependency and vulnerability that came with true love. Deeply committing oneself to another person was a scary thing in that it created the sense that we were not in full control of our lives, this the real reason why married people had affairs and/or ended up in divorce court. Love could and would endure if people were willing to accept the existential risks that came with it, but Mitchell had serious doubts about such a thing happening in our Me-First society.[13]

Our Most Intimate Institution

The possibility that love was simply an unsustainable proposition did little to stop Americans from seeking it via the Internet. Much had been made of those who had successfully found love online, not too surprising given the excitement that surrounded the medium while the dot-com bubble grew bigger and bigger in the late nineties. In March 2000, however, the bubble was seen as having burst, and with it had the mania for all things online. By early 2001, the limitations of the Internet were being increasingly recognized, including those related to romance. "The reality, for those seduced by the dream of finding the perfect mate on the Internet, is that the success stories are the rare and serendipitous exceptions," wrote Joyce Cohen for the *New York Times* in January of that year, with offline relationships turning out to be much more difficult to sustain than the flirtatious online chit-chat. Communicating in real life was quite a different thing than a dialogue via email or in a chat room, more psychologists were beginning to say, and the strong connection that many reported having with someone on a computer usually did not translate well to the analog world. First face-to-face meetings between cyberlovers were more often than not turning out to be complete busts, and a rude surprise to those who truly believed they had found Mr. or Ms. Right. "The medium sucks you in," explained Joseph Walther, a professor at Rensselaer Polytechnic Institute, thinking the accelerated pace of online dating was more of a negative than a positive.[14]

While many online daters were not giving up the technology completely in their love lives, they were typically curbing their enthusiasm about its potential outcomes. As always, the process was a numbers game, with heavy users often making thousands of initial contacts that likely led to email exchanges with a few hundred different people. From there it was phone conversations with perhaps a hundred different people, with that pool maybe generating a few dozen in-person meetings. One such heavy user in Manhattan reported a 10 percent chance of having a second date after a first in-person meeting, a less than impressive figure related to the enormity of the funnel. As with everything else, the Internet offered quantity but frequently not quality when it came to love, one could assume, as the technology was notoriously bad in providing that impossible to define but essential sense of chemistry or "vibe" between two people. Nonverbal communication—eye contact, gestures, facial expression, body language, and silence—was a key element of human interaction, after all, and something that no amount of email could offer those looking for love on the Internet.[15]

While those in the industry continued to maintain that meeting someone with potential was far more likely online than say, at the grocery store or library, critics hammered away at what was described as the false intimacy of text-based relationships. Words were just not enough, academics doing research in the burgeoning field argued, especially when some of the words were deceptive or downright untrue. Less flattering aspects of one's physical being and personality were often omitted from descriptions of oneself in order to work the odds. Given such carefully edited self-portrayals, should it have been surprising that just one out of every ten first dates led to a second? Absolutely not, communications experts said, as seeing and hearing someone in the flesh was an entirely different experience than reading words he or she wrote (or had commissioned from a more literary friend).[16]

New research centered on the brain helped to explain why so much of Internet-based romance was doomed to fail. The arrow from Cupid's bow was actually a powerful biological drive, more scientists were arguing, with our urge for love equivalent to that for food or sex. That love was a primal drive made considerable sense given the seemingly irrational things people did when afflicted with the condition, and the way that the emotion could essentially take over one's mind and body in the early stages of a relationship. "What we're seeing here is the biological drive to choose a mate, to focus on one person to the exclusion of all others," said the anthropologist Helen Fisher who was now at Rutgers University and had recently published her findings in the journal *Neuroendocrinology Letters*. Fisher and her team analyzed MRIs of eighteen college students who stated they were in love, with the brain scans taken while they looked at a picture of their respective heartthrob. This study was based on the one done in England that found that brains on love were unique from those in different emotional states. As previous studies had shown, dopamine kicked in when one was romantically attracted to someone else, explaining the feeling that one had more energy and less need for sleep or food when smitten.[17]

Despite more evidence that love was at its core a biological function, not everyone was convinced that the emotion was just a matter of brain chemistry. An editorial written by Robert Epstein in the June 2002 issue of *Psychology Today* suggested as much, and deservedly received much attention given that Epstein was the magazine's editor in chief. Epstein sought a woman with whom to "fall deeply in love" over a designated period of time, the quasi-personal ad read, this self-described "experiment" intended to reveal whether two people could intentionally learn to love each other. "This isn't a publicity stunt," he made clear, but rather "a serious, albeit small-scale challenge to a vexing myth," i.e., that each of us are destined to fall in love with just a single individual with whom we should spend the rest of our lives in marital bliss. Rather than leave matters to fate, in other words, Epstein was taking a scientific approach to finding love, and using himself as the human guinea pig. He and the winner of the contest (hundreds of applications immediately rolled in) would contractually agree to date each other exclusively, go to counseling as part of their tutorial in love, and then together write a book about the experience. Many people who knew him (including the man's mother) thought that the well-respected scholar with a Ph.D. from Harvard had lost his mind, but Epstein was as serious as can be about the unusual venture.[18]

Epstein's direct challenging of one of the fundamental beliefs of love—that people "fell" into it—took a fair share of the psychological community by storm. Taking a deliberate and methodical approach to finding true romance went against our basic instinct to let nature take its course in such matters, making the endeavor almost anathema. A panel was soon organized at the Smart Marriages conference in Reno to discuss Epstein's curious undertaking. "Is this pure heresy, or is it an idea that can revolutionize our current understanding of how love works?" wondered Jan Levine, a psychologist and relationships specialist who would moderate the panel of four experts. A year after his controversial editorial, Epstein (now West Coast editor of the magazine) was sticking to his guns, still claiming that Americans' formula for love had proved to be a failure. One didn't need to look far to realize that the live-happily-ever-after myth made a great fairy tale but was a mistake to practice, he argued, citing the number of unhappy marriages as prime evidence. Levine disagreed. "Love is a spontaneous act that cannot be tampered with," she declared, convinced that it could not be willed or designed.[19]

However, another member of the panel, John Gray of *Men Are from Mars* fame, believed Epstein was on to something important, and that he should be commended for his commitment to education in the field. "We have been relying on romantic myths rather than the relationships skills that make marriage work," the relationship guru stated, seconded by another panelist, the aptly named author Pat Love. Love agreed that Epstein's idea had merit given the fact that more than 50 percent of marriages in the world were arranged and, on average, they lasted longer than those of Americans. "Half the world believes that first you marry, then you fall in love," she said, of the mind that practicality followed by fondness could indeed serve as an effective path to the long-term development of romantic feelings.[20]

So was Epstein's bold experiment successful? More no than yes, I would say. None of the more than 1,000 responses he received was compelling enough for the experiment to move forward, for one thing, suggesting that finding a partner through a personal ad was probably not the best approach. He did ultimately meet someone but not through his advertorial (it was on an airplane) and, while the woman agreed to be part of the project, the fact that she lived in Venezuela and had children from a previous marriage who did not want to leave the country made it unlikely to succeed. Unfazed, Epstein planned to test his concept with multiple couples and, if the results were positive, develop relationship programs based on "structured" love.[21] Picking a mate based on passion was "like getting drunk and marrying someone in Las Vegas," he remarked, thinking the time was right for arranged marriages to make a big comeback.[22]

Although his colleagues and mother thought that the man should take some of his own psychological medicine, Epstein was on the right side of history with his unconventional ideas about love and marriage. Until the 19th century, as E.J. Graff discussed in his *What Is Marriage For?: The Strange Social History of Our Most Intimate Institution*, arranged marriages were customary in Europe, a means of fortifying inter-family relationships, safeguarding wealth, and strengthening community ties. Love was beside the point, a concept difficult to imagine in contemporary romance-obsessed Western culture.[23] Others who knew their history, however, wondered if individuals were better off having the freedom to choose his or her mate based on feelings. About half of marriages in the United States failed and many that did "succeed" were far from perfect, making some conclude that the prince or princess they had hand-picked was actually a well-disguised frog. "The major reasons that people find and get involved with somebody else are proximity and physical attraction," observed Alvin Cooper, a staff psychologist at Stanford University, considering these two factors to be "terrible predictors of long-term happiness in a relationship."[24]

A Great Change Agent

While neuroscience had begun to steal much of the thunder regarding love from psychology, psychologists like Cooper were still looked to as experts in the field who could offer sound advice to those in need. Another one of note was Ethel Person, a psychoanalyst and Columbia University professor whose work focused on love. Person was a loud and proud supporter of romantic love, seeing it as "a great change agent" that helped people realize parts of themselves that they otherwise would not. "We come to know ourselves in a different way when we fall in love," she said in 2004, of the mind that "we discover capacities that we didn't think we had." Even "failed" relationships were not truly failures, she felt, seeing them instead as "part of the growth process." Valuable experiences in life didn't require a happy ending, according to Person, challenging the notion that a relationship that went south was by definition a waste of time and energy. She also dismissed the idea that people fell in love once and only once in their lives, believing it was something that could happen in different ways at different stages of life.[25]

Because of their real world experience, marital or couples therapists often had useful theories about love that could never be revealed by an fMRI in the lab of a neuroscientist. Harville Hendrix, for example, argued that individuals subconsciously partnered with people who helped them heal some kind of trauma from the past, an interesting idea steeped in Freudianism. (This observation "changed the way I saw romantic love forever," Oprah Winfrey remarked years after he mentioned it on her show, quite an accolade given how much attention she gave to the subject on television and in her magazine.[26]) Hendrix also challenged the popular belief that people should seek out partners who were very much like themselves and were thus presumably a good fit. Rather, two people ideally created a kind of new space that existed between them, their mission to occupy that through their relationship. "The between-ness is the locale of love," he said in 2004, finding too many people claiming their own space and trying to have their partner move into it.[27]

Henry Grayson, a well-known New York psychologist, presented his own thoughts about love in his provocative book *Mindful Loving* and popular tape series *The New Physics of Love*. Relationships succeeded or failed based on how we thought of them, he argued, a thesis grounded in mind over matter or that perception was reality. Changing other people's behavior was a lost cause, according to Grayson, seeing an internal shift in attitude as a far superior avenue to realizing positive relationships. Like Hendrix, Grayson believed that egos drove many relationships, with the fear of losing that "special" person the impetus to try to control him or her. Through greater self-awareness, we were less likely to misinterpret others' actions, and more apt to come to the realization that it isn't "all about me." Love could and should be a path to enlightenment, he proposed, like others with a more spiritual bent perceiving the emotion as a means of fulfilling our true potential.[28]

Much of practicing psychologists' jobs centered around busting the myths that were part and parcel of romantic love. Songs and movies engrained the idea that a prince or princess would one day come along, rescue us from loneliness, and lead us to the happy life that we deserved. Psychotherapist Diana de Vegh termed this the "scarcity" model of love, i.e., that there was one and only one person who was capable of achieving such an ambitious mission. Decades earlier, de Vegh had an affair with a real life prince—President John Kennedy—giving her personal experience in fairy tale-like love. Fantasy-based romance was parental in nature, she believed, especially for women seeking someone who could offer paternal safety and maternal nurturance. Love became "corrupted" when one's self-worth was dependent on another, however, with no good to come from feeling powerless and vulnerable. Likewise, relying on one person to fill up one's life as much as possible was a dangerous path to go down, de Vegh advised her clients. The world was a big place, she reminded those wanting to spend every minute with their significant other, pointing out that different forms of love could be found in different places.[29]

Psychotherapist Michael Vincent Miller, meanwhile, found that the transition from romantic love to companionate love was often the biggest problem in long-term relationships. The degree of work involved in marriage and having a kid or two was a rude surprise to many couples thinking the glow and excitement of early love would last forever. Dining out, hot sex, and a full night's sleep frequently became distant memories after a few years, with that once blissful relationship now a breeding ground for resentments and accusations of all kinds. "The extraordinary experience of romantic love conveys the feeling that 'the two of us are as one,'" Miller wrote in 2006, "but the daily tasks of marriage can quickly disabuse a couple of the notion that they have found such a perfect union." The trick to enduring love resided in how well each partner could manage the gradual realization that one was not just half of something but was rather an individual, he posited, as well as how well to deal with any disappointments that came along the way.[30]

That all relationships were inherently imperfect was itself a major revelation to those expecting a "perfect union" based on pure romantic love. "Successful" marriages were those in which conflict was used to strengthen the bond between two people, those who had done such a thing told others. "It's fraught with tension, but that's good, that's how it's supposed to be," said a fortysomething man speaking about marriage, having accepted the fact that he and wife were very different people but were still very much in love. Couples who made it through rough patches often reported that their relationships had as a result become tighter, recalling the Nietzschean idea that what doesn't kill something makes it stronger. Just giving one's partner some space, as the saying went, could work wonders in a friction-filled marriage, especially when there was an abundance of trust.[31]

The outpouring of psychology-inspired advice on love in magazines such as *O: The Oprah Magazine*, *Glamour*, *Ladies' Home Journal*, and *Redbook* was obviously designed to help women and some men navigate the rocky terrain of romance. "What is this strange force that has so much power over us? Why does it have to be such a big mystery? And why do we have so much trouble giving it, accepting it, making it last?" Oprah herself asked in one of many issues of her magazine that was dedicated to the subject.[32] Answers to such good questions were deemed very relevant for those who didn't reject the emotion outright; love was a complicated affair but worth pursuing, the standard narrative went. Love had become more complex over the past half-century, all agreed, with the women's rights movement, sexual revolution, and greater focus on the "self" destabilizing what was now fondly remembered as a simple, straightforward process: boy meets girl, after which they go steady, become engaged, get married, and presumably live happily ever after. "It's not that romance didn't involve moments of heartache and anxiety, but it proceeded along a recognized, accepted, and very clear trajectory," wrote Amanda Robb for *O*. This linear model was now as dated as a sock hop, however, making love a more challenging journey on which to embark.[33]

Without those clearly delineated steps, explained psychologist Scott Stanley, the arc of love now often followed a more unmarked path that left individuals with no clear sense of place. Couples might sleep together after a couple of dates and then, in a few months, move in together, with the relationship continuing to evolve in an amorphous sort of way. The end game was usually not clear, creating a sense of uncertainty that frequently became the dominant theme of the relationship. "Commitment" emerged as the key issue, with one partner typically more interested in going to the next level, i.e., marriage and/or kids, than the other. Clinical counselor John Van Epp saw so many of his single clients, most of them seemingly smart people, fall into this trap that he created something called the PICK (Premarital Interpersonal Choices and Knowledge) Partner relationship education program to help them determine whether to stick it out or move on.[34]

An Evolutionary Miracle

The meandering of relationships in real life was perhaps a contributing factor for making absurdly condensed versions of love some of the most watched shows on television. Popular reality shows such as *The Bachelor*, *The Bachelorette*, and *Joe Millionaire* (as well as the thankfully short-lived *Married by America* and *Meet My Folks*) were each based on the premise of love blooming instantly or nearly so in a controlled setting while millions of viewers watched the proceedings. In such shows, a single contestant gets to choose from a couple of dozen potential mates, with marriage the stated goal. Candidates are eliminated over the course of a season (dates are set in romantic and exotic locations), with a proposal the climactic scene. (The shows had little to do with "reality," as they were carefully scripted and edited to make compelling television.) Most experts pooh-poohed the idea that genuine and lasting love could result from such overtly commercial and contrived situations, but others, notably Helen Fisher, believed the principles of love at first sight could apply.[35]

A major assumption about love, whether depicted in faux reality or as expressed in the authentic version, was that it was heavily based in the relative "compatibility" of a couple. When two people's respective lists of personal characteristics aligned, many authorities in the field believed, they made a good match, as it was obvious the couple had much in common and were thus likely to get along well together. Some experts advised, however, that this was a false assumption. Compatibility was not something a couple possessed but had to create over the course of their relationship, they pointed out, making it a process that evolved over time. Another false assumption about love was that it was largely dependent on the "chemistry" between two people, according to many experts. While chemistry—that undefinable spark between two people—was an attractive idea, it was more things like patience, respect, and compromise that typified good relationships over the long haul, they argued, as such a bond would guide a couple in good times and bad.[36]

Needless to say, the producers of the well-orchestrated romantic goings-on to be seen on *The Bachelor* likely did not review the latest scientific findings in the field. If they had, it and similar shows might have paired couples based not on who most dramatically accepted a red rose in the final episode but rather on things like shared physiological responses and biochemical programming. Each of us had a unique "love map," Helen Fisher discussed in her most recent book *Why We Love: The Nature and Chemistry of Romantic Love*, something that served as the subconscious image of our ideal mate. If someone fit the terrain of this psychic map and satisfied a variety of other criteria (such as having things in common), it was then when neurotransmitters like dopamine and serotonin took over to create the emotion that we called love. Reality and objectivity often went out the window once the brain mixed its chemical cocktail, according to Fisher (who was now being referred to as "the Queen Mum of romance research"), nature's original way to encourage two people to couple and ensure that the species would survive.[37] "We are coming to some understanding of the drive to love—and what an elegant design it is!," she wrote in the book, describing the process as "an evolutionary miracle designed to produce more humans."[38]

Indeed, if one didn't know better, an examination of the brain scans of young people in love could make one conclude that the lovebirds were suffering from sort of psychosis. Behavior suggesting as much, i.e., the mania and obsession that often characterized the early stages of love, was thus entirely consistent with the neurological activity taking place inside the brains of the newly lovestruck. How else could one explain a late-sleeper's recently acquired habit of arriving at a certain Starbucks promptly at 6 a.m., precisely when a certain lady or gentleman happened to enjoy his or her coffee? Friends and relatives of the newly besotted would wonder what had happened to the fun person they knew, confused about why he or she was suddenly unavailable for anything. "This drive for romantic love can be stronger than the will to live," Fisher stated after she and the co-authors of the study, Lucy Brown of the Albert Einstein College of Medicine and Arthur Aron of SUNY Stony Brook, published their findings.[39] One didn't have to be an expert in the field to appreciate the power of infatuation love. "It is the most forceful human emotion that drives us to do all sorts of things," said Toni Morrison in explaining why she decided to name her most recent novel simply *Love*.[40]

If love was primarily a function of biology, how then to account for the torrent of books and courses designed to help people find it in their lives? Books such as Bruce Brander's *Love That Works: The Art and Science of Giving*, Pepper Schwartz's *Finding Your Perfect Match: 8 Keys to Finding Lasting Love Through True Compatibility*, and David Givens's *Love Signals: A Practical Field Guide to the Body Language of Courtship* were just a few of the latest how-tos intended to assist folks who were seeking a relationship with a special someone in their lives. Scientists were saying that it was brain chemistry that determined who we could and could not fall in love with, however, bringing to mind the old nature versus nurture argument. Was love essentially a matter of meeting the right person in the right place at the right time, or could one make it happen via a better understanding of what it was and how it worked? The answer wasn't clear, leaving the subject of love as somewhat of a mystery despite all the attention given to it over the decades.

The most sensible explanation for the workings of love was that while chemistry provided its spark, successful long-term partnerships relied on the kind of advice being offered in self-help books. Dopamine, norepinephrine, and other neurotransmitters were programmed to stimulate the limbic system for just a short period of time, in other words, after which the more rational parts of the brain took over the progression of love. "Having a crush on someone is wonderful but our bodies can't be in that state all the time," explained Pamela C. Regan, a professor of psychology at California State University, Los Angeles, and author of *The Mating Game: A Primer on Love, Sex and Marriage*, adding that an endless stream of such chemicals would actually prove fatal. Problems ensued when those in the early stages of love could not adequately transition from the initial chemically induced rush to the mostly mundane day-to-day management of relationships, one could conclude, this perhaps a primary reason why so many couples broke up.[41]

As previously observed, many young adults had no intention of allowing themselves to be subjected to the temporary madness that came with a crush. "Love is constant effort," one woman in her early twenties told a reporter from the *Washington Post* on Valentine's Day 2007, with her friend chirping in "It's so annoying" and another that "It's a waste of time." Love was impractical, silly, and a sign of vulnerability, these and many other women around their age across the country believed, preferring flings and hookups to serious relationships in their romantic lives. The numbers bore out the fact that both young women and men had critical views of love. A national poll of 18-to-29-year-olds conducted by the Pew Research Center found that almost 60 percent of the respondents were not at the time in committed relationships and that most of them were not interested in being committed to anyone. Friends in serious relationships were contemptuously called "married" even though they remained single, another indication of their scorn for love. "Being emotionally dependent on a lover is what scares these young women the most," the *Post*'s reporter concluded after her chat with the three ladies who were determined not to fall into what they believed was a sorry state of childish fantasy and sentimentality.[42]

Given new research by the indefatigable Helen Fisher, one has to wonder if the taking of SSRIs or antidepressants was playing a role in young women's lack of interest in and even disdain for love. She and her collaborator, psychiatrist J. Anderson Thomson of the University of Virginia, were making the case that Prozac, Zoloft, Paxil, and other commonly used antidepressants modified the brain chemistry of those who might otherwise experience the "temporary insanity" of early love. The drugs not only diminished the euphoria induced by dopamine and other neurotransmitters, their theory (published as a chapter in the book *Evolutionary Cognitive Neuroscience*) went, but also reduced their users' desire for a partner and perhaps even the ability to fall in love. The effect of such drugs on sexual desire was well known as was their tendency to dampen emotions in general, but the possibility that SSRIs could compromise the biology undergirding romantic love was a new idea that carried serious potential consequences.[43] Married couples became a minority in American households in 2005, according to census data, perhaps in part due to the rise of "Prozac Nation."[44]

Drug-induced or not, the down-with-love climate of the early 21st century likely prompted the re-release of Nathaniel Branden's classic study of love, *The Psychology of Romantic Love*. Originally published in 1980, the updated book (now carrying the subtitle *Romantic Love in an Anti-Romantic Age*) retained its attempt to explain "what love is, why love was born, why it sometimes grows, and why it sometimes dies." In his practice as a psychologist (that focused on self-esteem), Branden had encountered many people who had concluded that love was simply no longer a viable proposition, a byproduct of the increasing complexity of life. Branden maintained that love was attainable for those who understood what it really was about and were willing to take on its challenges, however, perceiving it as a direct route to both great joy and deep self-awareness. Love uniquely satisfied many of our needs as human beings, he argued, perhaps the most compelling being "our need to share our excitement in being alive and to enjoy and be nourished by the excitement of another."[45]

Cristina Nehring's *A Vindication of Love* also made a strong case for romantic love despite all the good reasons to avoid it. Nehring made a plea for, as the book's subtitle went, "reclaiming romance for the twenty-first century," she too thinking many women (and men) did not want to expose themselves to the emotional risks that came with passionate love. The book in some ways echoed Steven A. Mitchell's argument that individuals were reluctant to plunge deep into a relationship because they believed that doing so meant giving up a part of oneself. Women in particular did not possess "the generous fault to put oneself entirely in another's hands," Nehring wrote, with loss of control and autonomy the underlying reason for holding back. Those who did so were missing out on one of the best things in life, she insisted, seeing love as not just an enriching experience in itself but as something that helped one become a more creative and spiritual person. Taking a fresh look at those in the past who got romantic love right, i.e., Mary Wollstonecraft, Jean-Paul Sartre, Simone de Beauvoir, Frida Kahlo and Diego Rivera, would go a long way towards reinventing the emotion for the future, she argued, if nothing else an interesting premise.[46]

This Most Ethereal of Emotions

While many Americans were purposely opting out of love because of the toll it could take on the rest of one's life, marketers were finding the emotion to be a compelling selling tool. Love had become "a sentiment enthralling Madison Avenue," according to Andrew Adam Newman of the *New York Times*, citing BlackBerry's new advertising campaign as the latest to tap into the latent power of the emotion. Commercials for the smartphone carried the slogan "Love What You Do" and employed the Beatles' song "All You Need Is Love" as the musical soundtrack, techniques to reference the love that users had for their devices. (Some Blackberry users confessed they kept their gadget under their pillow while they slept, just one reason the things were sometimes referred to as "Crackberries.") Other marketers smitten with love included Subaru ("Love. It's What Makes a Subaru a Subaru"), LensCrafters ("See What You Love, Love What You See."), and Payless ("'I [Heart] Shoes."), complementing long running campaigns for McDonald's ("I'm Lovin' It.") and Olay ("Love the Skin You're In."). "Emotional attachments really are a crucial factor in purchasing decisions," said Linda Kaplan Thaler, chief executive of the Kaplan Thaler Group, in explaining the love trend in advertising, although it was not exactly clear why more marketers were adopting the approach.[47]

Part of the reason that love was in the marketing air may have had to do with the increasing attention that love was getting in the media. Advances in neuroscience continued to inform our understanding of love, so much so that many were concluding that researchers in the field were on the brink of a breakthrough or perhaps had already realized it. The chemical goings-on in the brains of those in the initial, "manic" stage of love was by now well established, but new research was showing that there was a biological component to the emotion in the latter stages as well. It was oxytocin, the attachment or "bonding" chemical that kicked in after the early period characterized by infatuation and obsession, according to a study published in 2009, further defining love as a neurological event. Oxytocin (and vasopressin) helped encourage the desire for an individual to commit to and practice monogamy with a partner, it was believed, making them nature's way to foster long-term relationships. Was it a lack of oxytocin that helped explain why certain individuals fell out of love over time, making divorce at least in part a byproduct of brain chemistry? It was not yet clear, but some scientists were already raising the idea of the development of drugs designed to influence the neurological foundation of love.[48]

The finding that "companionate" love was not simply the result of a relationship becoming the same-old same-old over time but was rather neurologically programmed to encourage stability was an important one. "If partners are going to stay together for the years of care that children require, they need a love that bonds them to each other but without the passion that would be a distraction," Jeffrey Kluger wrote for *Time*'s special issue dedicated to love in 2008, good news for those thinking that their marriage could be finished because the spark that had lit it years before had gone out.[49] Another study co-led by Arthur Aron revealed that the brains scans of long-married people who said they were still in love with their respective spouse looked very similar to those who were recently love-struck. The generally accepted belief that romantic love lasted a year or at most two could be wrong, psychologists and neuroscientists were beginning to think after reviewing the study's findings. While romantic love could seemingly exist for decades, "older" expressions of the emotion were not characterized by the obsessiveness and anxiety that came with the initial stage. Rather, it was calmness and attachment that defined "mature" love, more good news for those not wanting to ever have to go through the temporary madness of infatuation again.[50]

Such findings added to the evidence that love was not merely a social construction that had been created by romantic poets in medieval days or, much later, by Hollywood screenwriters. (Postmodernists, particularly Michel Foucault, were attracted to the idea of love being a form of institutional power and control.) Cross-cultural studies revealed that love was a universal human experience, this too suggesting that there was a biological basis for the emotion.[51] The conclusion that the workings of love were located in the brain was deservedly seen as a historical breakthrough. "For the first time in the history of human mating, scientists may have found a way to pin down this most ethereal of emotions," A.J. Jacobs wrote for *Esquire* in 2009, thinking that "we're on the verge of dissecting this butterfly."[52]

From a broad perspective, the scientific dissection of love could be seen as running parallel with that of happiness, another positive emotion that until recently had been largely ignored by the psychological community. Wide use of fMRIs had opened up a whole new avenue towards the study of love, something that Fisher and a small group of other researchers were fully embracing. Love and happiness obviously played significant roles in the everyday lives of individuals, but both were commonly viewed as less deserving for serious study as "negative" emotions like fear, anger, anxiety, and depression.[53] With the mental health field oriented towards gaining a better understanding of problems and how to potentially remedy them, it can be seen how love had been allowed to languish in the margins of psychology and psychiatry for so long. Finally however, the mystery of love appeared to being solved, many in the mainstream media excitedly reported. "For decades, researchers have probed the origin of love, tediously mining questionnaires and surveys for clues as to how sparks fly (and which ones stay lit)," noted Julie Hanus in *Utne*, but "now they're making game-changing discoveries."[54]

For at least one journalist, however, no amount of research could solve the mystery of love, even that which he had for his own wife. "We have little in common, and certainly none of those hard-wired connections that dating services say married couples are supposed to share," Steve Lewis confessed in the *New York Times*, adding that after forty years of marriage (and seven children) he remained "drawn to her daily in vast unspeakable ways." His future wife was not at all his "type" when they first met and vice-versa, and even now a computer algorithm would likely not consider them to be a good match. People would often congratulate Lewis for his successful marriage, but the man was reluctant to take any credit since he himself did not know why it had worked. "Over the years I have tried in vain to explain what it is about the connections and the confusion and the ambivalence and the roots of this counterintuitive relationship that connect us in unspoken ways," he wrote, concluding that "perhaps it's best just to give up trying to explain."[55]

Researchers of love had no intention of giving up their attempt to solve the mystery of love, however. Now that some clues had come forth, big questions were being asked regarding the future possibilities. If the emotion really was a chemical concoction cooked up by the brain, for example, could a synthetic love potion be created to help lonelyhearts find each other? Conversely, could a tonic be designed to prevent incompatibles from getting together, perhaps ultimately reducing the country's divorce rate?[56] How about something to lessen the bummer of being rejected by someone one still loved (brain chemistry was especially powerful in those situations) or, for those who did not want their lives seriously disrupted, one that made an individual not susceptible to the mania that came with early love? "I doubt many people would want to permanently suppress love but a temporary vaccine could come in handy," John Tierney quipped, thinking an "anti-love drug may be a ticket to bliss."[57] Whatever the possibilities, it was clear that love as a field had entered a new era in its history, and that even keener insights likely lied ahead given the greater attention it was now receiving. Few people could predict that it would soon not be science but technology that would dominate the investigation of love in America, however, and that the subject itself was about to be revolutionized.

Chapter 6

Ex Machina, 2010–

> *"Love can be found on the Verizon Wireless 3G network this Valentine's Day."*
> —2010 Verizon Wireless PR release

A few days before Valentine's Day 2010, Verizon Wireless delivered a press release with some exciting news. Users of some smartphones and other devices could download a number of new apps designed to, in the company's words, "spark the love, share the love, and test your love." One app, AstroLove2, drew upon astrology to help guide users' romantic lives, while another, Hallmark Mobile Greetings, offered a choice of more than 550 animated expressions of love to send to one's sweetie. To find out if he or she was "the one," there was the AMA Love Test that determined how much of the emotion the user had for another person. Finally, there was the Love Calculator, an app that evaluated the compatibility of a couple via a "basic random algorithm based on a 'secret' internal recipe." With more than 91 million customers, Verizon Wireless managed the country's largest wireless voice and 3G data network, putting it in a unique position to facilitate love on Valentine's Day.[1]

The arrival of love apps is a telling sign of our increasingly digital times. Technology in various forms has infiltrating love over the past decade, just the beginnings of what will no doubt be a full-scale invasion in the future. If the scientific goings-on within the area of love have proved fascinating, those related to technology are positively incredible. "Can a human fall in love with a computer?" *Popular Science* asked in 2014, the answer seemingly so.[2] As depicted in movies such as *Her* (2013) and *Ex Machina* (2014), people can develop an emotional attachment with their machines, something perhaps not surprising given the amount of time many spend with their computers, tablets, and smart phones. Squabbles with one's operating system are less likely than with a human, after all, and artificial intelligence (AI) can make a machine behave startlingly real. "It will be awhile before we can have with computers the kind of complex emotional relationship we have with other people, but I imagine people having one-night stands with Androids will happen a lot sooner," noted Gary Marcus, a professor of psychology at NYU, in 2013, he and others quite sure that the future of love will be an interesting one.³

Leave It to Science

Until humans found their ideal operating system with which to settle down, they have had to find alternative ways to find and nurture romantic love. Eastern philosophies and practices have become mainstream over the past decade, with Buddhism, meditation, natural remedies, and acupuncture just a few ways that East is meeting West.⁴ Not surprisingly, then, Easternism is informing Americans' approach to love, as the Buddhist philosophy of "unconditional love" offers a more holistic means of interpreting and expressing the emotion.⁵ Feng shui is another example of how Eastern inspired thought has recently been applied by some in the States to nourish love. Given that it was now accepted wisdom that men were from Mars and women from Venus, the ancient art of placement was viewed by more New Agey types as a way to improve a couple's lines of communication. In 2010, feng shui expert Ellen Whitehurst advised readers of *Redbook* to put a bowl of uncooked rice with a pinch of sea salt under their beds for a few weeks to encourage harmonious conversations. (Feng shui enthusiasts consider salt and rice to be excellent absorbers of negative energy.) "It'll awaken positive relationship energies and agreeable and open communication," the magazine stated, a quick and easy solution to what was for many quite a complex problem.⁶

As they had for years, *Redbook* and other women's magazines like *Glamour*, *Good Housekeeping*, and *O* represented prime sources for advice on romantic love for a certain segment of the market, primarily middle-class moms. Although "old media," these magazines have acted as influential cheerleaders for love, showing readers ways in which they could enjoy committed but still passionate relationships with their significant other. With some work and dedication, marital bliss could be achieved, according to article after article, affirming our social order rooted in monogamy and family. Tips were provided to do just that, with successful relationships of ordinary couples often used as case studies of enduring yet exciting love. "Want a marriage complete with butterflies in your stomach, secret smiles, PDA, nooners (seriously!), and that feeling of 'Wow, we really click?,'" began one such article in *Redbook* from September 2010. The stories of "five crazy-in-love couples who prove it's possible" were then told, each of them proud to "work at their bond."

Famous couples who had had long marriages were commonly featured to illustrate the power of love (orchestrated of course for public relations purposes). "The Happy-Couple Hall of Fame" was showcased that issue, its members including George and Barbara Bush, Jada Pinkett Smith and Will Smith, Kevin Bacon and Kyra Sedgwick, Kelly Ripa and Mark Consuelos, Iman and David Bowie, and Barack and Michelle Obama.[7]

Alongside such boisterous support for romantic love has come a deeper exploration of its scientific underpinnings. More research has revealed the degree to which love is a matter of chemistry, a fact that some have found rather disquieting. "Leave it to science to take all the fun out of something as cosmically pure as love," wrote Jessica Pauline Ogilvie of the *Los Angeles Times* in reporting the news that romance appeared to be largely a function of chemistry. It was important to remember that while love was indeed now perceived as the cause (or perhaps result) of a certain kind of chemical cocktail in the brain, that wasn't always the case. Biologists had long made the case that love was rooted in the makeup of the human organism, while anthropologists had argued that the emotion existed in order to encourage the survival of the species. Attachment theorists, meanwhile, believed that love was a function of the relationship one had with caregivers as a child, just one branch of thought off the very big psychological tree. Even those in the health field were making claims on love based on the apparently strong connection between the emotion and one's physiology and medical condition.[8]

Whichever way the winds of love were blowing, researchers in the field typically justified their work on the supposition that possessing a greater understanding of the emotion would be beneficial to people's wellbeing. As well, all agreed that love was a powerful emotion, and that much more needed to be known about it in order to harness its full potential. Helen Fisher remained the field's loudest spokesperson, delivering her latest thoughts on the subject in her new book *Why Him? Why Her?* The purpose of love was to "win life's greatest prize—a mating partner for life," the biological anthropologist maintained, reiterating that the one-two punch of dopamine and oxytocin was responsible for creating a strong emotional bond between two people.[9] Fisher was now extending her theories of love in a more applied, self-helpish way, however, believing that complementary personality types were the key to a good match. "Once you discover your own type, you'll improve your chances of finding—and keeping—your soul mate," her new book promised readers, a good example of how research in the field could possibly be translated into useful and practical terms.[10]

Stan Tatkin's *Wired for Love* also made the case that understanding "your partner's brain and attachment style," as the book's subtitle went, could go a long way to creating successful relationships. "Every person is wired for love differently, with different habits, needs, and reactions to conflict," Tatkin wrote, the good news being that it was possible to "neurologically prime the brain for greater love and fewer conflicts." The remainder of the book showed readers how to do that by helping them perceive what their partner was thinking at any given moment, quite a thing if at all true. Tatkin, a couples therapist, also offered a learning program covering much of the same material on an audio CD that drew upon recent findings from neurobiology, attachment theory, and emotion regulation research. "Improve your brain, improve your relationships," he told readers, adding to the body of thought that love could be a controllable and manageable process.[11]

Buoyed by the appealing idea that we could control not just our own love but that of others, research in the field has marched on, much of it supporting a direct connection between mind and body. It had previously been learned that people in love were generally healthier than those who were not, but now the emotion was being shown to be an effective painkiller as well. The euphoria produced by brains in love—dopamine, oxytocin, vasopressin, and adrenaline—made people ignore pain, a study done at Stanford University and SUNY Stony Brook showed, a finding that acknowledged the full power of the emotion. Love and pain shared the same neural system, the researchers (which included Arthur Aron) reported, exciting news for the medical community. "I could just prescribe a passionate love affair for all my patients every six months," joked Sean Mackey, chief of the pain management division at the Stanford University School of Medicine who was one of the study's researchers, seeing actual applications of the findings down the road.[12]

The scientific community also rejoiced in the discovery of how the brain created the complex emotion of romantic love. "Cupid arrows, laced with neurotransmitters, find their marks," reported Mark Fischetti in *Scientific American* in 2011, adding that no less than a dozen regions of the brain were responsible for stirring up feelings of love. Knowing which chemicals did what in the brain could lead to all kinds of new pharmaceuticals, some were predicting. Besides the possibilities of painkillers and "love potions," drugs designed to lessen the sadness that came with a breakup could perhaps be developed, just the beginning of what could be a whole segment of passion generators and inhibitors. Most exciting, a greater understanding of the interaction between brain chemistry and cognition was emerging. Cognitive functions were "triggers that fully activate the love network," said Stephanie Ortigue, an assistant professor of psychology at Syracuse University; her research showed that there was a definite physiological component to the emotion.[13]

Barbara L. Fredrickson agreed that there was a strong physiological component to love. In her book *Love 2.0: How Our Supreme Emotion Affects Everything We Feel, Think, Do and Become*, Fredrickson discussed how the experience of love was physically measurable not only by brain chemistry but by cardiac vagal tone (or heart rate). "It's marked by a biobehavioral synchrony that unfolds across two bodies and brains at once," she rather poetically said in a 2013 interview, thinking love was a more powerful emotion than we recognized, if such a thing was possible. Fredrickson, who was director of the Positive Emotions and Psychophysiology Laboratory at the University of North Carolina, defined love as "any micromoment in which we share a positive emotion with another person," making it something that could regularly nurture both mind and body if we allowed it to. Love was not the "lightening-bolt moment" portrayed in pop culture, she made clear, seeing it instead as a "real-time sensory connection" that could be made in everyday interactions.[14]

Given that many people were spending more time on their computers and other devices, however, making such a sensory connection was becoming increasingly less likely. Technology was proving to be a barrier to her interpretation of love, as email and texting just did not permit the kind of "positivity resonance" that she assigned to the emotion.[15] Frederickson may have been right, at least with regard to the inverse relationship between the growth of online technology and how many Americans were getting married. By 2013, more than 35 percent of relationships began online while the nation's marriage rate had dipped to 31.1 percent, the lowest in more than a century, according to the Proceedings of the National Academy of Sciences and Bowling Green State University's National Center for Family and Marriage.[16] Was ever-encroaching technology actually a threat to marriage and, if so, what were the social implications as we spent more time online?

A Series of Simple Actions

Although fewer Americans were getting married, falling in love fortunately remained one of life's greatest experiences. In *Us: Americans Talk About Love*, editor John Bowe collected stories of romantic love from ordinary Americans, a refreshing break from its scientific examination and psychological parsing. The stories came from a cross-section of Americans, clearly illustrating that the emotion had no regard for our social divisions of race, age, gender, class, geography, or sexual preference. Bowe, a journalist, went around the country and asked people who he or she loved most, with the forthcoming answers revealing how many different forms romantic love can take. Bowe was reluctant to draw any grand conclusions from the collection of stories, but he did offer a prescription for what he considered to be "successful" expressions of love. At its best, love was "a series of simple actions, performed repeatedly in various forms," he thought, advising readers to "listen, affirm, accept, support, commit, share, be honest, and forgive" in their relationships.[17]

Such actions had little to do with the mania of early love, additional evidence that long-term relationships were more behavioral than chemical. Expressing one's love by saying those three little words also went a long way to assuring one's partner they had something real and special. Many Americans had a tough time getting the words out of their mouth when directed to another person, however, a function of our emotionally repressed society. We used the word all the time regarding our possessions but had difficulty saying it to other people "because many of us grew up in families where love, while present, was rarely expressed verbally," thought Elizabeth Bernstein of the *Wall Street Journal*. Saying, "I love you" the first time to a romantic interest was especially nerve racking, not only because it exposed one's deep feelings but because it was unknown whether the feelings were mutual. Some people ran away as quickly as possible upon hearing the words, in fact, making the decision to utter the declaration a risky one. Giving a gift or texting "XOXO" were commonly used as safe surrogates for saying, "I love you," but relationship experts advised that there was no substitute for the real, vocal thing.[18]

Americans' reluctance to put the love they felt for someone into spoken words was made clear in a 2011 advertising campaign for M&M's. The M&M character Red was featured in the Valentine's Day campaign, naturally, but it was clear that the male chocolate candy had intimacy issues. In one commercial, Red sat on a park bench alongside a pretty female M&M who says, "I love you" to him but he remains silent, an awkward situation that sadly happened with some frequency in real life. (Men were popularly believed to have more trouble uttering the phrase than women.) "Red has trouble showing his emotional side," explained Jason Lucas, senior creative director for BBDO New York, the ad agency that created the campaign, adding that "the only way he can say it is with the candies." Non-candy men were apt to give their romantic partners chocolate and flowers as symbols of their love, making the commercial a good example of art imitating life.[19]

A study published in the *Journal of Personality and Social Psychology* just a couple of months later, however, showed that it was actually women who took longer to tell their partner "I love you." Two-thirds of (heterosexual) couples surveyed reported that it was the man in the relationship who stated the phrase first, with the study also showing that men thought about declaring their love before women. The authors of the study were careful to add that the reasons for saying the words could vary for men and women. "Men may be more impulsive in the way they express love, but what love means to men and what love means to women may be very different," noted Josh Ackerman, assistant professor of marketing at MIT Sloan School of Management, who was one of the co-authors of the study. Men may consciously or unconsciously use the phrase to advance sexual activity, the researchers posited, suggesting that evolutionary forces based in gender differences (spreading genes versus getting pregnant) could be at work in how the three little words were or were not expressed.[20]

The pressure to "drop the 'L' bomb," as Heidi Stevens of the *Chicago Tribune* put it, often intensified as the duration of a relationship lengthened. Those who had been dating for some time would typically begin to wonder if or when they should formally declare their love, as the timing of it was critical. A premature announcement could instantly kill the relationship if the feeling was not reciprocal, while waiting too long could convey the sense that one felt that the whole thing was just a fling. Anxiety really kicked in during early February, as Valentine's Day was considered the ideal time to say the three words. Once they were spoken, whether by one or both individuals, the relationship was irrevocably altered, making the venture a risky proposition. "When one person turns to another and takes the risk of exposing themselves with 'I love you,' it's an invitation to a very special kind of connection," noted Sue Johnson, a couples therapist and author of *Love Sense: The Revolutionary New Science of Romantic Relationships*, thinking that it was the implication of exclusivity that made the statement so highly charged.[21]

To whom to say "I love you" and when to say it was, needless to say, a complex decision given all the psychological and neurological factors in play. On a physiological level, many parts of the brain and an array of interacting hormones were involved, many studies had shown, while on a psychological level there were a host of personality characteristics and values that played a large role in determining with whom we fell in love. Throwing a curve into the process of love was that young adults now tended to have sex with a partner before they felt the emotion for him or her. Historically, for the most part, it was the other way around, and researchers were still trying to figure out the psychological and physiological implications of sex before love. Sex was known to accelerate the feelings of intimacy and activate the pleasure centers of the brain that were each essential parts of falling in love, making the area of study worthy of further investigation. "Even though we don't have answers, we're starting to figure out what kind of questions we need to ask," said Kayt Sukel, author of *Dirty Minds: How Our Brains Influence Love, Sex, and Relationships,* thinking great strides were finally being made in the science of love.[22]

One interesting way that researchers were learning more about love was to ask people how it had gone wrong for them. Those who had gone through a divorce tended to think long and hard about the reasons their relationship failed, making them good subjects for determining the factors that likely contributed to enduring love. Terri Orbuch, a professor at the University of Michigan's Institute for Social Research and author of *Finding Love Again: 6 Simple Steps to a New and Happy Relationship,* was one researcher pursuing work in this largely neglected area. Her longitudinal study showed that there were five common reasons for a marriage to go south, one being a lack of "affective affirmation," i.e., the usual verbal and physical expressions of love. Money, both its earning and spending, was the biggest source of conflict, suggesting that sharing a similar perspective on financial matters was extremely important for a relationship to last. It was communication, however, or more accurately a lack of it, that caused marriages to fail, Orbuch found, confirming previous research showing that actively listening to what one's partner had to say was a key element in making the love one felt for another last.[23]

Marriage therapists were in agreement that when it came to love, it was indeed the little things that meant a lot. Much was made of big, spontaneous romantic displays in the media and in the entertainment world, but it was more the nuts and bolts of two people living together—the making and spending of money, the doing of chores, the frequency of sex, etc.—that governed the long-term viability of a relationship. More couples were signing "relationship contracts" before getting married or living together, in which the partners agreed to who would do what in order to avoid misunderstandings down the road. Therapists also emphasized that it was better to spend quality time together rather than spend as much time as possible together to counter the belief that couples should stay glued to the hip. Preserving a certain level of independence made relationships stronger, they told their clients, with going out with one's own friends or pursuing a particular interest healthy for all parties. Schedule sex rather than just allow it to happen (or more likely not happen), they added, as this too was a way for couples to know they were on the same page in that department.[24]

Love Is a Process

Rather than show one's love in little ways on a daily basis, however, many Americans chose to wait until February 14 to demonstrate it in a big way. For over a century, Valentine's Day had served as an opportune time for American newspaper editors to publish articles having something to do with love, as they knew that many readers had the emotion on their minds on that day. For Valentine's Day 2013, the *Washington Post* published a series of articles regarding the relationship between love and faith, an interesting angle to take. (Christian and Jewish publications often addressed love in relation to the precepts of their respective faiths, but the mainstream press tended to focus on less spiritual dimensions of the subject.) In addition to "A Mormon Guide to Love," "A Muslim Guide to Love," "A Hindu Guide to Love," "A Christian Guide to Love," "A Catholic Guide to Love," and "An Atheist Guide to Love," each of them written by an expert in that area, there was Deepak Chopra's "A Seeker's Guide to Love." Chopra had previously mined the topic of love; among his more than seventy books was *The Path to Love*, and he also had issued a music CD, *The Secrets of Love*.[25]

With this short piece, however, Chopra had a chance to consolidate his thoughts about love and how it could serve as a kind of spiritual force. Although it could be fairly said that he was one of the contemporary kings

Americans (and many other people around the world) have sent Valentine's Day cards to express their love for over a century. Postcards like this one were popular in the early decades of the 20th century, part of what has become a celebration of romantic love every February 14. Art and Picture Collection, The New York Public Library. "Love's greeting to my Valentine." *The New York Public Library Digital Collections.* http://digitalcollections.nypl.org/items/510d47e3-6198-a3d9-e040-e00a18064a99

Valentine's Day has become big business since this postcard was mailed in 1906. Americans were estimated to spend a total of $20.7 billion on (and increasingly leading up to) the day in 2019, according to the National Retail Federation. Art and Picture Collection, The New York Public Library. "In true love." *The New York Public Library Digital Collections.* 190-. http://digitalcollections.nypl.org/items/510d47e3-64ed-a3d9-e040-e00a18064a99

of self-help, Chopra resented the ways in which love was being treated in the media like, in his words, "a recipe for cinnamon buns." The Internet had made what had already been a formulaic approach to a very complex subject worse, he believed, as the medium (especially Twitter) was custom fit to cater to our shorter and shorter attention spans.[26] Chopra addressed this in a rather extraordinary passage in his seeker's guide to love:

> Love isn't a fact, formula, or definable in words. Love is a process, perhaps the most mysterious one in human psychology.... Love is transporting. It carries us beyond our everyday selves and makes reality shine with an inner light.[27]

Chopra begrudged not just the Internetization of love but the way in which science had come to dominate the public conversation about it. "If romance was only a heady brew of hormones, genetic inheritance and sex drive, all we'd need is better data to explain it," he wrote, arguing that "no one knows what creates love as a powerful bond that is so full of meaning."[28]

If anyone knew the secrets of love, it may have been Daniel Jones. Jones had been editor of the "Modern Love" column in the *New York Times* since 2005, during which time he had received about 50,000 submissions from readers having to say something about love. "Modern Love" was reportedly one of the most read columns in the world, with women especially keen to hear interesting, real-life stories of love. For his 2014 book *Love Illuminated: Exploring Life's Most Mystifying Subject (with the Help of 50,000 Strangers)*, Jones sifted through the published essays and sorted the most compelling into general categories such as "Pursuit," "Connection," "Monotony," and "Infidelity." Like Chopra, Jones was critical of the rush towards online dating, thinking algorithm-based search mechanisms were not a particularly good way to find a suitable match. He and his wife were not paired up when they each signed up on a popular site, evidence that love transcended demographic information and the other criteria that the models relied on.[29] "Love is about curiosity, not certainty," he wrote in the book, suggesting that what one didn't know about one's partner was more attractive than what one did know.[30]

Indeed, Jones's illumination of love illustrated that the emotion had little regard for anything to do with logic, rationalism, or what made sense on paper (or a computer screen). Many of the essays he received were of the Romeo and Juliet school, i.e., love affairs between people of different and often conflicting social or economic backgrounds. Love conquered the barriers of race, age, class, religion, political affiliation, and all other socially constructed divisions, it appeared, proof that the emotion was a truly universal one. Jones dismissed the idea that he was a "love guru," but his advice to readers to "embrace the complexity" of the emotion was about as wise as any ever offered on the subject. "There are so many people who have trouble in relationships and love who are trying to make it something simpler than it is," he said, thinking the better way to go would be to "approach love humbly enough to know that it's going to be hard sometimes."[31]

That was not a message one was likely to hear on the current poster child of online matchmaking: e-Harmony. The site claimed to have a "scientific approach" to finding one's soul mate (the latter a term many experts, including Jones, found to be without basis). Through its comprehensive questionnaire, algorithm based on "29 dimensions of compatibility," and psychological evaluations, e-Harmony did indeed appear to be uniquely equipped to pair two people who were destined to be together. The company maintained that more than 500 marriages a day resulted from its method, an amazing statistic if true. Although it was significantly higher than what other online dating sites charged, the $60 monthly fee seemed a bargain given the cost of pursuing relationships that were not likely to work out. One could easily see how many people looking for true love signed up, especially when it was not unusual to receive five possible candidates a day.[32]

Some people's experience with e-Harmony, however, suggested that the company's approach to matchmaking, while perhaps scientific, was unlikely to lead to marriage (or even a second date). After initially disappointing results, a good number of users adjusted their screening filters to hopefully deliver better results, but many remained unconvinced that the pool of matches they were sent were potential soul mates. One big problem was that e-Harmony and virtually all other online dating sites had no way of knowing whether their subscribers were telling the truth regarding, well, anything. Liberties were often taken when it came to appearance and economic status, making it no surprise that dissatisfaction often resulted when the analog version of a person turned out to be quite different from his or her digital profile. "The entire online dating market, despite its immense popularity, is a giant buyer-beware zone," wrote Shaila Dewan for the *New York Times Magazine* in 2014, a not too surprising thing given the volume of scamming on the Internet as a whole.[33]

An Emotional Obsession

The difficulty of establishing a meaningful and committed relationship online might have impelled some to seek alternative and perhaps extreme ways to find love. This was certainly true for Mandy Len Catron who, like Robert Epstein, was willing to use herself as a guinea pig to try to learn if love could be more than a randomly determined event. "What happens if you decide that love is not something that happens to you, but an action?" she asked, telling her interesting story in Jones's "Modern Love" column. Recalling an experiment conducted by Arthur Aron in the early 1990s, Catron decided to see if she could purposely fall in love with someone by their answering a series of personal questions. (It had worked in Aron's study, with the two subjects, who had been complete strangers, getting married six months later.) Catron and her willing male subject (with whom she was acquainted) answered the same thirty-six questions Aron had his subjects answer, although her study was conducted in a bar versus university psychology lab. By revealing such personal thoughts in such a condensed amount of time, the theory went, the normal span of a relationship could be vastly accelerated, quickly leading to love. The last part of the session was for the two subjects to stare into each other's eyes for four minutes without speaking, quite a powerful experience, Catron reported. Did she and her co-subject fall in love? They did indeed, Catron told readers, further raising the possibility that the emotion could be intentionally generated once feelings of trust and intimacy were established. "Love didn't happen to us," she explained, "we're in love because we each made the choice to be."[34]

Other efforts were being taken to determine if was possible to control or harness the power of love rather than simply allow it to operate unchecked. In 2016, a team of psychologists reported the results of a study supporting the existence of something they called "love regulation," in which people could utilize their thoughts to increase or decrease how much of the emotion they felt towards someone else. Thinking positive thoughts about a romantic partner while viewing photos of him or her increased the level of attachment they felt, according to the study published in a scientific journal, while thinking negative thoughts did the opposite. Scans of the subjects' brains echoed the findings, suggesting that people might have had more power over love than they probably believed. "People think they can't control love so they might not even try," explained Sandra Langeslag, lead researcher on the study and assistant professor in the department of psychological sciences at the University of Missouri, St. Louis, "but this study shows you that you can."[35]

Whether there was merit to the Pavlovian study or not, this kind of research prompted important questions about the nature of love itself. The possibility that love was not an emotion, or at least did not strongly resemble other emotions, was revisited; the psychological community remained divided on the issue. Like other emotions, love was complex and triggered physiological and psychological responses but, unlike others, was not transitory and did not have a specific cause, as did anger or joy. Love was possibly a blend of other emotions, some believed, a sign that much more research needed to be done to have a clear sense of what it was and wasn't. While those in the field continued to attempt to classify and characterize love, more experts were coming to believe that we were able to directly influence its range and expression. Susan David, a psychologist at Harvard Medical School and author of *Emotional Agility*, belonged to this school of thought, advising readers in relationships to think positively, make minor adjustments (as needed), smile at (and have sex with) their partner, broaden their perspective, try new things together, and "let it go" as ways to shape and manage their feelings of love.[36]

Basic research in the field was instrumental in allowing psychologists and therapists to offer such sound advice. Gender differences relative to love were of particular interest. In normal settings, for example, it was men who fell in love faster, researchers still believed, a function of their biological inclination towards reproduction. "Women are custodians of the egg, so they are more careful romantically," said Helen Fisher, who was now spending some of her time as senior research fellow at the Kinsey Institute for Research in

Sex, Gender and Reproduction. The romantic phase of love typically lasted eighteen months to three years, part of our evolutionary process designed to get two people together to have and raise a child. Romantic love was "an emotional obsession," she told the *Wall Street Journal* in 2015, and "an adaptive mechanism for attraction and to start the mating process quickly." Three things about a person were required for you to fall in love with him or her, according to Arthur Aron: physical attraction, desirable personality, and the belief that the other person liked you. The presence of all three accounted for the "love at first sight" phenomenon, he and Fisher agreed, making it an entirely real possibility.[37]

After her forty-plus years of studying love, Fisher had become somewhat of an academic celebrity, widely recognized for what was groundbreaking work in the field. Based at the Center for Human Evolutionary Studies in the Department of Anthropology at Rutgers, Fisher had updated her book *Anatomy of Love: A Natural History of Mating, Marriage, and Why We Stray*, which had originally been published in 1992 and was considered a classic in the subject. Most impressive, perhaps, was her ability to see consumer-friendly applications for what might have been just obscure scholarly findings. Match.com and its subsidiary, Chemistry.com, had adopted her Fisher Temperament Inventory, which sorted personality types into four general groups ("builders," "explorers," "directors," and "negotiators") based on the answers to fifty-six-questions. (By 2016, 14 million people had completed the questionnaire in hopes they could find love online.) An unapologetic workaholic, Fisher was on a mission to explain the mysteries of love, the most important being how we determine the person with whom we want to spend the rest of lives.[38]

A Healthy Dose of Persistence

Fisher's research, along with additional studies done by the handful of others exploring the hows and whys of love (particularly Aron), challenged many of the prevailing beliefs about it. Women were not more romantic than men, for example, as it was the latter who believed in the ideas of love at first sight and soul mates. It was thus men who more idealized their relationships and romantic partners, going against the grain of much of American popular culture. The *au courant* view that monogamy for humans was just a social construction, i.e., that we were naturally promiscuous like most animals, was also wrong, according to most experts. Although there were of course exceptions, there was a biological and social basis for monogamy, anthropologists generally agreed, a premise that diverged from the literally sexier notion that we were hardwired to sleep around. And while the initial, intense stage of romantic love typically averaged just a couple of years, long-term relationships did not have to slide into the more practical, rather dull state of compatibility. Some couples remained as passionate with their respective significant other as ever, although the obsession and mania of young love had thankfully ebbed.[39]

Recent research has shown that other popular myths about love are incorrect. "Opposites attract" has long explained why two people get together, but the truth is usually quite different. "While there are some examples of against-the-odds love, the odds actually indicate that you're most likely to get together with someone who's a lot like you," wrote Len Mandy in the *Washington Post* in 2016. In her book *Falling in Love: Why We Choose the Lovers We Choose*, Ayala Pines offered compelling evidence suggesting that the leading factor for who we love is geographic proximity. Although she had numbers to back that up, it is simply common sense that we are most likely to become acquainted and thus perhaps fall in love with someone who lives and/or works near us. Other studies have indicated that despite our increasingly multicultural and global society, we choose partners who are similar to us in terms of race, ethnicity, religion, class, income, and education. Harmonious personalities were likely the best predictor of the success of a relationship, as Fisher and others argued, but we still tended to gravitate to people of similar backgrounds.[40]

Yet another myth busted by psychologists specializing in love was that despite the famous line from the movie *Jerry McGuire* ("You complete me"), it was unlikely that any other person could make another feel whole or "finished." 88 percent of those surveyed in a 2010 Gallup survey believed in the idea of soul mates, i.e., that there was a "one and only" person whom they are fated to be with forever and who is waiting for them. While an attractive notion, soul mates were for the most part an imaginary concept steeped in romantic idealism, however, with no pairing capable of being or becoming perfect or "meant to be."[41]

In fact, researchers have found that having a perceived soul mate is detrimental to enjoying a happy long-term relationship, as there is the expectation that nothing would ever go wrong.[42] Ty Tashiro, author of *The Science of Happily Ever After: What Really Matters in the Quest for Enduring Love*, was one relationship expert who believed that having or striving for a soul mate was an obstacle to a healthy and lasting relationship. "The problem with soulmates is that people tend to think that fate is responsible for producing them," Tashiro told the *New York Observer* in 2018, explaining that "the reality is that enduring love is the byproduct of intentional, clear thought and action, as well as a healthy dose of persistence."[43]

Professionals' dismissal of the popular belief in soul mates was part of something bigger. Couples who approached love as a journey were happier than those who considered it a destination, research showed, more reason to leave the notion of soul mates to the movies and romance novels. More generally, psychologists were increasingly embracing the proposition that, rather than being at the mercy of the whims of Eros, individuals had to address love as a work in progress that required real and dedicated effort for it to succeed. Too many people believed that their partner could or should know what they were thinking, leading to communication breakdowns. Couples claiming to be kindred spirits sharing an almost psychic connection more likely and more simply displayed kind and caring behavior towards each other, whether they were aware of it or not.[44]

As it had for many years, deconstructing the narratives of love stemming from movies also made up a key part of therapists' job. Too many people took the standard plot of a Hollywood romantic comedy (seemingly often starring Hugh Grant) or romance novel seriously, thinking such things happened with some frequency in real life. Matt Huston of *Psychology Today* described the story as such:

> A man spots a woman across a crowded room and knows that they're meant to be together. He wins her heart, but then he makes a big mistake-or fate pulls them apart-and he is sure he's lost her forever. Talking with his closest friends, he realizes that she's still the only one for him. So he tracks her down and publicly declares his love (in song, perhaps), and they end up in each other's arms with a story to tell their kids.[45]

In an interesting exercise, Huston asked a group of experts to assess such a story from a professional perspective to determine "how conventional plot points of romantic fiction played out in the real world." Maryanne Fisher, a psychologist at Saint Mary's University, felt the love-at-first-sight aspect of the classic story (nicely illustrated by Jack's first sighting of Rose on the deck of the Titanic in the 1997 film of that name) was an "ill-advised dating strategy." Real-life Jacks might be missing out on other great potential partners by assuming their respective Roses were "the one," the professor argued, thinking it would be wiser for those instantly smitten to keep their options open. Love often blossomed without an initial bang, she explained, with regular open communication a more reliable predictor of healthy relationships than wordless connections across a room (or ill-fated ocean liner).[46]

The lengths to which fictional pursuers would prove their love, once they had realized it, certainly made good entertainment, but were a bad idea in actual practice, according to Julia Lippman, a communications researcher at the University of Michigan. In the 2004 film *The Notebook*, for example, the male protagonist plants a field of his love's favorite flowers and then renovates her house, each a way to show how much he cared for her. Doing such things in real life would probably make the pursued run for the hills, Lippman pointed out, as that kind of unsolicited behavior fell squarely in the general category of stalking. (A *YouTube* video that recuts the movie suggests as much.) One-sided romances are just that, she suggested, with more balanced ones more likely to lead to pairings that will last.[47]

Another tried-and-true trope in romantic fiction was the last minute race for the protagonist to declare his or her love for another who is resigned to the fact that the relationship is over. In films ranging from *The Graduate* to *Manhattan* to *When Harry Met Sally* to *Say Anything* to *The Wedding Singer*, a character moves in great haste to confess his or her ardor before it's too late, providing viewers and readers with an exciting conclusion. Galena Rhoades, a psychologist at the University of Denver, believed such dramatic scenes helped to instill the idea that meaningful relationships required a sense of urgency, a message that hurt the chances of real ones succeeding. Try to avoid speeding across town at reckless speeds to inform someone that you've realized you're in love with him or her, she advised, as those kind of gestures would probably be perceived as more frantic than romantic.[48]

Finally, counting on a single, emotionally charged moment to signify one's love for another, as often demonstrated by the passionate first kiss or marriage proposal in a movie or novel, would be a similarly misguided thing to do. True commitment was typically a long process involving many different steps, according to relationship experts, and most of them were far less exciting than smooching in the pouring rain or getting down on one knee while onlookers oohed and aahed. It was instead the mundane that better defined the mechanics of love, noted Sean Horan, a communications researcher at Texas State University, activities that likely did not make compelling viewing or reading. "You go to work, come home, spend the evening together watching TV, doing dishes, maybe having a glass of wine," he said, the minutia of couple's lives the glue that kept them together.[49]

An Irresistible Romance Algorithm

The formulaic nature of Hollywood movies suggests that it would be difficult or even impossible for a single film to alter the trajectory of a subject as immense as love, but Spike Jonze's 2013 *Her* did just that. In the film set in near future Los Angeles, boy (Theodore, played by Joaquin Phoenix) falls in love with girl (Samantha, played by Scarlett Johansson), not an usual story except for the fact that the latter happens to be the former's computer's operating system (the first to be equipped with artificial intelligence). What was also unusual was that the couple's relationship appeared to be perfect save for it being between a human and a machine, with none of the standard conflicts that served to move a film's plot forward and keep viewers engaged in the story. "I have never loved anyone the way I love you," Samantha tells Theodore, words that anyone in a committed relationship would want to hear. Was a body or a brain necessary in a romantic relationship? Did it matter that Samantha was not "real" if she made Theodore happy? Such questions challenged our basic assumptions about love, and likely made some viewers wonder if they had as good a relationship with their own (human) significant other. Jonze insisted the film was a "love story" rather than a commentary on technology, something apparent through his emphasis on the emotions the two feel or, in Samantha's case, appears to feel.[50]

While Samantha is not an ordinary operating system—she is an "intuitive entity" with exceptional empathic skills—real life love stories such as that depicted in *Her* may be in our future. Ray Kurzweil's theory of Singularity based in the humanization of machines and the mechanization of humans suggests that a person could one day fall in love with a computer and, perhaps, vice-versa.[51] In fact, it may be difficult to distinguish between people and machines in a few decades, according to Kurzweil, whose book *The Singularity Is Near* rocked the world by pronouncing that humans would be able to move beyond their biological makeup in the not so distant future. People and technology will merge in 2045, the inventor and futurist claimed, a literally life-changing event resulting from exponentially advanced artificial intelligence. Humans, or whatever we would be called, would comprise a new and different kind of species, not an easy idea to wrap one's head around, especially since it will supposedly take place in many of our lifetimes. The Singularity is "an era in which our intelligence will become increasingly nonbiological and trillions of times more powerful than it is today," Kurzweil proposed, with technological change leading to "the dawning of a new civilization that will enable us to transcend our biological limitations and amplify our creativity."[52]

Given such a (scary) scenario, it can easily be seen how the much less revolutionary concept of love between a human and machine is feasible. "It may seem far-fetched, but researchers say it's plausible," wrote Erik Sofge for *Popular Science* when *Her* was about to be released, explaining how "lovebots" programmed with "an irresistible romance algorithm" could possibly be created as computers got much smarter.[53] Many people already spend more time with their various devices than with other people, after all, something that will only increase in the future. Such an intimate relationship could lead users to fall in love with their machines, some are predicting. "For many of the psychologists, social scientists, and experts in artificial intelligence who study this kind of relationship, it's not a matter of if, but when," wrote Ben Popper of theverge.com in 2013, the key being that the machines in question will have to have a mind, or something like it, of their own. Should this happen sometime in the decades ahead, the idea of love itself will morph, it's safe to say, marking a new era in the history of the subject.[54]

The 2015 film *Ex Machina* also featured love between a human and a machine, suggesting that the idea appears to be becoming part of the cultural zeitgeist as its reality grows. (A number of films, notably the 1927 *Metropolis* and 1982 *Blade Runner*, had visited this terrain over the decades, but it is only recently that such relationships seem entirely possible and even probable because of advances in artificial intelligence.) *Ex Machina* revolved around the Turing test, i.e., the hypothesis put forth by the British computer scientist Alan Turing concerning whether a machine was capable of thinking like a human. In the film, the protagonist, Caleb, falls in love with Ava, an artificially intelligent robot owned by Caleb's billionaire boss, Nathan, and mayhem naturally ensues. Long story short, the movie echoed the message of *Her*, i.e., that it is entirely plausible for a human to love a machine, although it is much less clear whether the reverse can hold true.

The increasingly intimate relationship between humans and machines is likely helping to create a longing for things and experiences that are perceived as real and authentic. Indeed, a sweeping backlash against encroaching digital technology in general appears to be escalating, a phenomenon masterfully discussed in David Sax's 2016 book *The Revenge of Analog: Real Things and Why They Matter*.[55] Love appears to be part of this yearning for experiences that are not delivered in bits and bytes, as there are elements of romance that cannot be satisfied by texting, Skyping, and the universe-unto-itself of online dating. While there is no shortage of websites allowing users to meet someone anywhere at anytime for anything, it's safe to say that, like everything having to do with the Internet, it is matter of quantity over quality. (A 2016 study by Pew Research Center found that a third of the people using dating apps never meet anyone in person.[56])

Some with the time and money, for example, are hiring personalized matchmakers to find that special someone, a practice that goes back thousands of years. ("Choosing a life partner was often viewed as far too complicated a decision for young people on their own, and from Aztec civilization to ancient Greece and China, their elders [often women] intervened to make sure they had the 'right' kind of suitor," wrote JR Thorpe for bustle.com in 2016.[57]) Those in the business argue that dating apps are great for hookups but something much different is required to be introduced to a person that could be a life partner. High-end matchmaking services such as New York–based Lasting Connections consider themselves to be "highly-trained romantic-compatibility experts whose primary goal is finding clients a passionate, fulfilling, and long-lasting relationship," an appealing concept to certain busy business executives.[58]

Another response to the digitalization of romance is a minor revival of the love letter. As anachronistic as a quill pen, a love letter offers a means of communicating thoughts in a way impossible in an email or text, something augmented by the tangibility and handcrafted quality of putting and reading ink on paper. "A letter has a remarkable way of transpiring feelings, emotions, honesty, sincerity and authenticity," observed Sonia Cancian, an assistant professor of history at Zayed University in Dubai, after studying hundreds of them in her research. The ideal love letter mixed the poetic with the mundane, according to Cancian, giving the reader a clear sense of whatever was taking place in the writer's world. Take one's time and direct the letter to an audience of one, she advised those wanting to take a stab at such a thing, the only rule being that the chosen words had to be heartfelt.[59]

While romance between humans and machines may be just the stuff of futurism, our contemporary technological landscape also presents certain challenges and opportunities with regard to love that Americans of generations past never had to deal with. "Technology has allowed people to come together in a whole new way," observed Emily Dieckman, a student at California State University at Fullerton, in 2016. Dieckman's boyfriend lived hundreds of miles away, reason for them to rely heavily on texting and video chatting to stay in touch. Couples separated by distance had for centuries communicated by letters and, more recently, by telephone, of course, but the digital revolution had led to forms of contact that people of the not so recent past could hardly imagine. The smartphone, and what it connects to, has without question altered the ways in which those in a relationship interact, although one cannot say for sure whether it is for the better or worse. (Historians of the future will have to determine the social significance of a couple's posting photos of themselves, all of them seemingly in a state of near ecstasy, on Facebook or Instagram.[60])

Because she was in a long-distance relationship and was fluent in all of the available digital avenues of communication, Dieckman had keen insights regarding the intersection of technology and love. Dieckman wisely recognized that despite all the new gadgets and explosion of social media, the fundamental nature of love had not changed. "No matter how much we text and Skype, I think there's one thing—the most important thing—that has stayed the same, and that is love itself," she observed for her college newspaper, *The Daily Titan*. "It sounds cheesy, and it is, but there's something really comforting about it to me," she continued, thinking that "in a time where everything around us seems to be changing and shifting so quickly, knowing that we experience the same feeling as people thousands of years ago, offers a sense of peace." Dieckman's profound words serve as an important reminder that the more that changes about love, the more that it seems to remain the same, a reassuring thought as technology plays an ever-increasing role in our everyday lives.[61]

Conclusion

"Love is a smoke raised with the fumes of sighs," Romeo says in the very beginning of *Romeo and Juliet*, expressing his misery that Rosaline does not love him back. Shakespeare's words written four centuries and change ago resonate today, and speak to the emotional rollercoaster on which love can take one. Rather than be perceived as a simple joy of life, as one might expect, romantic love has been considered a problem and nuisance in America over the past century, we repeatedly hear in tracing its history. Much like its emotional sibling, happiness, love has proved to be a challenging and frustrating pursuit, filled with complexities and contradictions. Many, perhaps most, Americans have struggled to find and preserve love, while others have rejected the emotion wholesale, not wanting or willing to take on the commitment it requires. The heartache that comes with losing love is just as or even more powerful as that comes with having it, research shows, reason enough for a fair number of people to think of it in negative terms or decide to opt out.

Alongside this widespread dismissal of romantic love has been, paradoxically, the recognition that it is the deepest and richest experience of which we are capable. Much of the stuff of life pales in comparison to being in love, we've been told, a conclusion that many of us who have taken the plunge can attest. Love is a polarized emotion, it is clear, both revered and loathed because of its intensity. Collectively, we both seek love out and avoid it, fully aware of its rewards and risks. Which we choose to do as individuals has much to do with what is going in our lives at a particular moment in time. Timing is everything in life, one can say, especially when it comes to love. Love means different things at different points in one's life, part of the ephemeralness and evanescence of the emotion. The tendency of love to come and go as it likes is one of its most confounding aspects, and evidence that we are not in full control of the emotion.

The idea that we are not in charge of love—that we "fall" into it or out of it as circumstances dictate—reflects our inclination to view it as a mysterious, almost supernatural force that can never be truly understood. Although we are a more religious people than many others around the world (most of us believe in God), we are also a largely rational people, drawn to logic, practicality, and common sense. Falling in love is not at all a rational act, yet most of us are willing to fully invest ourselves in what some have called a mental pathology or temporary state of insanity. We often fight the feeling ("I wish I wasn't so in love with you" is a refrain heard often in fiction and I believe real life), but still ultimately give in or succumb to the emotion. Love is thus a leap of faith that we had not intended on taking, and a concession of sorts to a higher power that dictates how we will spend much of the rest of our lives.

This willingness to enter into a kind of altered state of consciousness is largely a result of the training in love we receive in our youth. Americans learn the narrative of romantic love at an early age, something that will serve as a central part of one's personal identity over the course of a lifetime. (At age six, my daughter announced her intention to marry a certain classmate when she became an adult. It is not unusual for kindergarteners to pair off as "boyfriend" and "girlfriend" and consider themselves engaged.) This seeding of love is a direct result of children both mirroring their parents and embracing the live-happily-ever-after endings embedded in books, movies, and television shows. The oft-mentioned observation that romantic love is a fairy tale thus has much truth to it. Marketers of entertainment aimed at kids have taken the trope of romantic love and ran with it, reinforcing the idea that meeting and settling down with a special person is the key to a happy, fulfilling life. The notion that there is one and only one person who is truly capable of serving as a life partner has helped to locate love within the realm of destiny and fate and to define the experience as one that is somehow divinely ordained.

Our biology also obviously has played a major role in encouraging that we gravitate towards love throughout our lives. Love is there for a reason, scientists and anthropologists have reminded us, a central part of the grand design of our species. Nature dangles the carrot of love through brain chemistry, making it a tempting force that is difficult to resist. The joy and euphoria to be had by a brain in early love can by matched only by strong opiates, this alone making it understandable why so many of us are seduced by the emotion. The "discovery" of love in the brain has justifiably been recognized as an important scientific breakthrough, perhaps even analogous to those made by Copernicus and Newton in their attempts to learn the physical laws of the universe. The ability to see love via fMRI scans shifted the study of love towards neuroscience, and offered a means to more quantifiably evaluate theories offered by psychologists, sociologists, and others in the social sciences and medicine. Viewing the physical properties of an emotion was not unlike peeking inside the body through x-rays in the late 19th century, a very exciting historical development that helped to advance (and publicize) the field.

Also revolutionary was the collapsing or integration of love with marriage that took place in the United States in the early decades of the 20th century. Scholars of love have taken great effort to point out that the American interpretation and expression of the emotion is for the most part an aberration or anomaly, historically speaking, an exception to how it has generally been articulated in other times and in other places. Love, American-style is thus a radical concept, it's fair to say, something of which most of us are unaware because we associate it heavily with the common social institution of marriage. Our bold experiment with the domestication of love has had mixed results, with many pointing to the nation's high divorce rate and incidence of extramarital affairs as evidence that love and marriage do not go together like as a horse and carriage. I disagree with such a sweeping conclusion, however, as there are obviously many "successful" marriages built on a foundation of love, whether passionate or "compatible." As well, a committed relationship offers the opportunity to be part of something bigger than oneself, and realize the kind of joy that can only come with having a family. (See my histories of fatherhood, aging, and happiness for more on that.)

From a long view, we can see that romantic love in America over the past century followed two disciplinary paths that occasionally crossed. One could be called philosophical, carrying on a long tradition of great and not so great minds musing on the nature of love. With the development of modern psychology and sociology between the world wars, love as a subject became more formalized and legitimized, blessed by the methods of the social sciences. Out of this process, science emerged as the second main path love would take, with a handful of dedicated researchers pursuing work in the field at any given time. While some argued that approaching love as a science was misguided, a subversion of nature, academics were determined to uncover some of the mysteries that had cloaked the subject for millennia. Pharmacology and biotechnology promise to dominate the future of the field, we can safely say, with love potions and killer apps merging man and machine perhaps waiting in the wings.

While no doubt a risky venture, filled with uncertainty and unknowns, love embodies the very essence of life itself, I argue after becoming a devout student of it, finding myself side with those who have throughout history recognized its power and its glory. There are no bigger stakes than sharing one's life with another person and, perhaps, having a child with him or her, making love arguably the ultimate emotional experience one can have. It is entirely understandable how the more prudent are passing on relationships predicated on love (I first got married at age 58), as the sacrifices and compromises involved with one are enormous. Many millennials are doing just that, not wanting to take on the commitment and responsibility that comes with anything or anyone requiring a long-term investment. (They are also shunning ownership of cars, homes, and full-time jobs, making their apathy towards or aversion to love wholly consistent with their freelance lifestyles.) With many millennials up to their ears in college debt and the children of divorced parents, love is often perceived by members of that generation as a luxury they cannot afford or as a foolish enterprise on which to embark.

Still, I cannot help but align with others of the pro-love school who have suggested that those who rebuff the emotion are missing out on a big part of life. Like other highly charged sites such as religion or spirituality, love offers the possibility of adding significant meaning and purpose to one's life, inscribing it with a layer of existentiality otherwise unobtainable. No institutional authority governs love, making it something that demonstrates our fundamental liberties and free will. Rather than act as a threat to individual autonomy, love at its best augments the self, bringing out dimensions of one's personality that would instead lay dormant. Good numbers of both men and women have rejected such a view, however, seeing love as a prime limiter of and constraint on the classic American values of individuality, freedom, and independence. Feminist movements in particular have put a damper on romantic love, with many women seeing their fight for equality as mutually exclusive with a committed relationship with a man. More anti-authoritarian men too have resisted the draw of love, perceiving it as a learned social construct that the majority of Americans were mistakenly believing was innate and natural. A running theme in this book has in fact been Americans' critical view of love, making one wonder if the emotion really is a chemically-induced fantasy being taken much too seriously and one that runs counter to our basic national character rooted in self-determination.

Whatever one's view of love, there can be no dispute that it is a complex emotion rooted in both brain activity and social behavior. This dualistic quality of love has packed a one-two punch that has proved to be irresistible to most of us, making it not surprising that the emotion has taken on such cultural significance. Myths, especially the idea of a "soul mate," have only reinforced the potency of love, putting the emotion squarely in the center of everyday life. Love is woven into a wide variety of major cultural influences including movies, television, and the ever-expanding online universe, notably dating services and apps. Popular culture has heavily shaped Americans' expectations in their romantic relationships (and not for the better), this book has showed, with the ascent of mass media after World War I exerting tremendous influence on both the perception and reality of love for many Americans. While more a history of how love has been perceived in the country over time, the experience of the emotion, i.e., what it is, why it exists, and how it is expressed, has been a big part of the story.

While not intended to be a tutorial in love, readers hopefully have gained some useful insights into how to best accommodate the emotion in their life. I certainly have in writing the book, finding in the literature many valuable tips relating to ways to improve the dynamics of and lessen the conflict in a long-term relationship, especially marriage. Love and marriage are two very different things, experts of all stripes have consistently maintained, the former an emotion and the latter an arrangement requiring a host of organizational skills. Managing each at the same time is a careful balancing act, the connubially experienced know all too well, a reminder that the American endeavor of fusing love and marriage has been a daring one. Some of this has to do with the fact that we are simply not taught how to love (or be married, for that matter) as part of our formal education. We learn more about the Pythagorean theorem and the Treaty of Ghent in school than about love, an odd thing given how much more the latter subject will likely play in our lives. Love is an improvisational act, we can conclude, and when applied a work in process that demands a set of skills different from any other for it to, for lack of a better word, succeed.

Sadly, however, Americans have seemingly displayed a glaring lack of skill in managing romantic love over the past century, something no shortage of authorities in the field have made note of. While fictional expressions of love have been hailed as triumphant realizations of the human spirit, the real thing has often been perceived as a pernicious problem in this country. Love is a troublesome emotion that more often than wreaks havoc on the lives of those who unwittingly enter into it, we hear over and over, with bad breakups and much time spent in therapists' offices clear evidence of such. Americans' penchant of viewing love as a destination rather than as a journey has certainly not helped matters, and our orientation towards and fondness of accomplishing goals have encouraged some to treat the emotion as a task that has to be completed. Attempts to eliminate the randomness of love through supposedly scientific methodologies have not been resounding successes, suggesting that there is something about the emotion that goes beyond full human comprehension. Failure in love has carried serious consequences, notably psychic trauma, distressed children, and high legal bills.

What precisely is wrong with love in America? Why do so many relationships initially overflowing with the emotion end? Are individuals' expectations too high, or does boredom naturally set in after a certain amount of time? Are too many couples simply mismatched, or are the pressures of modern life too high for many relationships to endure? Or are Americans basically a dissatisfied and restless lot, always thinking something else and better is waiting around the corner? Thousands of psychologists and sociologists have offered perfectly reasonable explanations to such questions, but there are of course no definitive answers. Our tendency to frame relationships, and especially marriage, as "work" perhaps offers a clue to why love has been so problematic since the Wilson administration. Only Americans could view love as a job; our obsession with values like progress, achievement, improvement and success is not at all consistent with the makeup of such an unreliable, immeasurable emotion. More flexible and making no demands to be perfect, Europeans' traditional concept of and approach to love seems better suited to the waywardness of the emotion, as it recognizes the fallibility of ordinary people.

Relatedly, nowhere else in the world is romantic love such an important part of the economy. Love is the centerpiece of the domestic, consumerist American way of life, if one thinks about it, the vital spark that sets off a chain events geared around the consumption-based lifestyle that is common to marriage and family. Love helps to keep the wheels of capitalism spinning, and in this respect functions as a facilitator of cultural norms and social order. Love is a corporately endorsed product marketed and sold to Americans, as it is very good for business. Besides serving as the engine that drives much of the earning and spending of money required to raise kids, the expression of love itself represents a significant chunk of the economy. Many businesses such as flowers, candy, jewelry, and hospitality (restaurants and travel) are heavily dependent on the desire of one person to demonstrate his or her love to another person, especially on Valentine's Day and during the holiday season. Dating and "keeping the romance alive" are expensive propositions, as is the perceived need to appear attractive to one's mate via beauty products and services. Love in this country is thus, like virtually everything else, really about money, making the emotion as American as mom, apple pie, and Chevrolet.

As Russell Baker keenly observed, choosing not to participate in love is viewed as a suspicious and somewhat subversive act in the United States, in part because it is opposition to our consumerist lifestyle and our commitment to economic growth. Avoiding romantic entanglements is considered not just unnatural but un–American, a violation of our national creed grounded in the making and spending of money. Skirting love also goes against the grain of the dominant narrative of American popular culture, further marginalizing those who prefer to fly solo in their personal lives. Since they each came into being, the movie and music industries have used love as a primary device to tell stories and entertain, in the process instilling the idea that happiness is dependent upon finding Mr. or Ms. Right. With this kind of compelling, repetitive storytelling, it is not surprising that a huge business has sprung up around the acquiring or repairing of romantic love. Love is either coming or going or be too little or too much in quantity, it appears, very rarely the right kind in the right amount. Always in need of overhauls or tune-ups, love is a constantly renewable resource, and an ideal business model for the billion of dollars self-help business and our therapeutic culture in general.

Against this rather critical and perhaps cynical backdrop, however, is the irrefutable beauty and wonder of love that have led some to refer to it as the "supreme" emotion. Love is hard and probably impossible to define but, like pornography, one knows it when one sees or feels it. If love was not real, or at least didn't appear to be real, it would never have been possible for it to realize the degree of status it has assumed in popular and consumer culture. It is an unmistakable sensation that is like nothing else and impossible to replicate, ensuring that the anti-love movement can gain only a certain amount of traction. The magic of love has continually befuddled scientists, with all efforts to slice and dice it over the years falling short in some respect. The hundreds of studies parsing the who, what, where, when, and why of love have without a doubt added much to our understanding of the dynamics of love, but no kind of research design can ever capture the mystical aspects of the emotion or even the operative laws of attraction. In short, the workings of Cupid's arrows defy full scientific analysis and the methodology of any algorithm, for me a very good thing as I personally like the idea of a behind-the-scenes force existing beyond our corporeal world.

Upon considerable reflection, the story of love in America has made quite a good love story itself. We are a heavily myth-based culture, making it perfectly sensible that we've been strongly attracted to fables and parables involving romance. Academics of various persuasions from both the humanities and social sciences have been drawn to the field because of the obvious challenges the investigation of love presents. As well, it is undeniably cool to say you specialize in the study of love, and more than one researcher has probably ventured into the area thinking doing so could advance their career or perhaps land them a book deal. The fact that love is a timeless and universal subject also works to its advantage; it is never going to be considered passé or become obsolete. Love is fundamentally immune to social, political, and economic upheavals, this too ensuring that it remains a topic of interest to many across the spectrums of time and space. Like other emotions such as fear and anger, love is a staple human experience; while its interpretation and expression may differ based on where one happens to live, its essence transcends cultural diversity. Unlike many other arenas, love is never really "in" or "out" or "up" or "down," making it largely resistant to the constantly shifting winds of change.

Much of the cultural currency of love is based on its rare ability to straddle what may appear to be opposing or contradictory forces. From a psychological perspective, love is located in both the conscious and unconscious, for example, crossing over the recognized mental boundaries of awareness and unawareness. It combines both left- and right-brain thinking to form a cognitive mash-up of sentiment and logic. It operates on both a macro and micro level, its universality matched by its individuality. It is both learned and instinctive, a unique forging of nurture and nature. From a disciplinary view, love is both an art and a science, supported by a rich history of the philosophical and a generous dose of sound, data-driven research. Finally, romantic love is characterized by both great joy and great despair, its druglike emotional high matched by a very deep low should things go south in a serious relationship. Love is a prime example of the Chinese concept of yin and yang, one might reasonably conclude, illustrating that seemingly conflicting principles can be complementary, interconnected, and interdependent.

The Zelig–like nature of love and its insistence to make its presence known at any time and any place has endowed the emotion with a special form of power. Despite widespread criticism and concerted efforts by many to crush it out of their lives, love has of course survived, with little reason to think it will ever disappear. With the rise of individualism over the last half-millennium and triumph of the self over the past century, one might have thought that a practice based on the interests of two people would recede. But exactly the reverse has happened, an indication that it is those things in which experiences are shared that will stand the test of time. Like friendship, community, volunteering, and philanthropy, love is humanity at its best, I think, a collective activity that is characterized by kindness, empathy, and caring. More of all kinds of love, romantic and otherwise, is a very good thing, I hope we can all agree, as any activity in which the interests of others are prioritized would make the world a better place. The future of love in this country is unknown, but I have no doubt that the emotion will continue to contribute abundant purpose and meaning to our everyday lives.

Chapter Notes

Preface

1. See Simon May's *Love: A History* for an excellent of love from ancient times, and Marilyn Yalom's *The Amorous Heart: An Unconventional History of Love*, Kristin Celello's *Making Marriage Work: A History of Marriage and Divorce in the Twentieth-Century United States*, and Leila J. Rupp's *A Desired Past: A Short History of Same-Sex Love in America* for more detailed explorations of different aspects of romantic love. As well, Irving Singer's trilogy on the nature of love is a true tour de force of the subject, and *A General Theory of Love* by Thomas Lewis, Fari Amini, and Richard Lannon is very worthwhile reading. Simon May, *Love: A History* (New Haven, CT: Yale University Press, 2011; Marilyn Yalom, *The Amorous Heart: An Unconventional History of Love* (New York: Basic, 2018); Kristin Celello, *Making Marriage Work: A History of Marriage and Divorce in the Twentieth-Century United States* (Chapel Hill, NC: University of North Carolina Press, 2009); Leila J. Rupp, *A Desired Past: A Short History of Same-Sex Love in America* (Chicago: University of Chicago Press, 2002); Irving Singer, *The Nature of Love: Plato to Luther* (Boston, MA: The MIT Press, 1984); Irving Singer, *The Nature of Love: Courtly and Romantic* (Chicago, IL: University of Chicago Press, 1987); Irving Singer, *The Nature of Love: The Modern World* (Chicago, IL: University of Chicago Press, 1987); Thomas Lewis, Fari Amini, and Richard Lannon, *A General Theory of Love* (New York: Random House, 2000).

2. Susan J. Matt, and Peter N. Stearns, eds., *Doing Emotions History* (Champaign, IL: University of Illinois Press, 2014; Rob Boddice, *The History of Emotions* (Manchester, UK: Manchester University Press, 2018); Barbara Rosenwein and Riccardo Cristiani, *What Is the History of Emotions?* (Cambridge, UK: Polity, 2018); Jan Plamper, *The History of Emotions: An Introduction* (New York: Oxford University Press, 2015); Barbara H. Rosenwein, *Generations of Feeling: A History of Emotions, 600–1700* (New York: Cambridge University Press, 2015); William M. Reddy, *The Navigation of Feeling: A Framework for the History of Emotions* (New York: Cambridge University Press, 2001).

3. Peter N. Stearns, *Shame: A Brief History* (Champaign, IL: University of Illinois Press, 2017); Rob Boddice, *The Science of Sympathy: Morality, Evolution, and Victorian Civilization* (Champaign, IL: University of Illinois Press, 2016); Guenter B. Risse, *Driven By Fear: Epidemics and Isolation in San Francisco's House of Pestilence* (Champaign, IL: University of Illinois Press, 2016); Lawrence R. Samuel, *Happiness in America* (Lanham, MD: Rowman & Littlefield, 2018).

4. Needless to say, making same-sex love visible and socially acceptable was one of the most important social movements of the latter decades of the twentieth century. Those interested in how race influenced marriage in the interwar years might consult Anastasia Curwood's *Stormy Weather: Middle-Class African Marriages between the Two World Wars* (Chapel Hill, NC: University of North Carolina Press, 2010).

Introduction

1. Arthur Schlesinger, Jr., "An Informal History of Love U.S.A.," *Saturday Evening Post*, December 31, 1966, 30.

2. Stephanie Coontz, *Marriage, a History: How Love Conquered Marriage* (New York: Penguin, 2006) 15. See Rebecca Davis 's *More Perfect Unions: The American Search for Marital Bliss* (Cambridge, MA: Harvard University Press, 2010) for a thorough analysis of how Americans' attitudes about marriage changed dramatically between the 1930s and 1970s.

3. "An Informal History of Love U.S.A."
4. Richard Stengel, "No More MoonJune: Love's Out," *New York Times*, August 5, 1979, E21.
5. Kenneth Gergen, and Mary Gergen, "It's a Love Story," *Psychology Today*, December 1988, 48–49.
6. Jack Flam, "A History of Love," *Wall Street Journal*, January 28, 1993, A12; Stephen Kern, *The Culture of Love: Victorians to Moderns* (Cambridge, MA: Harvard University Press, 1993).
7. Theodore Hendrik Van de Velde, *Ideal Marriage: Its Physiology and Technique* (New York: Random House, 1930).
8. Coontz, 205.
9. Florence Shinkle, "Searching for the Right One," *St. Louis Post-Dispatch*, February 14, 1999, D1.
10. Liesl Schillinger, "The Lost Art of the Love Affair," *New York Times Book Review*, February 14, 1999, 35; Doris Langley Moore, *The Technique of the Love Affair* (New York: Simon & Schuster, 1928).
11. Hara Estroff Marano, "The Truth About Compatibility," *Psychology Today*, September/October 2004, 52.
12. Judith Hertog, "Against Romance: An Un-Valentine," nytimes.com, February 8, 2019.
13. Pepper Schwartz, *Love Between Equals: How Peer Marriage Really Works* (New York: Touchstone Books, 1995).
14. Laura Sessions Stepp," "Love's Labor Lost," *Washington Post*, February 14, 2007, C1.
15. Maria Popova, "The First Kiss in Cinema: How Thomas Edison Scandalized the World in 1896," brainpickings.org, January 20, 2102.
16. Carlise Jones, "The New Love-Making School: Kiss Me Now, Save a Lot of Time," *New York Herald Tribune*, August 27, 1939, E3.
17. Caryn James, "At Its Best, Love Is Far From a Fairy Tale," *New York Times*, March 4, 1990, H13.
18. Caryn James, "Love With Improper Strangers," *New York Times*, April 22, 1990, H1.
19. Don Oldenburg, "When Your Love Life Reads Like a Movie Script," *Washington Post*, July 23, 2001, C8; Marcia Millman, *The Seven Stories of Love: And How to Choose Your Own Happy Ending* (New York: William Morrow, 2001).
20. Patricia Corrigan, "Love Hollywood-Style," *St. Louis Post-Dispatch*, June 25, 2003, E1; James Robert Parish, *The Hollywood Book of Love: An Irreverent Guide to the Films that Raised Our Romantic Expectations* (Chicago, IL: Contemporary Books, 2003).

21. Rachel Abramowitz, "Not in the Mood for Love," *Los Angeles Times*, February 11 2007, E1.
22. Howard Reich, "A Little Romance, Please," *Chicago Tribune*, February 14, 1999, 5.
23. gap.com.
24. subaru.com.
25. Laura Kipnis, *Against Love: A Polemic* (New York: Pantheon, 2003) 195.

Chapter 1

1. "Einstein Holds Love Not Due to Gravity," *New York Times*, July 25, 1933, 21.
2. "Einstein Holds Love Not Due to Gravity."
3. "The Sorrows of Free Love," *Living Age*, May 8, 1920, 342–5. See John C. Spurlock's *Free Love Marriage and Middle-Class Radicalism in America* for more on that movement. John C. Spurlock, *Free Love Marriage and Middle-Class Radicalism in America* (New York: NYU Press, 1988).
4. Gilbert Frankau, "Can the Modern Girl Love?" *Forum*, November 1922, 917.
5. "Can the Modern Girl Love?" 919.
6. George Humphrey, "Falling in Love," *Collier's*, December 20, 1924, 27.
7. "Falling in Love."
8. "Mrs. Lydig Warns of Loveless Unions," *New York Times*, September 10, 1926, 14.
9. "Mrs. Lydig Warns of Loveless Unions"; See my *Rich: The Rise and Fall of American Wealth Culture* (AMACOM, 2013) for more on the desire of titles among wealthy young American women.
10. Rose Macauley, "Love," *Forum*, July 1926, 109.
11. "What Is Love?," *Forum*, August 1927, 269.
12. "What Is Love?"
13. Joseph Wood Krutch, "Love—Or the Life and Death of a Value," *Atlantic Monthly*, August 1928, 199–210.
14. "Blue Days for the Scribes," *Los Angeles Times*, February 27, 1921, III13.
15. "Flays Hollywood as Free-Love City," *Washington Post*, June 30, 1922, 9.
16. "Love Colony Head is Held," *Los Angeles Times*, September 23, 1922, I11.
17. "Woman Author Arrested," *Los Angeles Times*, February 1, 1925, 11.
18. "Love-Cult Head in Martyr Role," *Los Angeles Times*, November 10, 1925, A5.
19. "Hurley Demands Arrests in Every 'Triangle' Suit," *Chicago Daily Tribune*, January 7, 1923, 5.

20. "Says 'Bootleg Love' Permeates Nation," *New York Times*, January 15, 1927, 6.
21. "Judge Lindsey Denies Advocating Free Love," *New York Times*, January 31, 1927, 11.
22. "Marriages Discussed by Lindsey," *Los Angeles Times*, August 13, 1927, A8.
23. Himkon Strunskey, "About Books, More or Less: We Experiment," *New York Times*, November 27, 1927, BR4.
24. "Free Love Out-Worn, Declares Dr. Cabot," *Boston Daily Globe*, March 29, 1927, 5.
25. "'Jungle Age' Is Assailed at Endeavor Convention," *Atlanta Constitution*, July 8, 1927, 4.
26. "Assails Free Love and Trail Marriage," *New York Times*, September 26, 1927, 23.
27. "Manning Condemns Free Love Discussion," *New York Times*, April 4, 1928, 26.
28. "Dr. Gates Refuses to Debate Lindsey," *New York Times*, December 5, 1930, 27.
29. "Spread of Free Love Attacked," *Los Angeles Times*, November 4, 1927, 2.
30. "Youth Group Denounced by D.A.R. Official," *Baltimore Sun*, March 21, 1930, 30.
31. "Author Attacks Radical Teaching," *Washington Post*, January 3, 1931, 7.
32. See Larry Ceplair's *Anti-Communism in Twentieth-Century America* (Praeger, 2011) for a solid history of both "official" and "unofficial" anti-communism in the United States between the world wars. For more on the American way of life, see my *The American Way of Life: A Cultural History* (Fairleigh Dickenson University Press, 2017).
33. "'Free Love' Teaching Denied by Columbia," *New York Times*, March 4, 1932, 7.
34. "Study Love Affairs of Wedded Persons," *New York Times*, July 20, 1928, 19.
35. "Study Love Affairs of Wedded Persons."
36. Mary Garden, "Love and Marriage," *Ladies' Home Journal*, September 1930, 9.
37. "Love and Marriage."
38. "Love and Marriage."
39. "Love and Marriage."
40. "Love and Marriage."
41. "Love and Marriage."
42. Anonymous, "The American Girl Misses the Man She Wants," *Saturday Evening Post*, February 11, 1933, 8.
43. Robert C. Binkley, "Should We Leave Romance Out of Marriage?," *Forum*, February 1930, 72.
44. "Should We Leave Romance Out of Marriage?"
45. "Should We Leave Romance Out of Marriage?"
46. Jessica G. Cosgrave, "The Problem of the Affections," *Good Housekeeping*, March 1928, 27.
47. W. Beran Wolfe, M.D., "Romance vs. Marriage," *Forum*, September 1931, 166.
48. "Romance vs. Marriage."
49. Henry Morton Robinson, "Sons as Lovers," *North American Review*, March 1934, 233.
50. Clemence Dane, "What Is Love?," *Forum*, December 1935, 335.
51. Raoul de Roussy de Sales, "Love in America," *Atlantic Monthly*, May 1938, 645.
52. "Love in America," 645–646.
53. "Love in America," 646–647.
54. "Love in America," 650–651.
55. Carlise Jones, "The New Love-Making School: Kiss Me Now, Save a Lot of Time," *New York Herald Tribune*, August 27, 1939, E3.

Chapter 2

1. Nell Giles said much the same thing about falling in love and falling out of love. The former, she observed in *Ladies' Home Journal* in 1944, "is a strictly emotional process and therefore the most fun in the world," while the latter "takes brains and is therefore about as much fun as doing an algebra problem." Nell Giles, "How to Fall Out of Love," *Ladies' Home Journal*, October 1944, 4.
2. Arthur Gordon, "Never Marry for Love," *Good Housekeeping*, October 1940, 37.
3. "Love: America's No. 1 Problem?," *Science Digest*, August 1943, 19–24.
4. Harold Hefferman, "Many Film Romances Result in Marriages," *Hartford Courant*, August 18, 1940, A6.
5. "Many Film Romances Result in Marriages."
6. Hedda Hopper, "Love Will Have Its Way!," *Chicago Tribune*, December 5, 1943, F3.
7. Hope Ridings Miller, "Author of 'Love in America' Turns Attention to, and Gives Advice on the Wooing of Women Warworkers," *Washington Post*, November 24, 1943, B3.
8. Dorothy Hillyer, "Best Books of the Season," *Daily Boston Globe*, May 20, 1943, 18; David L. Cohn, *Love in America: An Informal Study of Manners and Morals in American Marriage* (New York: Simon & Schuster, 1943).
9. Beatrice Sherman, "American Love Scene," *New York Times*, May 23, 1943, BR8.
10. Dorothy Dunbar Bromley, "What's Wrong with Women? Bold Male Risks an Answer," *New York Herald Tribune*, May 30, 1943, D1.
11. Albert Lernard, "Lonely Hearts Dept.," *Washington Post*, June 13, 1943, L5.

12. "Movie Versus True Love and the Angry London Bishop," *Baltimore Sun*, April 4, 1947, 14.
13. "Movie Versus True Love and the Angry London Bishop."
14. "Movie Versus True Love and the Angry London Bishop."
15. Judith Chase Churchill, "What Do You Know About Love?," *Woman's Home Companion*, August 1947, 36.
16. "What Do You Know About Love?"
17. Betty Di Pesa, "Why Mother of Three Gives Course on Love," *Daily Boston Globe*, November 9, 1947, A10.
18. Waverly Root, "Plain Talk About Romantic Love," *American Mercury*, November 1947, 543.
19. John E. Gibson, "Science Looks at Love," *Ladies' Home Journal*, June 1948, 69.
20. "Science Looks at Love."
21. F. Alexander Magoun, *Love and Marriage* (New York: Harper and Brothers, 1948).
22. Roald Dahl, "I Love You," *Ladies' Home Journal*, May 1949, 44.
23. Murray Campbell, "Five Faces of Love," *Woman's Home Companion*, November 1949, 38.
24. Howard Whitman, "Science Discovers Real Love," *Reader's Digest*, September 1950, 115–118.
25. "Science Discovers Real Love."
26. "Authority Says Marriage Needs to Be Practical," *Norfolk New Journal and Guide*, July 8, 1950, D2.
27. Marynia Farnham, "More Love, Less Sex," *Coronet*, July 1950, 62.
28. Hubbard Hoover, and Isabelle Macrae Hoover, "European Idea of Marriage Puts Home and Family First," *Chicago Daily Tribune*, January 10, 1951, a3.
29. "Romance Alone Held No Basis for Marriage," *Los Angeles Times*, April 16, 1951, A9.
30. "Romantic Love Nearly Passe, Says Babs, with 4th Divorce," *Atlanta Journal and Constitution*, July 22, 1951, 8A.
31. "Marriages Cannot Last If Based on Love Alone, Says Professor," *Hartford Courant*, September 10, 1952, 19c.
32. "Do You Really Want a Romantic Husband?," *McCall's*, January 1953, 34.
33. "Love Among the Commies," *Life*, February 23, 1953, 30.
34. Zelda Popkin, "What Do You Know About Love?," *Coronet*, April 1953, 138.
35. Dr. Anna K. Daniels, *The Mature Woman* (New York: Prentice-Hall, 1953).
36. John Kord Lageman, "Romance Can Ruin Your Marriage," *Cosmopolitan*, March 1954, 60.
37. Paul H. Landis, "Don't Expect Too Much of Sex in Marriage," *Reader's Digest*, December 1954, 28.
38. Hannah Lees, "What Every Husband Needs," *Reader's Digest*, October 1957, 139.
39. Dorothy Thompson, "Do We Misunderstand Romantic Love?," *Ladies' Home Journal*, December 1955, 11.
40. M. Holmes, "What Became of the Man I Married?," *Better Homes & Gardens*, May 1952, 6.
41. Margaret Blair Johnstone, "You Can't Get Away with Marital Infidelity!," *Coronet*, March 1952, 35.
42. Morton Sontheimer, "How Much Do You Love Each Other?," *McCall's*, March 1954, 21.
43. Smiley Blanton, *Love or Perish* (New York: Simon & Schuster, 1956).
44. Erich Fromm, *The Art of Loving* (New York: Harper & Row, 1956).
45. George Walsh, "Your Mind and Love," *Cosmopolitan*, September 1957, 46.
46. T.F. James, "The Truth About Falling in Love," *Cosmopolitan*, June 1958, 24.
47. Dorothy Barclay, "Loving Wisely and Well," *New York Times Magazine*, September 28, 1958, SM45.
48. William Ridley, and Laura Ridley, "Love and Science," *Ladies' Home Journal*, February 1959, 14; See Sorokin's *The Ways and Power of Love: Techniques of Moral Transformation* (Templeton Press, 2002) and, to place it in historical context, Jay Weinstein, *Social and Cultural Change: Social Science for a Dynamic World* (Rowman & Littlefield, 2005). For the definitive account of family life during the Cold War, see Elaine Tyler May's *Homeward Bound: American Families in the Cold War Era* (New York: Basic Books, 1988).
49. Jessamyn West, "Love Is Not What You Think," *Ladies' Home Journal*, June 1959, 46.
50. Edith Kermit Roosevelt, "A Housewife Sounds Off," *Austin American*, July 26, 1959, B3.
51. Morton M. Hunt, "In Defense of Romantic Love," *New York Times Magazine*, September 27, 1959, SM22.
52. "In Defense of Romantic Love."
53. "In Defense of Romantic Love."
54. "In Defense of Romantic Love."
55. "In Defense of Romantic Love."
56. "In Defense of Romantic Love."
57. "Love: The Elixir of the Good Life," *Life*, December 28, 1959, 174.

Chapter 3

1. "'Love' Redefined for Red Chinese," *New York Times*, September 4, 1960, 22.

2. Herbert Hendin, "Revolt Against Love," *Harper's*, August 1975, 20.
3. D. Trilling, "What Ever Became of Romantic Love?," *Look*, February 16, 1960, 60.
4. Russell Maguire, "What Is Love," *American Mercury*, August 1960, 61.
5. John G. Fuller, "Trade Winds," *Saturday Review*, March 26, 1960, 6.
6. John E. Gibson, "Love Makes the World Go 'Round," *Today's Health*, February 1960, 4–5.
7. "Love Makes the World Go 'Round."
8. Hans J. Morgenthau, "Love and Power," *Commentary*, March 1962, 247.
9. Morton M. Hunt, "Can Husbands and Wives Stay in Love?," *Redbook*, April 1962, 40–1.
10. Morton M. Hunt, *The Natural History of Love* (New York: Grove Press, 1959).
11. M. Scarbrough, "Cupid on the Couch," *Seventeen*, February 1963, 156.
12. "Poetry Called Vital to Love," *New York Times*, February 15, 1962, 22.
13. Emma Harrison, "Total Love Held Need in Marriage," *New York Times*, June 28, 1962, 34.
14. Ernest van den Haag, "Love or Marriage?," *Harper's*, May 1962, 43.
15. J.B. Priestley, "Eroticism, Sex and Love," *Saturday Evening Post*, April 27, 1963, 10.
16. Robert Graves, "Are Women More Romantic Than Men?," *Life*, October 15, 1965, 126.
17. "Love in America," *Saturday Evening Post*, December 31, 1966, 3.
18. Russell Baker, "Love, Your Magic Spell Is Everywhere, Dammit," *Saturday Evening Post*, December 31, 1966, 8.
19. "Love, Your Magic Spell Is Everywhere, Dammit."
20. "Love, Your Magic Spell Is Everywhere, Dammit."
21. "Love, Your Magic Spell Is Everywhere, Dammit."
22. "Love, Your Magic Spell Is Everywhere, Dammit."
23. Sandford Brown, "'May I Ask You a Few Questions About Love?,'" *Saturday Evening Post*, December 31, 1966, 24.
24. "'May I Ask You a Few Questions About Love?'"
25. "Yes, Yes, Yes, Yes," *Saturday Evening Post*, December 31, 1966, 78.
26. Max Gunther, "The Merchants of Venus," *Saturday Evening Post*, December 31, 1966, 74.
27. "The Merchants of Venus."
28. "The Merchants of Venus."
29. Wilfrid Sheed, "We Overrate Love," *Saturday Evening Post*, March 25, 1967, 10.
30. "We Overrate Love."
31. L. Keast, "How to Fall Madly Out of Love," *Mademoiselle*, June 1968, 137.
32. M. Evans, "How Little Love Means," *Redbook*, September 1968, 65.
33. Dr. Joyce Brothers, "Will Liberalized Sex Kill Romantic Love?" *Good Housekeeping*, June 1971, 62.
34. "Yes Begins with a No," *Time*, June 22, 1970, 68; Rollo May, *Love and Will* (New York: W.W. Norton, 1969).
35. Richard Corliss, "Who Says All the World Loves a 'Love Story'?," *New York Times*, January 10, 1971, D11.
36. Henry Raymont, "Book Unit Rejects 'Love Story,'" *New York Times*, January 22, 1971, 16.
37. Thomas Meehan, "The Yale Faculty Makes the Scene," *New York Times Magazine*, February 7, 1971, SM12.
38. "New Texas Airline 'Loves' Its Passengers," *New York Times*, August 8, 1971, 56.
39. John D. Morris, "Seat Belts Advertised With Love," *New York Times*, December 3, 1972, S13.
40. Marek-Marsel Mesulam, and Jon Perry, "The Diagnosis of Love Sickness," *Psychophysiology*, September 1972.
41. "Love at First Sight? Dr. Murstein Says No," *Philadelphia Tribune*, October 14, 1972, 11.
42. Russell Baker, "Love and Potatoes," *New York Times*, November 26, 1974, 39.
43. Barbara Grizzuti Harrison, "Is Romance Dead?," *Ms.*, July 1974, 39.
44. "Is Romance Dead?"
45. Stanton Peele, and Archie Brodsky, "Love Can Be an Addiction," *Psychology Today*, August 1974, 22.
46. John Alan Lee, "The Styles of Loving," *Psychology Today*, October 1974, 44.
47. John Alan Lee, "Graph Your Own Style of Loving," *Psychology Today*, October 1974, 51.
48. Michael Vincent Miller, "Intimate Terrorism," *Psychology Today*, April 1977, 79.
49. James Reston, "Proxmire on Love," *New York Times*, March 14, 1975, 39.
50. "Proxmire on Love."
51. Helen Bevington, "Love Stories," *New York Times*, December 21, 1975, 227; Martin Levin, ed., *Love Stories* (New York: Quadrangle/The New York Times Book Co., 1975).
52. Anatole Broyard, "Whistling in the Dark," *New York Times*, October 5, 1976, 43; Robert Brain, *Friends and Lovers* (New York: Basic Books, 1976).
53. Erica Jong, "Speaking of Love," *Newsweek*, February 21, 1977, 11.
54. Russell Baker, "Meaningful Relation-

ships," *New York Times Magazine*, March 19, 1978, SM5.

55. Leslie Bennetts, "A Scientist's Love Story: Research on Passion and Beyond," *New York Times*, July 28, 1978, A12.

56. "A Scientist's Love Story: Research on Passion and Beyond."

57. Joy Gould Boyum, "Still in Love with Love Stories," *Wall Street Journal*, May 11, 1979, 21.

58. Richard Stengel, "No More MoonJune: Love's Out," *New York Times*, August 5, 1979, E21.

59. "No More MoonJune: Love's Out." Arranged marriages were and remain common in many countries around the world.

60. Maureen Howard, "Women with Men," *New York Times*, September 30, 1979, BR4; Jill Tweedie, *In the Name of Love* (New York: Pantheon Books, 1979).

Chapter 4

1. "20 Cents Worth of Love," *New York Times*, March 12, 1984, B11.

2. K.R. Gertz, "Romance: The Return of Love & Marriage," *Harper's Bazaar*, June 1980, 24.

3. C. Calvert, "Are You Loveable?" *Mademoiselle*, May 1980, 208.

4. B.J. Raphael, "Why Love Makes Us Feel Fat," *Glamour*, November 1980, 248.

5. Jerry Adler, "The Science of Love," *Newsweek*, February 25, 1980, 89; Dorothy Tennov, *Love and Limerence: The Experience of Being in Love* (New York: Stein and Day, 1979).

6. Carol Wallace, "Harlequin Presents Pulsating Love Stories That Are Selling," *Boston Globe*, November 26, 1980, 1.

7. "Harlequin Presents Pulsating Love Stories That Are Selling."

8. John S. Wilson, "They're Singing Songs of Love in All the Clubs for Valentine's Day," *New York Times*, February 13, 1981, 41.

9. Linda Matchan, "Balancing Love and Work—It May Save Your Life," *Boston Globe*, October 8, 1980, 1.

10. Judy Klemesrud, "Learning to Mix Love and Money," *New York Times*, February 16, 1981, B6.

11. Diane White, "Love Conquers All; Later Anything Conquers Love," *Boston Globe*, February 14, 1981, 1.

12. Michael Blowen, "Has Hollywood Jilted Romance? Love Does Not Conquer All in Contemporary Cinema," *Boston Globe*, February 12, 1981, 1.

13. Lawrence Eisenberg, "Cruising with the Love Boat," *Boston Globe*, December 26, 1982, 1.

14. John J. O'Connor, "Bash Aboard 'Love Boat,'" *New York Times*, February 26, 1982, C23.

15. William F. Doherty, "Questions 4 of Love, Matter of Money," *Boston Globe*, March 27, 1981, 1.

16. Michael deCourcy Hinds, "They Fell in Love at First Sight," *New York Times*, February 14, 1981, 15.

17. Nathan Cobb, "Get Personal: Looking for Love Among the Classified," *Boston Globe*, December 12, 1982, 1.

18. Alfie Kohn, "Is Love Really Chemistry After All?," *Boston Globe*, February 13, 1983, 1.

19. Glenn Collins, "Chemical Connections: Pathways of Love," *New York Times*, February 14, 1983, B6.

20. L. Draegin, "Are You in Love with Love?" *Mademoiselle*, December 1982, 91; J. DeLynn, "Passion Junkies," *Mademoiselle*, October 1983, 108.

21. "Hooked on Love," *Omni*, May 1984, 78; "Watch Out for the Career Lover," *Glamour*, December 1984, 114.

22. Robin Norwood, *Women Who Love Too Much: When You Keep Wishing and Hoping He'll Change* (New York: Pocket, 1985).

23. Ellen Goodman, "When Love Enters the Executive Suite," *Boston Globe*, September 27, 1983, 1.

24. Fred Bayles, "A Hard Line on Corporate Love Affairs," *Boston Globe*, August 23, 1983, 1.

25. Daniel Goleman, "Psychologists Start to Take the Measure of Love," *New York Times*, November 20, 1984, C1.

26. Daniel Goleman, "Patterns of Love Charted in Studies," *New York Times*, September 10, 1985, C1.

27. Daniel Goleman, "Psychologists Pursue the Irrational Aspects of Love," *New York Times*, July 22, 1986, C1.

28. Sandra Salmans, "What's New in Romance: Living on Love—and Marketing It, Too," *New York Times*, December 4, 1988, A13.

29. Leo Buscaglia, *Living, Loving & Learning* (New York: Holt, Rinehart and Winston, 1982); Lynn Langway, "Dr. Hug Will Uplift You," *Newsweek*, May 9, 1983, 85.

30. George Leonard, *Adventures in Monogamy: Exploring the Creative Possibilities of Love, Sexuality and Commitment* (New York: Tarcher, 1988).

31. Sandra Salmans, "What's New in Romance: Living on Love—and Marketing It, Too," *New York Times*, December 4, 1988, A13.

32. Sandra Salmans, "What's New in Ro-

mance: Want to Meet a Mate? Spend More Time at Work," *New York Times*, December 4, 1988, A13.

33. Kenneth Gergen, and Mary Gergen, "It's a Love Story," *Psychology Today*, December 1988, 48–49.

34. Daniel Goleman, "After Kinship and Marriage, Anthropology Discovers Love," *New York Times*, November 24, 1992, C1.

35. Kay S. Hymowitz, "Where Has Our Love Gone?," *Wall Street Journal*, April 6, 1995, A16. See Peter N. Stearns and Carol Z. Stearns, "Emotionology: Clarifying the History of Emotions and Emotional Standards," *The American Historical Review* (1985), 813–830.

36. Thomas Sowell, "Love and Other Four-Letter Words," *Forbes*, January 1, 1996, 64.

37. M.S. Mason, "Family Plays a Starring Role in Romantic Comedies of the '90s," *Christian Science Monitor*, February 14, 1997, 10:3.

38. Devra Maza, "Ode to a First Kiss," *Los Angeles Times*, February 12, 1998, 6.

39. Laurent Belsie, "Can Folks Find Their Valentine On-line?," *Christian Science Monitor*, February 14, 1997, 3:4.

40. "Can Folks Find Their Valentine On-line?"

41. "Love and Marriage on the Internet," *PR Newswire*, June 9, 1998, 1.

42. Jennifer Wolcott, "Click Here for Romance," *Christian Science Monitor*, January 13, 1999, 11.

43. Rita Elkins, "Use 'Net to Stock Up on Valentine Goodies," *Florida Today*, February 10, 1999, pNA.

44. Martha Mendoza, "Internet Romances Thrive Internationally, and So Do Related Sales," *Chicago Tribune*, February 12, 1999, 2. Twenty years later, Valentine's Day is a bigger than ever bonanza for marketers. Americans were estimated to spend a total of $20.7 billion for Valentine's Day in 2019, according to the National Retail Federation, while a survey by Bankrate found that each of us forked out an average of $267 to celebrate the day. Men spend more than five times what women spend for the holiday, the research also showed. "Take Out Your Wallet, It's Valentine's," linkedin.com, February 14, 2019.

45. Ellen Creager, "How Do I Love Thee?," *Detroit Free Press*, February 12, 1999, G1.

46. Judith Martin, "Love's Progress," *Wall Street Journal*, February 12, 1999, W13.

47. Julie Deardorff, "Classes Courting Students Looking for Lessons in Love," *Chicago Tribune*, February 14, 1999, 1.

48. Pamela Gerhardt, "Sex, Lies & E-mail," *Washington Post*, July 27, 1999, Z12.

49. Nancy Bearden Henderson, "Publishers Need More Romance—Novels, That Is," *Chicago Tribune*, June 16, 1998, 1.

50. "Publishers Need More Romance—Novels, That Is."

51. "Publishers Need More Romance—Novels, That Is."

52. Kirsten Schamberg, "Chicago Puts Romance Writers in the Mood," *Chicago Tribune*, July 30, 1999, 1.

53. "Chicago Puts Romance Writers in the Mood."

54. Renee Graham, "Rose-Colored Glasses," *Boston Globe*, October 4, 1998, 6.

55. "Rose-Colored Glasses."

56. Martin Arnold, "Count the Ways: How, Not Why," *New York Times*, February 4, 1999, E3.

57. Chris Erskine, "For a Fact, Fiction Is Ruining His Romance," *Los Angeles Times*, February 10, 1999, 1.

58. Florence Shinkle, "Searching for the Right One," *St. Louis Post-Dispatch*, February 14, 1999, D1.

Chapter 5

1. Dave Eggers, "Like You, I Am Unhappy, Outraged Even, with the Decline of True Love in Society," *New York Times Magazine*, May 7, 2000, SM77.

2. Antonio Regaldo, "Researchers Looking for Love in All of the Brain's Right Places," *Wall Street Journal*, November 8, 2000, B2.

3. Josh Fischman, "Why We Fall in Love," *U.S. News & World Report*, February 7, 2000, 42.

4. Vanessa E. Jones, "Love's Scholar Feminist Theorist bell hooks Offers a New Look at an Old Subject," *Boston Globe*, January 12, 2000, C1; bell hooks, *All About Love: New Visions* (New York: William Morrow, 1999).

5. Karen S. Peterson, "Love at First Sight," *USA Today*, February 14, 2001, D09.

6. Karen S. Peterson, "The Reality of 'Instant' Love," *USA Today*, January 16, 2003, D12.

7. Laura Kipnis, "Against Love," *New York Times Magazine*, October 14, 2001, SM98; Laura Kipnis, *Against Love: A Polemic* (New York: Pantheon, 2003).

8. Andrew Sullivan, "The Love Bloat," *New York Times Magazine*, February 11, 2001, SM23.

9. "The Love Bloat."

10. Matthew Klam, "Love in the 21st Century," *New York Times Magazine*, October 14, 2001, SM71.

11. Frances Parnes, "Suddenly, Love in a Hurry," *New York Times*, November 4, 2001, WE1.

12. Arthur Allen, "Love Is the Airwaves," *Washington Post*, February 10, 2002, WMAG28.
13. Martin Duberman, "Gayness Becomes You," *The Nation*, May 20, 2002, 49; Stephen A. Mitchell, *Can Love Last?: The Fate of Romance Over Time* (New York: Norton, 2002).
14. Joyce Cohen, "On the Internet, Love Really Is Blind," *New York Times*, January 18, 2001, C1.
15. "On the Internet, Love Really Is Blind."
16. "On the Internet, Love Really Is Blind."
17. Benedict Carey, "The Brain in Love," *Los Angeles Times*, December 16, 2002, F1.
18. Karen S. Peterson, "Personal Ad: 'We'll Learn to Love Each Other,'" *USA Today*, June 20, 2002, D01.
19. Karen S. Peterson, "Falling in Love by Design," *USA Today*, June 26, 2003, D08.
20. "Falling in Love by Design."
21. "Falling in Love by Design."
22. Anjula Razdan, "What's Love Got to Do With It?," *Utne*, May/June 2003, 69–71.
23. E.J. Graff, *What Is Marriage For?: The Strange Social History of Our Most Intimate Institution* (Boston: Beacon Press, 1999).
24. "What's Love Got to Do With It?"
25. Cathleen Medwick, "Radical Romance," *O: The Oprah Magazine*, February 2004, 172.
26. Oprah Winfrey, "The Real Thing," *O: The Oprah Magazine*, February 2004, 25.
27. Dawn Raffel, "Love: The Verb," *O: The Oprah Magazine*, February 2004, 174.
28. Mark Matousek, "Love: It's All in Your Head," *O: The Oprah Magazine*, April 2004, 93; Henry Grayson, Ph.D., *Mindful Loving: 10 Practices for Creating Deeper Connections* (New York: Gotham, 2003).
29. Dawn Raffel, "Love Myths," *O: The Oprah Magazine*, January 2005, 51.
30. Michael Vincent Miller, "After the Beginning," *O: The Oprah Magazine*, February 2006, 168.
31. Anonymous, "Love: The Reality Show," *O: The Oprah Magazine*, February 2006, 170.
32. "Aspects of Love," *O: The Oprah Magazine*, October 2008, 244.
33. Amanda Robb, "What's Timing Got to Do With It?," *O: The Oprah Magazine*, February 2006, 174.
34. "What's Timing Got to Do with It?"
35. Karen S. Peterson, "The Reality of 'Instant' Love," *USA Today*, January 16, 2003, D12.
36. Hara Estroff Marano, "The Truth About Compatibility," *Psychology Today*, September/October 2004, 52.
37. Henry Jackson, Jr., "What's Love Got to Do With It?," *St. Louis Post-Dispatch*, February 9, 2004, HF1.
38. Helen Fisher, *Why We Love: The Nature and Chemistry of Romantic Love* (New York: Henry Holt, 2004).
39. Benedict Carey, "Watching New Love As It Sears The Brain," *New York Times*, May 31, 2005, F1.
40. Teresa K. Weaver, "Morrison's New *Love*," *Atlanta Journal-Constitution*, October 26, 2003, M1.
41. Neely Tucker, "An Affair of the Head," *Washington Post*, February 13, 2007, C1.
42. Laura Sessions Stepp," "Love's Labor Lost," *Washington Post*, February 14, 2007, C1.
43. Susan Brink, "Are Antidepressants Taking the Edge Off Love?," *Los Angeles Times*, July 30, 2007, F8.
44. Leon Alligood, "Dr. Love Keeps Marriage Sparks Alive," *Nashville Tennessean*, February 14, 2008.
45. Nathaniel Branden, *The Psychology of Romantic Love: Romantic Love in an Anti-Romantic Age* (New York: Tarcher/Penguin, 2008) xix.
46. Martha C. Nussbaum, "The Passion Fashion," *The New Republic*, September 23, 2009, 43; Cristina Nehring, *A Vindication of Love: Reclaiming Romance for the Twenty-First Century* (New York: Harper, 2009).
47. Andrew Adam Newman, "For Marketers, Love Is in the Air," *New York Times*, December 28, 2009, B3.
48. Judy Foreman, "Dear, I Love You with All My Brain," *Los Angeles Times*, June 22, 2009, E1.
49. Jeffrey Kluger, "Why We Love," *Time*, January 28, 2008, 54–60.
50. Sharon Jayson, "Proof's in the Brain Scan," *USA Today*, November 17, 2008, D6.
51. Steven Pinker, "Crazy Love," *Time*, January 28, 2008, 82.
52. A.J. Jacobs, "Do I Love My Wife?," *Esquire*, June 2009, 120.
53. "Do I Love My Wife?"
54. Julie Hanus, "Hunka Hunka Burnin' Nerves," *Utne*, July/August 2009, 81.
55. Steve Lewis, "Love Conquers All. Even Life's Mysteries," *New York Times*, February 8, 2009, R4.
56. "Do I Love My Wife?"
57. John Tierney, "Anti-Love Drug May Be Ticket to Bliss," *New York Times*, January 13, 2009, D1.

Chapter 6

1. "That's Amore," PRNewswire.com, February 9, 2010.
2. Erik Sofge, "Can a Human Fall in Love

with a Computer?," PopularScience.com, December 17, 2013.

3. Ben Popper, "The Science of Her," theverge.com, December 16, 2013.

4. Lawrence R. Samuel, *Future Trends: A Guide to Decision Making and Leadership in Business* (Lanham, MD: Rowman & Littlefield, 2018).

5. Dharmavidya David Brazier, "Unconditional Love," *Tricycle*, Summer 2013, 30l; Anne C. Klein, "The Four Immeasurables," *Tricycle*, Fall 2014, 82.

6. "Get Lucky in Love," *Redbook*, February 2010, 74.

7. Jennifer Benjamin, "How to Love Him Like You Just Met Him!," *Redbook*, September 2010, 190.

8. Jessica Pauline Ogilvie, "Why I Get a Kick Out of You," *Los Angeles Times*, February 8, 2010, E1.

9. "Why I Get a Kick Out of You."

10. Helen Fisher, *Why Him? Why Her?: Finding Real Love by Understanding Your Personality Type* (New York: Henry Holt, 2009).

11. Stan Tatkin, *Wired for Love: How Understanding Your Partner's Brain and Attachment Style Can Help You Defuse Conflict and Build a Secure Relationship* (Oakland, CA: Danerhouse, 2012).

12. Sandeep Ravindran, "Study Shows People in Love Feel Less Pain," newsok.com, January 7, 2011.

13. Mark Fischetti, "Your Brain in Love," *Scientific American*, February 2011, 92.

14. Wendy Donahue, "Love Is … Not What a Lot of Us Think," *Chicago Tribune*, March 17, 2013, 6.22; Barbara L. Fredrickson, *Love 2.0: How Our Supreme Emotion Affects Everything We Feel, Think, Do and Become* (New York: Hudson Street Press, 2013).

15. "Love Is … Not What a Lot of Us Think."

16. Catherine Godbey, "Love at First Sight," decaturdaily.com, September 17, 2013.

17. Carmela Ciuraru, "Review: 'Us: Americans Talk About Love,'" csmonitor.com, February 13, 2010, 21; John Bowe, ed., *Us: Americans Talk About Love* (New York: Farrar, Straus and Giroux, 2010).

18. Elizabeth Bernstein, "I Just Called to Say, Ahem, I, Uhh, Love You," *Wall Street Journal*, February 8, 2011, D1.

19. Tanzina Vega, "Campaigns for a Holiday That Marketers Love," *New York Times*, February 14, 2011, B3.

20. Alexia Elejalde-Ruiz, "Timing, Meaning of 'I Love You' Differs by Gender," *Chicago Tribune*, April 24, 2011, 31.

21. Heidi Stevens, "Dropping the 'L' Bomb," *Chicago Tribune*, February 9, 2014, 6.4.

22. Karen Weintraub, "The Heart of the Matter," *Boston Globe*, February 6, 2012, G13; Kayt Sukel, *Dirty Minds: How Our Brains Influence Love, Sex, and Relationships* (New York: Free Press, 2012).

23. Elizabeth Bernstein, "Divorce's Guide to Marriage—Study Tracks People Who Split Up for Best Ways to Stay Together," *Wall Street Journal*, July 24, 2012, D1.

24. K. Aleisha Fetters, "When Less Romance Is More," *Women's Health*, November 2012, 105.

25. Deepak Chopra, "A Seeker's Guide to Love," Washingtonpost.com, February 14, 2013.

26. "A Seeker's Guide to Love."

27. "A Seeker's Guide to Love."

28. "A Seeker's Guide to Love."

29. Daniel Jones, "Modern Love Illuminated," *Forward*, February 14, 2014, 2.

30. Daniel Jones, *Love Illuminated: Exploring Life's Most Mystifying Subject (with the Help of 50,000 Strangers)* (New York: William Morrow, 2014).

31. "Modern Love Illuminated."

32. Shaila Dewan, "Who Wants Free Love Anyway?," *New York Times Magazine*, June 1, 2014, SM15–16.

33. "Who Wants Free Love Anyway?"

34. Mandy Len Catron, "To Fall in Love with Anyone, Do This," *New York Times*, January 11, 2015, ST6.

35. Elizabeth Bernstein, "How to Fall Back in Love," *Wall Street Journal*, December 20, 2016, A19.

36. "How to Fall Back in Love."

37. Elizabeth Bernstein, "Love at First Sight," wsj.com, April 21, 2015, D1.

38. Chuck O'Donnell, "Researchers Wrote the Book on Love," *Bridgewater (NJ) Courier-News*, February 8, 2016, A1.

39. Len Mandy, "Five Myths About Love," Washingtonpost.com, February 12, 2016.

40. "Five Myths About Love."

41. "Five Myths About Love."

42. "Five Myths About Love."

43. Francesca Friday, "Science Confirms the Search for a Soulmate May Prevent True Love," observer.com, February 20, 2018.

44. "Science Confirms the Search for a Soulmate May Prevent True Love."

45. Matt Huston, "What Love Really Looks Like," *Psychology Today*, January/February 2017, 9.

46. "What Love Really Looks Like."

47. "What Love Really Looks Like."

48. "What Love Really Looks Like."

49. "What Love Really Looks Like."
50. Caryn James, "What 'Her' Gets Right About Technology and Love," dailybeast.com, December 17, 2013.
51. "A Man and His Machine, Finding Out What Love Is," npr.org, December 20, 2013.
52. Howard Lear, "Technological Singularity: What's the Future of Artificial Intelligence?," clicksoftware.com, January 18, 2016.
53. "Can a Human Fall In Love with a Computer?"
54. Ben Popper, "The Science of Her."
55. David Sax, *The Revenge of Analog: Real Things and Why They Matter* (New York: Public Affairs, 2016).
56. "Elite Matchmaker Sameera Sullivan Helps Singles Find Real-Life Love in a Hi-Tech World This Valentine's Day," PRNewswire.com, January 31, 2017.
57. JR Thorpe, "The History of Matchmaking, in 7 Strange Facts," bustle.com, August 31, 2016.
58. "Elite Matchmaker Sameera Sullivan Helps Singles Find Real-Life Love in a Hi-Tech World This Valentine's Day."
59. Malia Wollan, "How to Write a Love Letter," *New York Times Magazine*, September 3, 2017, SM 25.
60. Emily Dieckman, "Pixelated Love," *University Wire*, May 15, 2016.
61. "Pixelated Love."

Bibliography

Baber, Ray Erwin. *Marriage and the Family*. New York: McGraw-Hill, 1939.

Blanton, Smiley. *Love or Perish*. New York: Simon & Schuster, 1956.

Boddice, Rob. *The History of Emotions*. Manchester, UK: Manchester University Press, 2018.

———. *The Science of Sympathy: Morality, Evolution, and Victorian Civilization*. Champaign, IL: University of Illinois Press, 2016.

Bowe, John, ed., *Us: Americans Talk About Love*. New York: Farrar, Straus and Giroux, 2010.

Brain, Robert. *Friends and Lovers*. New York: Basic Books, 1976.

Branden, Nathaniel. *The Psychology of Romantic Love: Romantic Love in an Anti-Romantic Age*. New York: Tarcher/Penguin, 2008.

Buscaglia, Leo. *Living, Loving & Learning*. New York: Holt, Rinehart and Winston, 1982.

Celello, Kristin. *Making Marriage Work: A History of Marriage and Divorce in the Twentieth-Century United States*. Chapel Hill, NC: University of North Carolina Press, 2009.

Chopra, Deepak. *The Path to Love*. New York: Harmony Books, 1996.

Cohn, David L. *Love in America: An Informal Study of Manners and Morals in American Marriage*. New York: Simon & Schuster, 1943.

Coontz, Stephanie. *Marriage, a History: How Love Conquered Marriage*. New York: Penguin, 2006.

Curwood, Anastasia. *Stormy Weather: Middle-Class African Marriages between the Two World Wars*. Chapel Hill, NC: University of North Carolina Press, 2010. Daniels, Dr. Anna K. *The Mature Woman*. New York: Prentice-Hall, 1953.

Davis, Rebecca. *More Perfect Unions: The American Search for Marital Bliss*. Cambridge, MA: Harvard University Press, 2010.

Ellis, Albert. *The American Sexual Tragedy*. New York: Twayne Publishing, 1959.

Fisher, Helen. *Anatomy of Love: A Natural History of Mating, Marriage, and Why We Stray*. New York: W.W. Norton, 2016.

———. *Why Him? Why Her? Finding Real Love by Understanding Your Personality Type*. New York: Henry Holt, 2009.

———. *Why We Love: The Nature and Chemistry of Romantic Love*. New York: Henry Holt, 2004.

Fredrickson, Barbara L. *Love 2.0: How Our Supreme Emotion Affects Everything We Feel, Think, Do and Become*. New York: Hudson Street Press, 2013.

Fromm, Erich. *The Art of Loving*. New York: Harper & Row, 1956.

Graff, E.J. *What Is Marriage For? The Strange Social History of Our Most Intimate Institution*. Boston: Beacon Press, 1999.

Grayson, Ph.D., Henry. *Mindful Loving: 10 Practices for Creating Deeper Connections*: New York: Gotham, 2003.

hooks, bell. *All About Love: New Visions*. New York: William Morrow, 1999.

Hunt, Morton M. *The Natural History of Love*. New York: Grove Press, 1959.

Johnson, Dr. Sue. *Love Sense: The Revolutionary New Science of Romantic Relationships*. Boston, MA: Little, Brown and Company, 2013.

Jones, Daniel. *Love Illuminated: Exploring Life's Most Mystifying Subject (with the Help of 50,000 Strangers)*. New York: William Morrow, 2014.

Kent, Margaret. *How to Marry the Man of Your Choice*. New York: Warner Books, 1987.

———. *Love at Work*. New York: Grand Central, 1988.

Kern, Stephen. *The Culture of Love: Victorians to Moderns*. Cambridge, MA: Harvard University Press, 1993.

Kipnis, Laura. *Against Love: A Polemic*. New York: Pantheon, 2003.

Leibowitz, Michael R. *The Chemistry of Love*. Boston, MA: Little, Brown, 1983.

Leonard, George. *Adventures in Monogamy: Exploring the Creative Possibilities of Love, Sexuality and Commitment.* New York: Tarcher, 1988.

Levin, Martin, ed. *Love Stories.* New York: Quadrangle/The New York Times Book Co., 1975.

Lewis, Thomas, Fari Amini, and Richard Lannon. *A General Theory of Love.* New York: Random House, 2000.

Magoun, F. Alexander. *Love and Marriage.* New York: Harper and Brothers, 1948.

Markman, Howard, ed. *Why Do Fools Fall in Love? Experiencing the Magic, Mystery, and Meaning of Successful Relationships.* Hoboken, NJ: Jossey-Bass, 2000.

Matt, Susan J., and Peter N. Stearns, eds. *Doing Emotions History.* Champaign, IL: University of Illinois Press, 2014.

May, Elaine Tyler. *Homeward Bound: American Families in the Cold War Era.* New York: Basic Books, 1988.

May, Rollo. *Love and Will.* New York: W.W. Norton, 1969.

May, Simon. *Love: A History.* New Haven, CT: Yale University Press, 2011.

Millman, Marcia. *The Seven Stories of Love: And How to Choose Your Own Happy Ending.* New York: William Morrow, 2001.

Mitchell, Stephen A. *Can Love Last? The Fate of Romance Over Time.* New York: W.W. Norton, 2002.

Moore, Doris Langley. *The Technique of the Love Affair.* New York: Simon & Schuster, 1928.

Nehring, Cristina. *A Vindication of Love: Reclaiming Romance for the Twenty-First Century.* New York: Harper, 2009.

Norwood, Robin. *Women Who Love Too Much: When You Keep Wishing and Hoping He'll Change.* New York: Pocket, 1985.

Orbuch, Terri. *Finding Love Again: 6 Simple Steps to a New and Happy Relationship.* Naperville, IL: Sourcebooks Casablanca, 2002.

Parish, James Robert. *The Hollywood Book of Love: An Irreverent Guide to the Films that Raised Our Romantic Expectations.* Chicago, IL: Contemporary Books, 2003.

Pines, Ayala. *Falling in Love: Why We Choose the Lovers We Choose.* New York: Routledge, 1999.

Plamper, Jan. *The History of Emotions: An Introduction.* New York: Oxford University Press, 2015.

Reddy, William M. *The Navigation of Feeling: A Framework for the History of Emotions.* New York: Cambridge University Press, 2001.

Regan, Pamela C. *The Mating Game: A Primer on Love, Sex and Marriage.* Thousand Oaks, CA: SAGE, 2008.

Risse, Guenter B. *Driven by Fear: Epidemics and Isolation in San Francisco's House of Pestilence.* Champaign, IL: University of Illinois Press, 2016.

Rohrlich, Jay B., M.D. *Work and Love: The Crucial Balance.* Orangeville, ON (Canada): Summit Books, 1980.

Rosenwein, Barbara H. *Generations of Feeling: A History of Emotions, 600–1700.* New York: Cambridge University Press, 2015.

Rosenwein, Barbara, and Riccardo Cristiani, *What is the History of Emotions?* Cambridge, UK: Polity, 2018.

Rupp, Leila J. *A Desired Past: A Short History of Same-Sex Love in America.* Chicago: University of Chicago Press, 2002.

Samuel, Lawrence R. *Happiness in America: A Cultural History.* Lanham, MD: Rowman & Littlefield, 2018.

Sax, David. *The Revenge of Analog: Real Things and Why They Matter.* New York: Public Affairs, 2016.

Schwartz, Pepper. *Love Between Equals: How Peer Marriage Really Works.* New York: Touchstone Books, 1995.

Segal, Erich. *Love Story.* New York: Harper & Row, 1970.

Singer, Irving. *The Nature of Love: Courtly and Romantic.* Chicago, IL: University of Chicago Press, 1987.

———. *The Nature of Love: Plato to Luther.* Boston, MA: The MIT Press, 1984.

———. *The Nature of Love: The Modern World.* Chicago, IL: University of Chicago Press, 1987.

Sorokin, Pitirim. *The Ways and Power of Love: Techniques of Moral Transformation.* West Conshohocken, PA: Templeton Press, 2002.

Spurlock, John C. *Free Love Marriage and Middle-Class Radicalism in America.* New York: NYU Press, 1988.

Stearns, Peter N. *Shame: A Brief History.* Champaign, IL: University of Illinois Press, 2017.

Sukel, Kayt. *Dirty Minds: How Our Brains Influence Love, Sex, and Relationships.* New York: Free Press, 2012.

Tashiro, Ty. *The Science of Happily Ever After: What Really Matters in the Quest for Enduring Love.* Toronto, ON (Canada): Harlequin, 2014.

Tatkin, Stan. *Wired for Love: How Understanding Your Partner's Brain and Attachment Style Can Help You Defuse Conflict and Build a Secure Relationship.* Oakland, CA: Danerhouse, 2012.

Tennov, Dorothy. *Love and Limerence: The Experience of Being in Love*. New York: Stein and Day, 1979.

Tweedie, Jill. *In the Name of Love*. New York: Pantheon Books, 1979.

Van de Velde, Theodore Hendrik. *Ideal Marriage: Its Physiology and Technique*. New York: Random House, 1930.

Walster, Elaine Hatfield, and William Walster. *A New Look at Love*. Boston, MA: Addison-Wesley, 1978.

Winch, Robert Francis. *The Modern Family*. Evanston, IL: Northwestern University Press, 1952.

Yalom, Marilyn. *The Amorous Heart: An Unconventional History of Love*. New York: Basic, 2018.

Index

Cold War 46, 48, 51, 64
Communism 24–25, 46, 56
consumer culture 6, 33, 39, 47, 61, 145; advertising 32, 45, 53, 115, 124; digital 92, 94, 119; marketing 13–14, 60, 64–65, 67–68
contraception (birth control) 6, 23, 24, 45

death 66–67
divorce 43, 45, 51, 58, 72, 104, 126, 142; and brain chemistry 116–117; and "companionate marriage" 23- 24; and feminists 70; and Hollywood 36–37, 40; and loveless marriages 18, 30; and marital infidelity 16, 22; millennials 143; and pre-nups 81; rising rate of 41, 47–49, 54, 57, 60, 76, 86; and romance novels 95
drugs 70–71, 83–84, 100, 114, 116–117, 122, 141–142, 147

feminism 2, 6, 8–9, 28, 56, 66–67, 70, 76, 88, 101, 143
"free love" 16, 20–26
friendship 73, 85, 88, 91, 102, 113, 147
Freudian psychology 6, 33, 44, 54, 59, 62, 108

Great Depression 2, 29, 37, 69

happiness 3, 29, 32, 43, 61, 102, 104, 142; and brain chemistry 84; marketing 13; and marriage 26, 108; and popular culture 82, 146; and psychology 85, 116–117; pursuit of 56, 140
Hollywood 8–12, 20, 32, 34, 36–37, 40, 42, 53, 81–82, 89, 96–97, 100, 116, 134–135; *see also* movies

"I love you" 12, 68, 97, 124–125

"love at first sight" 28, 58, 69, 82–83, 101, 111, 132, 134

love letters 102, 138
"lovebots" 136

matchmakers 7, 92, 93, 137–138
millennials 2, 8, 143
movies 2, 16, 29, 31–34, 36–38, 47–48, 75–76, 91, 109, 119, 136–137, 141; *Love Story* 67; in the 1920s 3, 6, 20–21; stars 60; *see also* Hollywood
music (songs) 2, 6, 9, 12–14, 29, 33, 40, 62, 69, 80, 100, 103

neuroscience 3, 79, 99–100, 108, 115, 116, 141
novels (fiction) 6, 11, 29, 32, 39–40, 53, 67, 73–74, 80, 87, 94–97, 134, 141

"opposites attract" 42, 58, 75, 133

radio 3, 33, 40, 103
religion 2, 20–26, 30, 44–45, 49, 89, 127, 143

self-help 7, 56, 62, 74, 84, 96–97, 100, 103, 113, 121, 128, 143, 146
sexual revolution 2, 12, 31, 47, 56, 66, 67, 70, 86, 110
social media 128, 138
socialism 25
"soul mates" 30, 47, 49, 58, 121, 129–130, 132–134

television 2, 12, 47, 76, 81–82, 108, 111

Valentine's Day 1, 8, 13, 67, 80, 89, 92, 96–97, 113, 119, 124–128, 145

work 6, 45, 63, 80–81, 84–85, 87, 145
World War I 3, 6, 7, 16, 19–20, 78, 144
World War II 2, 35, 37–40